D1093968

THE PRODIGAL GENIUS

OTHER BOOKS BY NOEL B. GERSON

Fiction

SUNDAY HEROES
DOUBLE VISION
TEMPTATION TO STEAL
ISLAND IN THE WIND
TALK SHOW
CLEAR FOR ACTION
WARHEAD
THE CRUSADER
MIRROR, MIRROR
TR
THE GOLDEN GHETTO
SAM HOUSTON
JEFFERSON SQUARE
I'LL STORM HELL
THE ANTHEM
THE SWAMP FOX
GIVE ME LIBERTY
YANKEE DOODLE DANDY
THE SLENDER REED
OLD HICKORY
THE LAND IS BRIGHT
THE HITTITE
THE YANKEE FROM TENNESSEE
THE EMPEROR'S LADIES
THE GOLDEN LYRE
THE TROJAN
DAUGHTER OF EVE
THE SILVER LION
THE CONQUEROR'S WIFE
THAT EGYPTIAN WOMAN
THE HIGHWAYMAN
THE FOREST LORD
THE IMPOSTOR
THE GOLDEN EAGLE
THE CUMBERLAND RIFLES
THE MOHAWK LADDER
SAVAGE GENTLEMAN

Nonfiction

BECAUSE I LOVED HIM
FREE AND INDEPENDENT
THE EDICT OF NANTES
P.J., MY FRIEND
FRANKLIN: AMERICA'S LOST STATE
PASSAGE TO THE WEST
SURVIVAL JAMESTOWN
LIGHT-HORSE HARRY
MR. MADISON'S WAR
KIT CARSON
NATHAN HALE
SEX AND THE ADULT WOMAN (WITH ELLEN F. BIRCHALL, M.D.)
BELGIUM: FUTURE, PRESENT, PAST
ROCK OF FREEDOM
SEX AND THE MATURE MAN (WITH LOUIS P. SAXE, M.D.)
FOOD
VALLEY FORGE
THE LEGEND OF POCAHONTAS

THE PRODIGAL GENIUS

The Life and Times of Honoré de Balzac

BY NOEL B. GERSON

1972

DOUBLEDAY & COMPANY INC., GARDEN CITY, NEW YORK

Library of Congress Catalog Card Number: 78–175376

Printed in the United States of America
First Edition

For
Sandy Richardson

LIST OF ILLUSTRATIONS

Following page 62

Following page 134

Following page 230

Following page 302

Endpaper illustration courtesy of Historical Pictures Service, Chicago

THE PRODIGAL GENIUS

I

The family name was Balssa, and persists to the present day. There are hundreds of peasant families in Auvergne who call themselves Balssa, Balsan, Balsac and Balza, the name meaning, in the ancient Celtic of the region, a sharp-edged boulder. According to educated guesses, the peasants who lived in the little town of Balsac, near the larger town of Brioude, were scattered during one of the many invasions that made life intolerable for the people of what had once been a semi-independent land.

No Balssa achieved anything of consequence until one Bernard, a miser who spent every penny he earned acquiring grazing land, farms and other property. For more than forty years, until his death in 1778, he, his wife and their eleven children slept in a single room on straw pallets. Their home, such as it was, stood near the tiny village of Nougayrié in an area of strong natural contrasts. To the east lay the Alps, to the west stood the Auvergne

Mountains that bisect south-central France. Nougayrié was surrounded by fertile valleys and bleak pasture lands. Few men who lived in that day ever rose from poverty to affluence, but Bernard Balssa possessed extraordinary qualities. He not only became a landowner of some consequence, but was determined to give his eldest son an education. Bernard-François not only labored in the fields and vineyards with his father, but, thanks to the local priest, became the first Balssa to learn to read and write. Even more ambitious than his father, Bernard-François found employment with an attorney in the town of Canezac, and there taught himself so much about the drafting of legal documents that he became an expert on the subject.

Bernard-François worked for a time in Toulouse, and then, while still in his twenties, went to Paris, where he changed the spelling of his name to Balzac to adapt it to the oddly distinctive pronunciations of people in the capital. There, with little but his intelligence and drive to aid him, he obtained a job serving as clerk to the Public Prosecutor. Later he became principal bailiff in the Court of Common Pleas, and finally secretary of the King's Council. Not only was he a man of great ambition and ability, but he was also politically agile. He jumped to the Republican side during the French Revolution which erupted in 1789. Two years later, he was Commissioner of the Police Tribunal, one of three men in charge of the Paris police. In this post he made enemies, and his past made him suspect, so a year later he found it wise to leave Paris and take up temporary residence in Valenciennes. Never one to remain idle, he made use of old friendships and won an appointment as supply-master for the Republican Army of the North.

In this post he was in charge of all procurement for a force of more than fifty thousand men. He bought food for the men and fodder for their horses; he purchased canvas for tents, medicines, blankets, and even chose the wines consumed by officers. Farmers and manufacturers eager to sell to the Army of the North found it convenient to line the purse of the supply-master, and Bernard-François, while always discreet, was never a man to refuse cash. He lived for a time in Brest, then was transferred to Tours, where he arrived in 1797.

Still a bachelor at fifty-one, he was handsome, broad-shouldered and, by middle-class standards, the possessor of a comfortable fortune. He knew enough of the world not to consider himself wealthy, yet he was rich far beyond the standards of his peasant father. There were others who found him attractive, among them the Sallambier family, deeply entrenched members of the bourgeoisie, who had manufactured brocades and other cloth since the time of Henry IV.

Before Bernard-François quite knew what was happening to him, he found himself married to dark-haired Laure Sallambier, an exceptionally attractive girl of nineteen. Reared in a strict household, she accepted the marriage without objection.

Bernard-François felt no qualms about marrying a girl thirty-two years his junior. A self-proclaimed follower of Rousseau, he was convinced he would survive to the age of one hundred, and lived in accordance with strict rules he had made up for himself. He arose at dawn and retired soon after sunset, he walked a minimum of ten miles per day, and each day he drank a quart of a "secret elixir" he concocted from the sap of trees. A student of Chinese philosophy, he believed in living a simple life, but, in view of his origins, he was a surprisingly complex man. Reared as a Catholic, he had absorbed the principles of the Revolution and had left the Church, finding it too authoritarian. Nevertheless he was a student of Roman Catholic history, and could lecture by the hour on the papacy and on heresies.

Above all Bernard-François was a moderate. He deplored the excesses of the Revolution and became a follower of Napoleon because he believed in the individual liberties the Emperor promulgated. He endorsed freedom of religion and speech, but vehemently opposed violence in any form. A voracious reader, he had studied Voltaire, Montaigne, Erasmus and Descartes, but he liked to think he had evolved his own philosophy and approach to life. He was concerned with what he called the "equilibrium of vital forces" which manifested themselves physically, and he observed a regimen that allowed him to balance reading, physical exercise, rest and eating. It is not surprising that he became known in Tours as an eccentric.

He and his wife proved to be remarkably ill-matched. Laure Balzac was as arrogant as she was pretty, as remotely disdainful as her husband was passionate, and she felt compelled to argue with any view he might express. Unfortunately for him, she had received an unusually good education at a Paris convent, and was far more intellectual than most middle-class women. In spite of her learning, however, she was a believer in the occult, and had a great weakness for fortunetellers. Her husband decried this trait, as did her children in later years, but it is not surprising that the eldest of her living children, Honoré, should have followed secretly in her footsteps and consulted fortunetellers until the last year of his life.

The first child born to Laure and Bernard-François was a boy who lived only three weeks, and his mother was so exhausted trying to care for him that she fell ill and almost lost her own life. So, when her second child was born on May 20, 1799, she named him Honoré and promptly sent him to the home of a wet nurse who lived in a nearby village. This woman was kind and sympathetic, but her husband, a policeman, drank heavily, and the atmosphere in their little cottage was stormy.

Sixteen months after Honoré's birth he was joined by a baby sister, Laure, and the two children remained with the nurse. Their father paid them frequent visits, brought them gifts and took them for carriage rides. But, according to Honoré, he did not set eyes on his mother until he and his sister were returned to the family home when he was four years old. Even granting that Mme. Balzac was a cold woman who displayed little love for her children over a period of many years, it is difficult to believe she ignored them completely for so long a time.

Did Honoré exaggerate, as he did in so many things? It is difficult, if not impossible, to ferret out the truth. Laure indicates in her correspondence that her mother paid little attention to her, to her older brother or to a baby sister, Laurence, who was born in 1802. But she says nothing that either corroborates or disproves her brother's astonishing claim.

What is true is that Honoré hated his mother for having ignored him, and spent his life simultaneously despising her and trying to win her approval. Aware of his contempt from early childhood, she withheld the love and praise he craved. This attitude was in large part responsible for making him an emotional cripple, but it also endowed him with the furious compulsive drives that made him a great novelist.

When Honoré and Laure joined their parents in a new, large house, Bernard-François had become deputy mayor of Tours, and the family lived in great style. But the boy soon wished he could return to the cottage of his nurse. His mother was stern, quick to punish and quicker to scold, and was wrapped up in her own desire to live a life of luxury. She rarely showed any sign of affection to her husband, her son or her daughters. In fact, according to another of Honoré's claims, his mother literally never kissed him, never hugged him, never held him on her lap. Yet his assertion might not be solely the product of his imagination. Laure, in her correspondence with her sister after both were grown and married, referred frequently to their mother's extraordinary coldness.

The birth of Laurence marked an interesting change in the family's status. For the first time Bernard-François and Laure called themselves *de* Balzac, adding the prefix to indicate that their antecedents were noble. Thereafter they were rarely consistent, sometimes calling themselves de Balzac, sometimes contenting themselves with the simpler Balzac. Honoré was subjected to incessant criticism and ridicule in later years when, midway through his career, he started calling himself de Balzac, but there was a family precedent for his pretensions, and the blame belonged more to his mother than to him.

The children's life was made even more complicated when one Mademoiselle Dalahaye was hired as their governess. Strict and unrelenting, she added to their burdens and squelched their enthusiasms. Bernard-François bought his son a toy violin, and Honoré liked to saw on it by the hour, pretending he was actually playing it, but he had to retire to the nursery for the purpose, and was punished if either his mother or the governess heard a note.

When the boy was five he and the elder of his sisters were taken to Paris for a visit with their Sallambier grandparents, and Honoré remembered the trip all of his life. Specifically, he said, he fell in love with Paris and decided he wanted to live there when he grew up. It is possible, of course, that he actually entertained this precocious wish and remembered it, but it is equally possible that, as a world-renowned author, he wanted to add gloss to his biography. One of the fascinations of Balzac's life is that of separating fact from the fiction he wrote with such conviction.

Two basic changes interrupted the normal flow of life in the Balzac household. Grandpa Sallambier died a few months after the children's visit to Paris, and Grandma Sallambier came to Tours to live with her daughter and son-in-law. At last Honoré had a champion. His grandmother gave him sweets and spending money when his parents denied him both. It was she who sparked his interest in reading, which she unfailingly encouraged. It was also she who taught him to swear, and to play cards for money; she invariably contrived to lose, which was her way of giving him a few francs. And she entertained him with stories of Parisian high life, giving him an appetite for glamour. He did not know that her tales were based on hearsay and her own vivid imagination.

The other change was equally far-reaching. Mme. Balzac fell in love with a neighbor, Jean de Margonne, one of the wealthiest and most handsome men in Tours, who was approximately her own age. She had an affair with him, and when Honoré was eight she gave birth to another son, whom she called Henry, using the English rather than the French spelling. Bernard-François knew nothing of his wife's deception, but the rest of the family always believed that Henry was the illegitimate son of Mme. Balzac and Margonne.

Certainly her treatment of her youngest child was unique. Clearly her favorite from the time of his birth, she petted and spoiled him, often overwhelming him with demonstrations of affection. Honoré and Laure, who had good reason to be jealous, despised Henry until the end of his tragic life; Laurence, more nearly his own age, managed to tolerate her younger half brother.

It was not accidental that, with the arrival of a new son, Mme. Balzac made it her business to dispose of the elder. Within a month of the baby's arrival, Honoré was sent off to a boarding school, the Collège de Vendôme. In 1807 this institution undoubtedly qualified as the most unusual in France.

It was owned and operated by an order of priests, known as the Oratorians, who had rightly acquired reputations as radicals. The headmaster and his assistant, both devoted priests, were married, and many members of the faculty also had wives. They paid lip service to Napoleon, of course, as their property would have been confiscated had they opposed the Empire, but they made no secret of their strong pacifist beliefs, and openly criticized the Emperor's never-ending military ventures.

Their charges lived lives that were simultaneously restricted and permissive. There were no holidays, the pupils never went home for visits and their parents were forbidden to visit them more than once a year. Every hour of a boy's day was organized, and the usual punishment for infractions of the rules consisted of a beating on the open palms of one's hands with a thick leather strap. All incoming and outgoing mail was censored, and a boy who tried to complain to his parents received an extra thrashing. The worst of punishments was confinement in a cell known as "the alcove," and additional cells for miscreants were located at one end of each dormitory.

Under no circumstances were the boys permitted to go into the town of Vendôme, but they did enjoy a number of privileges that were unique. They were allowed to converse at meals, provided they discussed intellectual subjects. Two hours were devoted to violent physical sports each day, and on one day each week classes went off with a master on hikes that began at dawn and lasted until sunset. The boys were allowed to purchase candy and other treats with the allowances sent to them by their parents, and during the recreation hour each day, when many played games, a boy who elected to read was permitted to take any volume he wanted from the school library, including books elsewhere restricted to adults.

Honoré enjoyed few of the school's benefits, however. He received no spending money from his parents, a fact which Laure corroborated, and his fellows naturally refused to share their sweets with him. In the six years he spent at the Collège, from 1807 to 1813, he was the only child in the entire school of more than two hundred boys whose parents did not come for the celebrations on the annual prize day. Honoré literally did not see his father for six years, and his mother visited the school only once. Bernard-François believed he had to observe his own regimen in order to prolong his life to the magic age of one hundred, and therefore could not travel. Mme. Balzac not only lacked the interest in her eldest child, but presumably did not want to be separated from her lover, either.

So Honoré, a sallow, pinch-faced boy who was the better part of a head shorter than his classmates, thought of himself as an abandoned orphan. He was so shy he made few friendships, and rapidly developed into what would become known, in a later time, as a loner. Since no one cared about him, he did not try to achieve high grades, and only when he was in danger of failing did either of his parents bother to send him a curt note of admonition.

Only one letter he wrote home during his six years at the Collège has been preserved, and it indicates his loneliness:

Vendôme,
1 May, 1809

My dear Mother,

I think Papa was very unhappy when he heard that I had been put in the alcove. To console him please tell him that I have got a second prize in Latin. It is a history of Charles XII of Sweden, and it says many things of interest about him.

I do not forget to clean my teeth with my handkerchief.

I have a new exercise book in which I make fair copies of my exercises and I get good marks and that is how I hope to please you.

I embrace you warmly and all the family and all the gentlemen of my acquaintance. These are the names I know of boys who have won prizes and come from Tours:

Boislecompte.

He is the only one I can remember.

Balzac Honoré,

Your obedient and affectionate son.

One of the masters, a Father Lefebvre, took pity on the lonely boy, and tutored him privately in mathematics, in which Honoré was particularly weak. The priest himself had eclectic tastes in reading and loved literature, which he was fond of discussing with his pupil. He had noted that Honoré spent his time reading during the recreation hour, and one day the boy confided that he had deliberately misbehaved so he would be confined in the alcove. There, he said, he could read undisturbed.

The priest promptly made his own library available to him. Father Lefebvre didn't know it, but he was doing literature a favor, even though Honoré's compulsive traits were growing worse. He read constantly, and when the strain made his eyes water, he daydreamed. He was Hamlet and Romeo, Antony and Macbeth and Iago, whose character he found far more absorbing than that of the more phlegmatic Othello.

This was the period during which the Empire of Napoleon Bonaparte reached its zenith of power, size and influence. The good fathers were careful to give the Emperor his due, much though they disliked his military conquests. So Honoré was steeped in Napoleonic fact and legend. It is impossible to comprehend and appreciate the erratic life and monumental achievements of Honoré de Balzac unless one realizes that, during his loneliest and most impressionable years, Napoleon became his idol. Some day he, too, would perform prodigious feats, and then the parents who ignored him would be sorry they hadn't cherished him.

Honoré was also exposed to the works of Voltaire, and Vendôme may have been the only Roman Catholic school in France where the works of the master iconoclast could be found. The cynical, ultra-realistic view that Voltaire took of the human race made an indelible mark on the mind of a boy who had no reason to believe that people were other than selfish, cruel and grasping. Man was an opportunist who cheated and lied to get what he wanted, Voltaire had said, and the young Balzac had cause to agree.

Like so many precocious adolescents through the ages, Honoré tried to write poetry. He himself admitted in later years that his efforts were miserable, and his schoolmates teased him unmercifully, calling him The Poet. But his creative drive was already asserting itself, and each failure produced a greater expenditure of energy. Finally the headmaster decided to call a halt, and after trying in vain to convince him that he was no poet, forbade him to write more verse.

Years later, in the person of Louis Lambert, the most autobiographical of Balzac's many thousands of characters, he explained the curious theological concepts he developed while a student at the Collège. The strict disciplines imposed by the priests caused him to reject formal Catholicism, yet he clung to many of its features, which appealed to him, and he enlarged on them in a mind that shrank from the harsh realities of the world around him and caused him to create a dream world of his own.

He believed in God and called himself a Christian, although he seriously questioned the basic theological concepts of the Trinity and the Virgin Birth. God guided man, but was too busy to concern Himself with the day-to-day affairs of an individual, and therefore appointed angels to perform these tasks for Him. Since there were too few angels to look after the world's rapidly growing population, one had to perform extraordinary deeds in order to attract the attention of a guardian, whose help was always temporary. Therefore one had to perform great deeds repeatedly, or the angels would ignore him in the same way one's parents paid no attention to him.

There was another, more subtle way a person could attract an angel and obtain his help, and that was through the occult. Honoré had an unwavering, lifelong conviction that miracles occurred regularly, and it has been suggested that his own situation, already hopeless, was to become so much worse that he felt he could survive and prosper only if the Almighty, nudged by a sympathetic angel or two, performed some miracles on his behalf. This could be accomplished if one knew the future and acted accordingly, a belief that caused Honoré to form a lifelong dependency on fortunetellers and soothsayers. Angels also responded to the calls of witches and other special persons who were capable of occult communication, so he sometimes paid large sums to various charlatans for help.

The boy's pseudo-theology did not appeal to his masters, who urged him to concentrate on his schoolwork, but they discovered there was no way they could induce him to labor for higher grades. They could not help but be impressed by the breadth of his learning, however, and many years later Father Lefebvre wrote that Balzac Honoré was the only boy at Vendôme who could debate with the priests on any subject and at their own intellectual level.

An unverified story has it that Honoré, at the age of twelve, wrote a pungent, seventy-thousand-word treatise entitled *Thesis on Will Power*. According to the tale it was so advanced, so polished that the headmaster refused to believe he had composed it himself, and destroyed it. The origins of the story are obscure, but the finger of suspicion, as usual, points in the direction of the mature Balzac, who never denied its authenticity.

Honoré's description of Louis Lambert at the age of twelve or thirteen is as significant as it is illuminating, explaining in a few words the sort of boy he had been:

He devoured books of every kind, indiscriminately gulping down religion, history, philosophy and physics. He grasped seven or eight lines at a time, and his mind absorbed their meaning as rapidly as his eyes moved; often a single word in a sentence sufficed to tell him its content. His memory was as retentive of what he read as it was of the notions inspired by his own reflections or in conversation.

At the age of twelve his imagination, stimulated by the constant exercise of his faculties, had developed to such a point that the things he learned through reading were as vividly imprinted on his mind as if he had actually seen them; whether because he proceeded by analogy or was endowed with a kind of second sight, by means of which his mind encompassed all created things.

It quickly becomes evident to the modern reader that the neuroses implanted in the boy at a very early age had rooted and flowered. He was not merely an unrecognized genius, but a badly maladjusted young genius.

One of the more curious aspects of the life and career of Balzac is that he had no burning boyhood ambition to become a writer. Almost without exception the great authors, in the literature of virtually every civilized country, began writing as children and continued to write despite the obstacles that confronted them. Honoré de Balzac, however, was determined to become a powerful, famous and respected man.

Neither while he was a student at the Collège nor in the long, repeatedly disappointing years that followed, during which he suffered one failure after another in a variety of enterprises, did he think of himself primarily as a writer. Had one of his business ventures succeeded, he would have been content to become wealthy and renowned in that field. His own testimony, corroborated by his sister, his mistress of many years, and his few close friends, points to this conclusion. Balzac sought wealth and power and found them with his pen only because all other avenues were successively closed to him.

To be sure, it can be argued that his many frustrations, beginning in earliest childhood, made it inevitable that he would find release by putting his thoughts on paper. But, as will be seen in a subsequent chapter, his writing career began more or less by accident, and another decade was to pass before he took himself seriously as a writer.

The many confusions of his difficult childhood emphasize and help to explain this paradox. The most brilliant of Vendôme's students was snubbed by his parents, ridiculed by his peers and was not appreciated by his teachers. Honoré lived exclusively in the world of books, and seemed pleased when his classmates paid no attention to him, withdrawing even further into his own shell.

The Oratorian fathers, who had regarded him as lazy and intractable, became alarmed when he lost his appetite, ate little and failed to reply when someone spoke to him. Unable to cope with him, they sent him home in mid-April 1813, before the end of the school year.

His sister Laure later described his homecoming in detail. He was incredibly pale, she said, and was so thin she failed to recognize him when he walked into the house. What struck her most forcibly were his eyes, which looked enormous in his pinched face; he never focused on anyone, but stared vacantly into space, groping like a sleepwalker when he moved. He rarely replied when someone addressed him, and he seemed unaware of his surroundings. It is obvious that he was in a state of emotional collapse.

Bernard-François was angry and upset, and Grandma Sallambier was bitter. "So this is what that school has done to the healthy boy we sent them," Laure quoted her as saying.

If Mme. Balzac reacted to her son's pitiful state, she did not mention it to him or anyone else. She continued to devote most of her attention to her precious Henry, and scarcely seemed to acknowledge that her eldest child had returned home.

Honoré was so stung by his mother's continuing indifference that he began to recover. Other factors were at work, too. He was reunited with the sisters he loved and who showed him great affection. He spent time each day with his grandmother, who fattened him by saving choice morsels from the dinner table and slipping them to him in secret. Within a few months the boy regained his weight, his health and his ebullience.

As he became more aware of the world around him, he realized how many changes had taken place in six years. His father, increasingly eccentric and argumentative, was feuding with half of Tours's officialdom. His mother, who had drifted away from Jean de Margonne, had alienated most of the city's good ladies, who avoided her, and her increasing isolation made her more waspish and hypercritical than ever. Only Grandma Sallambier, who was aging rapidly, remained sympathetic and interested in the growing boy.

A month or two after Honoré's fourteenth birthday he returned to school, this time to classes in Tours as a day student. But he learned far more from his father, who delivered daily monologues on subjects ranging from the building of the Great Wall of China to the moral problems caused by the betrayal of young girls. The boy discovered many books in his father's library, some of them salacious, that the priests at the Collège hadn't owned, and new vistas began to open.

The events of 1814 in the great world beyond Tours stunned Honoré. The Emperor Napoleon, whom he worshiped, was sent off to Elba in exile. All of the values the boy held dear crumbled on that dreadful April day, and he was left with only his schoolwork as a pillar to which he could cling. He applied himself so diligently to his studies that, to his own surprise as well as that of his parents, he received an award in the autumn of 1814 as an honor student.

There was no improvement in his financial status, however. His parents remained miserly, and did not give him one sou for spending money. Other boys, the sons of officials less prominent than his father, bought their lunch from vendors, and relished the delicacies they purchased. Honoré brought a little bread and cheese with him from home. Once again he felt humiliated and rejected.

It might be noted that there was no change in his situation in the years that followed, after the family moved to Paris and Honoré was sent off to a boarding school there. In one of his major novels, *La Peau de chagrin*, Balzac put his feelings into an observation made by Rafael:

The sufferings I had endured at home among my own family and at school were now renewed during my sojourn at the Pension Lèpître. My father had not given me any pocket money whatsoever. My parents were completely content at the thought that I was being fed, clothed and stuffed full of Latin and Greek. While living in boarding schools I came to know some thousand or so schoolmates, but I cannot recall in any single case ever having come across a similar instance of utter unconcern on the part of a boy's parents.

The family was still well-to-do, but Bernard-François had so many arguments with his colleagues that he was afraid they might denounce him to the restored Bourbon monarchist authorities as an incorrigible Bonapartist. Wanting to put some distance between himself and his enemies, he moved his family to Paris, and the Balzacs took up residence in the Marais quarter, where the Sallambier family had lived for more than a century.

Honoré was given little opportunity to taste the joys of Paris, however. Almost immediately after the family arrival he was sent to the Pension Lèpître, a boarding school owned and operated by one Jacques-François Lèpître, who had achieved a measure of distinction during the Terror of the Revolution by taking an active part in a plot to rescue Marie Antoinette. This effort had won Lèpître a measure of respectability with the Bourbon adherents, and his school was considered one of the most fashionable in Paris.

Young Balzac, with no pocket money of his own, promptly went into debt, borrowing from the school's porter in order to taste such forbidden joys as pipe smoking. But he could only dream of visiting the brothels in the vicinity of the Place Royal, which were frequented by his wealthier schoolmates. Their exaggerated stories of the erotic joys they had tasted whetted his appetites, but for the present they remained unfulfilled. As he himself later said, it was small wonder that, when he finally began to indulge in affairs, he made up for lost time.

In mid-March 1815, Napoleon returned from exile, marched on

Paris and the exciting Hundred Days began. Until the Emperor's final defeat at Waterloo in June, the Bonapartist supporters at the school were exhilarated beyond measure. Honoré shared the pleasure of his peers, but his experiences had made him wary, and he kept his mouth shut, letting the others cheer.

His caution paid dividends. The Bonapartists were expelled from the school in July, but Lèpître did not suspect that he entertained similar enthusiasms, and he received a certificate of graduation at the end of September. His parents were disappointed because he failed to win any honors, and sent him to still another school which had a reputation for strictness. It was operated by one Abbé Ganser, a German-born priest, who ran a militarylike institution with Teutonic thoroughness.

Honoré remained there a year, and in the autumn of 1816, at the age of seventeen, he stood thirty-second in a class of sixty. His mother, never satisfied with his efforts, sent him a letter which is a perfect illustration of her unvarying attitude toward him:

> *My dear Honoré,*
>
> *I can find no words strong enough to describe to you the grief which you are causing me. You are making me really unhappy, though I am doing all I can for my children and ought to expect that they should make me happy!*
>
> *The good and worthy Father Ganser has informed me that you have dropped down to the thirty-second place in translation!!! So all the pleasure I had promised myself tomorrow has again been spoiled.*
>
> *We were to have met tomorrow at eight o'clock. We should have had our midday meal and supper together, and we could have had such a nice talk together and told one another all sorts of things. But your lack of industry, your wantonness, your neglect of your studies compel me to leave you to your just punishment. How empty my heart is now! How long the journey will seem to me! I am keeping from your father the fact that you have received such a bad place in your class, for you certainly won't be allowed to go out on*

Monday, though your day off from school was intended to serve a useful purpose and by no means merely your personal pleasure.

The dancing master is coming tomorrow at half past four. I will have you fetched and taken back after your lesson.

I should be remiss in the duty imposed on me by my love for my children if I were to treat you any different.

I am,

Your heartbroken mother,

Laure de Balzac

Honoré's mother continued to show him the same cold, self-pitying attitude throughout his life, and no matter what he did or failed to do she found reason to criticize him and, when within her power, punish him. He was almost fifty when he first discovered Coleridge's *Ancient Mariner*, and told Laure, "Mama is the albatross hanging from my neck, and has been since the day I was unfortunate enough to be brought into the world as her son."

In spite of his mother's scorn, however, the youth received his final certificate on graduation in November 1816. His parents had already decided his future for him. Bernard-François had always wanted to be a lawyer, so Honoré was entered in the School of Jurisprudence at the University of Paris. He was given no voice in the matter.

Unlike others of his age, who attained a degree of freedom and dignity when they became university students, Honoré continued to suffer restrictions. He would live at home rather than board at the university. He would receive no spending money, and was expected to find part-time employment so he could contribute room and board to his family.

There was no financial basis for their parsimony. Although Bernard-François was on the verge of retirement, the family's investments brought them a comfortable living of fifteen thousand francs per year, and Grandma Sallambier contributed another five thousand, although she protested that her food and lodging actually cost no more than half that sum. Laure and Laurence were attending a boarding school, and Henry, who remained at home, was given whatever he wanted in the way of elegant clothes, spending money and luxuries. The boy even had his own horse, a privilege that no one else in the family enjoyed.

Honoré's life was a compounded misery. He hated law school, and his mother made his home life a hell on earth. Nothing he said or did satisfied her, and she nagged at him so constantly that his grandmother retired to her own room so she wouldn't hear the tirades. Bernard-François was so absorbed in his health regimen that he was oblivious to everything else. Unfortunately for the family, he decided that affairs with young girls still in their teens would keep him vigorous and assure him the full century of life he sought. His wife, who was aware of his escapades, closed her eyes to them.

Honoré attended classes by day, and at night he worked in the offices of an advocate, Guyonnet de Merville, a friend of the Sallambier family. Thanks to the arrangements made by his mother, her son's wages were paid directly to her, and Honoré was still completely without funds. After spending two years with De Merville, Honoré moved to a similar position as a clerk with a lawyer named Passez, who handled his parents' legal affairs. Mme. Balzac was pleased that her son obtained a raise in pay, all of which she pocketed.

The only person, other than Grandma Sallambier, who showed Honoré any sympathy or understanding was the family physician, Jean-Baptiste Nacquart, who became his lifelong friend. Dr. Nacquart was a pioneer in the field of psychology, and wrote a number of treatises on the influences the mind and the emotions exerted on the body; neither he nor Honoré realized it, but the influence he exerted on the thinking of the young Balzac was enormous.

The years spent in the offices of De Merville were not wasted, either. The attorney was one of the most prominent members of his profession in Paris, and by copying his briefs Honoré learned much about civil law that would be useful when he wrote his great novels about domestic travail.

Miraculously, his home life and the grinding labors that kept him busy day and night did not dampen his spirits. He became the comedian in the large office of De Merville clerks, and kept the place in an uproar. His influence on his colleagues was so great that one day the chief clerk sent him a brief note, which was delivered to him in a classroom. It read, "*M. Balzac is requested not to come to work tonight because there is a great deal of work to be done.*"

Honoré's ability to absorb vast quantities of information very swiftly was a great help to him. He mastered his subjects in law very quickly, and this gave him the time to attend other classes at the university, which he did without his parents' knowledge. He spent an entire year studying natural history, he took several courses in philosophy, one in economics and another in theology. Although he didn't yet realize it, he was fascinated by man's knowledge of himself and his beliefs on the subject of God.

Whenever Balzac had an hour or two to spare, he played cards with Grandma Sallambier, who still allowed him to win. Balzac suspected she knew he spent this money on the prostitutes of the Place Royal, but carefully refrained from discussing the subject with her. He was so secretive, in fact, that these initial forays into the world of sex remained unknown to anyone for more than a century, and not until the end of World War II, when a valuable cache of family papers was found, including several hundred letters written by Honoré's sister, Laure, did the facts emerge. Until then most Balzac biographers assumed he remained a frustrated virgin until he became involved in the first great romance of his life.

Grandma Sallambier could not be kept in the dark forever, and eventually she discovered that Balzac had become a man in every sense. Although considered strait-laced by her daughter and son-in-law, the old lady had her own salacious sense of humor. According to a story told with considerable relish by Laure, her brother became sexually attracted to one of the more handsome young women of Paris, an unnamed lady who had social position and wealth.

Teasing the young man, Grandma bet him the sum of one hundred francs that he could not take the young woman to bed. Balzac didn't have one franc to his name, but accepted the wager—and won. His grandmother was delighted to pay.

One of the seemingly great mysteries of Honoré de Balzac's life is what made him attractive to a woman, any woman. By the time he was twenty he had stopped growing, and was only five feet, three inches tall. His head was large, and sat on a bull-like neck above exceptionally broad shoulders and a thick torso. He was already displaying the proclivities of a gourmand that would eventually make him so hopelessly overweight that he would pant when he climbed a single flight of stairs, and his round face was puffy. His dark hair, hanging below his ears, was carelessly combed, and was thickly plastered with the pomade he used all of his life.

He was also an exceptionally sloppy dresser, even in later years, when he owned a wardrobe as dazzling as it was expensive. Often his coat was spotted, and one or two buttons of his brocaded vest usually were undone. His stockings were wrinkled on his thick calves and ankles, and the correspondence of virtually everyone who knew him mentions the fact that one or both of his shoelaces usually were untied.

Apparently his secret lay in his eyes, although his portraits and the crude daguerreotypes of his final years reveal nothing extraordinary. Even the many people who had good cause to dislike him commented on the way he came alive when his eyes flashed, and he appears to have exerted an almost hypnotic influence on women, particularly those who were neurotically inclined. Even as a young man he was a compulsive talker who dominated a conversation, and it appeared that when romance was on his mind, his cascade of words could sweep a woman into a horizontal position. He was aided in his maturity, of course, by the conviction held by many of his feminine readers that he was the only living writer who thoroughly understood women.

In his youth, however, before his fame bolstered him, he presented a sad, somewhat pathetic spectacle, and no one knew he dreamed of emulating his idol, Napoleon. It was dangerous in the years of the Bourbon restoration, when the conservative Louis XVIII and his equally conservative successors sat on the throne of France, for anyone to admire the exiled Emperor, who was living out his days in the custody of the British on the distant island of St. Helena.

The world in which Balzac came to manhood was an uncertain one. France, already bankrupted by Napoleon's military campaigns, suffered the additional burden of paying the reparations exacted by her conquerors. Prices were exorbitant, there was a shortage of manpower, farmers were just beginning to produce food in sufficient volume to satisfy the nation's physical wants, and the Industrial Revolution, already in evidence in Great Britain, the German states and the Low Countries, had not yet influenced the French economy.

Nevertheless there was a ferment, as yet imperceptible, that was taking place in France, particularly in Paris. Within the next two decades the city would become the intellectual and cultural capital of the world, exerting as much influence in these spheres as she had in the military and political realms when Napoleon had been the master of Europe. A new generation was growing to adulthood, and not many years would pass before the thinking and feeling of literate people everywhere, on both sides of the Atlantic, would come under the spell of Victor Hugo and Honoré de Balzac, Alexandre Dumas the elder, Stendhal and George Sand, Théophile Gautier and even the pedantic Charles-Augustin Sainte-Beuve. The wealth of talent was such that Eugène Sue was considered second-rate by his contemporaries, and Flaubert and Zola, who followed in the footsteps of the great, had to struggle long and hard to find original ways for the expression of their own genius.

At the beginning of the nineteenth century's second decade, Paris enjoyed advantages of which few other major cities in continental Europe could boast. She had escaped the physical ravages of war and could concentrate on expansion as her population once again began to grow, without being forced to rebuild. Even more important, although the Bourbons and their supporters tried to turn back the clock, France—her capital even more than the provinces—had absorbed the principles of her great Revolution and of the Napoleonic Empire that had followed it. Most of Paris' one and a half million inhabitants believed passionately in liberty and equality, although they elected to fraternize selectively on the basis of class distinctions that, far from disappearing, had become somewhat more rigid again. Above all, Parisians believed in the personal freedoms that had flowered under Napoleon: freedom of speech, including the right to criticize the regime; freedom of religion, including the right to reject God, if one wished; freedom of assemblage; freedom to rise from one's caste, if one possessed the agility and ability; and freedom of the press.

This last was the most difficult to achieve. Nineteenth-century governments in France, including the republics established at various times, kept tight reins on the written word. Like Napoleon, the Bourbons and Republicans alike considered the written word the most dangerous to the stability of any government, and a censorship of newspapers, books, magazines and the theatre was maintained. No one, not even Hugo and Balzac, who raised their voices in a clamor for freedom of the press, quite realized the true meaning of such freedom. Even they, like their countrymen, were so imbued with the principle of the need for controls of some sort that they did not advocate the total freedom enjoyed in the young United States of America. There were no Washingtons and Adamses, Jeffersons and Madisons, Monroes and Jacksons in France.

The physical expansion of Paris was spectacular, even in the decades preceding the wholesale beautification enterprise carried out so successfully by Baron Haussmann under the aegis of Napoleon III. Expensive homes and apartment buildings sprang into being in the Champs Élysées district, where farmers had pastured their cattle only a few years earlier. In the older sections of the city, to be sure, in Montmartre on the Right Bank and Montparnasse on the Left, the poor were crowded into increasingly cramped quarters as the city grew at a rate of more than one hundred thousand persons per decade, a rate regarded as phenomenal at the time.

In the nineteenth century the French restaurant, café and bistro, became an important part of Parisian social life. In England men enjoyed their private clubs, some hundreds of which were founded, but in France the eating and drinking establishments proliferated. The café, or coffeehouse, had arrived in Paris one hundred years earlier, in the 1720s, by way of Turkey, and Voltaire had been a habitué of one of the oldest, the Procopé, in the theatrical district.

But it was not until the 1820s that new eating and drinking houses were established by the hundreds, then the thousands, at a rate so rapid one could scarcely keep track of the new ones. Members of every profession and vocation, every economic and political and social group, had their own favorites.

Newspapermen and authors favored inexpensive and colorful places where they could make their cynical observations on the current regime without fear of being overheard by government spies. Monarchists frequented their own cafés and restaurants, and others became the gathering places of Bonapartists, Republicans, Socialists and, eventually, Communists. Plumbers, stevedores, carpenters, printers, shoemakers and perfumers all had their own spots, where they could meet their colleagues, drink wine and appreciate the cuisine that had become the nation's pride.

Women continued to lead more restricted lives. Most of the cafés and neighborhood bistros were closed to them. A lady could dine at the Grand Vefour, the favorite of both Hugo and Balzac, provided she was escorted by a gentleman, but if unaccompanied she was barred. Yet there were exceptions to the general rule. Actresses were permitted to occupy tables in some of the cafés near the theatres, and mannequins from the House of Worth, and other dressmaking establishments, had their own meeting places, but they were not considered ladies. The prostitutes of Paris, said to number five thousand, had their own cafés in various quarters of the city, where they went to relax. It was an unwritten law that men did not disturb a streetwalker when she was dining and drinking with her colleagues.

The cultural explosion of the 1820s and 1830s was astonishing. In 1810, when Napoleon's power was at its zenith, there were five theatres in Paris that produced plays throughout the calendar year. By 1840 there were forty, and four decades later there were fifty. People who wanted to know what was happening in Paris, in France and, perhaps, in the world, had their choice of anywhere from fifteen to thirty Paris newspapers. The less successful appeared and vanished with regularity, but new publications sprang into existence overnight to take their places. There were magazines too numerous to count, including those that specialized in literary criticism, art criticism, and music criticism. There were poetry magazines by the score, most of them appearing for only a few issues. A few hardy survivors catered to the general public and began to include short stories, novellae and serials.

They succeeded so well that the newspapers began to serialize fiction, printing either daily or weekly installments of new novels. When an important novel by Hugo, Dumas or Balzac appeared, the circulation of the magazine soared, and the serial became an important—perhaps the most important—source of a professional writer's income. The same phenomenon was taking place in England, where the appearance of a novel by Charles Dickens caused lines two and three blocks long to form in front of newsstands.

One of the prime benefits of the Revolution and the Empire was the vast increase in education. In 1789, when the Revolution erupted, only the aristocrats, some members of the clergy and a sprinkling of the bourgeoisie could read and write. In three decades the base had undergone enormous growth, and schooling had become one of the country's most flourishing industries. Not only were all of the upper classes, male and female alike, now literate, but so were the middle classes of both sexes, and the educational revolution was drawing in masses of the peasants and urban poor as well.

This growth vastly increased the reading public, and produced a seemingly overnight growth in the market for the written word. Men wanted to read about politics, while women wanted fiction, and this hunger was the direct cause of the appearance of newspapers, magazines and books in large numbers.

It was also responsible, by the 1820s, for the appearance of a new product to satisfy the expanding market. The use of the word "product" here is intentional. There was a great demand for what can only be classified as cheap fiction, which consisted of romances, adventure, and the horror-suspense-mystery stories that came to be known as Gothic novels. Their writers were men of no standing or reputation, and they churned out these stories so rapidly, not bothering in any way with literary taste or style, that the authors preferred, in the main, to write under pseudonyms. Publishers paid them flat fees for their labors, usually very small sums, and the books were printed, bound and distributed as inexpensively as possible. In a general sense, such efforts were the equivalent of the paperback original fiction that began to appear in ever-increasing volume after World War II.

This, then, was the world into which Honoré de Balzac was graduated in January 1819, when he received his law degree and went to work as a very junior partner in the offices of Maître Passez, who lived in the apartment directly above that of his parents. His wages were larger than they had been when he had been a clerk, but were still tiny, and he received nothing himself, his mother having arranged with Passez for the benefit of her own purse.

The young man was beginning to know Paris. A cup of coffee in a café cost very little, and a small coin would buy one of the cheap books on sale everywhere. He sat at a sidewalk table to watch the city stroll past him, and he read large numbers of these works of fiction, no one knows how many.

In the spring of 1819, he celebrated his twentieth birthday, and one day soon thereafter he closed his desk, packed up his law books, his pen and his inkwell, and went home. He had no intention of pursuing a career as a lawyer, he told his stunned family, but intended to become an author instead.

II

It seems to be an immutable law of human nature that every younger generation rebels against its elders, a law of which parents living in the final third of the twentieth century are even more painfully aware than were their predecessors. Seen in this light, the sudden, volcanic rejection of his future by Honoré de Balzac was not surprising, but his parents, not unexpectedly, were unable to appreciate it. All they knew was that the most downtrodden and meek of family mice was not only roaring like a lion, but meant every bellow from the depths of his repressed psyche.

Honoré's rebellion could not have come at a more inconvenient time, from his parents' point of view. In the spring of 1819, just before the young man made his great decision, Bernard-François had unexpectedly been retired from the civil service by an ungrateful government, and his pension amounted to only one quarter of his salary. His wife had her own income from various properties she owned, to be sure, and they also had a number of investments that would enable them to continue living comfortably. But they sensibly decided to retrench and leave Paris, where rents, food, clothing, servants and other living costs were far more expensive than in other parts of the country. A Sallambier cousin agreed to buy a house in the little village of Villeparisis and rent it to them for a nominal sum. Located on the main stagecoach route that linked Paris and the military garrison town of Metz, near the German border to the northeast, Villeparisis existed only because it was a livery station where stagecoaches changed horses. It boasted a half-dozen small, dreary inns, and double that number of stables. Mme. Balzac found it a convenient place to live because she could take a commercial coach to Paris at almost any hour of the day or night.

Her son's decision shocked her. Honoré had been supported by his parents all of his life, and had received a superb higher education. Now, when he was in a position to practice law and help his family financially, he elected to desert an honorable profession and join the ranks of poverty-stricken mountebanks. She found the prospect unbearable.

But the idea fascinated the self-educated Bernard-François, who had always respected the written word. He was willing to grant that not many authors had ever been able to support themselves, but there were a few who had achieved both riches and renown. He admitted that his son had shown no talent with a pen, but he was willing to take a chance on the youth, provided there were restrictions placed on him.

Mme. Balzac, for all of her stern and unyielding approach to life, was still her mother's daughter, and had inherited something of a gambler's willingness to take risks, provided the odds against her were not too great. There was always the possibility that her elder son, whom she had so long disliked, might become rich. So she agreed to work out a contract with him. Many of Balzac's biographers agree that a secret reason motivated her. When her tears and tantrums would not budge him from his adamant stand, she resolved to make Honoré's life as uncomfortable and unpleasant as possible, in the hope that he would abandon his foolish notion and return to the practice of law, where he belonged.

Maître Passez drew up a remarkable contract, and Honoré was so eager to break the parental chains binding him that he signed it. His mother and father agreed to support him for two years, paying him the starvation wages of seven hundred and fifty francs per year for this time. He obligated himself to write plays and novels for two years, and to pay his parents 50 per cent of the gross income he received in return.

Only a desperate youth would have accepted such terms. A poor, illiterate day laborer in Paris could not support himself on much less than two thousand francs per year, no matter how frugal his tastes. Not only was the sum of seven hundred and fifty francs cruelly insufficient, but Balzac had rarely attended the theatre, knew nothing about the book business and lacked even a nodding acquaintance with theatrical producers and playwrights, publishers and authors.

Mme. Balzac returned to Paris from Villeparisis and went apartment-hunting on his behalf. The place she selected for him, at 9 Rue Lesdiguières, in a dismal working-class district, may have been the most drab, inadequate living quarters in Paris. If there were worse, his mother failed in her efforts to find them.

Balzac lived on the top floor of a building so aged and wretched that it had to be torn down as unsafe and uninhabitable a few years later. He paid the sum of sixty francs per year for the questionable privilege of living there. He described the place in feeling detail in *La Peau de chagrin*, and those who saw the garret, his sisters and Dr. Nacquart among them, agreed that he did not exaggerate.

He climbed five flights up a dark, creaking staircase, the well so foul-smelling that one gasped for a breath of fresh air. The door to the apartment had been broken and had been repaired with a few rough-hewn planks, leaving gaps that allowed the stench to seep in. The attic had such a low ceiling that even the short Balzac could barely stand erect in it, and was so dark that he needed artificial light even on the brightest days. In summer the garret was suffocatingly hot, and in winter it was frigid. It was "a hole, worthy to be compared with the leads of Venice," Balzac said, and it had been vacant for several years because the proprietress had been unable to persuade anyone to live there, in spite of the low rental. The author's own description best conveys his feelings:

There could be nothing more detestable than this garret with its dirty yellow walls that reeked of misery. The roof slanted almost to the floor, and the sky was visible through loose tiles, but the window set in the ceiling was so small and dirty that it was impossible to distinguish day from night, rain from sunshine.

My lodging cost me three sous a day, and the oil I burned at night cost another three sous. I looked after the room myself. I wore flannel shirts because I could not afford the two sous a day for laundry. I used coal for heating, the cost of which spread over the whole year worked out at about two sous a day.

All these expenditures together did not amount to more than eighteen sous, leaving me two sous for unforeseen expenses. I do not remember during this long and wretched sojourn in the Pont des Arts ever having paid for the water I used. I fetched it for myself every morning, winter and summer, from the fountain in the Place St. Michel.

During all of my monastic solitude I lived in this way in poverty and seclusion, my own master and my own servant. With indescribable ardor I lived the life of a Diogenes.

Balzac was so poor he bought bread which was twenty-four to forty-eight hours old, a condition that even the paupers of Paris shunned, since they shared the conviction of those more comfortably situated that bread was swill unless eaten the day it was baked. In order to make the crusts palatable Balzac soaked them in either milk or water, and for the entire time he lived in the attic he ate nothing else.

His furniture was deplorably inadequate, and his mother, who gave various items of furniture to friends in Paris rather than have them transported to her new home, provided him with nothing. He had to buy the few items he possessed out of his first year's seven hundred and fifty francs. His bed was hard and flat, an unyielding cot that, he said, resembled "a miserable trestle." His desk was very old and leather-topped, but the leather was so ragged that he had to tear it off. He became so fond of this little table, four feet long and three feet deep, that he kept it for the rest of his life, carrying it with him on all of his travels and refusing to write on anything else. In his later years, Balzac admitted he found the table cramped, but continued to use it because of a superstitious feeling his talent would abandon him if he gave it away or sold it. His desk chair was straight-backed, without arms, and creaked, "providing me a lullaby to which I soon became so accustomed that I did not hear the noise." He also bought an old easy chair in which he sat when he read, and a broken crate he salvaged from someone's garbage held his few clothes.

An author although he did not yet know it, Balzac possessed the ability to rise above the squalor of his hermit's life. Another citation from *La Peau de chagrin* illustrates this trait:

When the weather was fine I could open my window. I remember how I joyfully dipped my bread in my bowl of milk as I sat before my window and breathed in the fresh air. My eyes roamed over a landscape of brown, red and light gray roofs of slate or tiles covered with green or yellowish moss. At first this prospect struck me as monotonous, but soon I discovered peculiar beauties in it. There was the evening illumined by the rays of the sun, with the ill-fitting shutters of the windows outlined as black hollows in this strange landscape, or the pale gleam of the street lamps which down below cast their yellowish reflections through the fog, and with their faint accusing light mirrored the undulations of the crowded roofs on the pavements like a misty sea of architecture.

Now and then queer figures emerged in the heart of this gloomy wilderness. Amid the flowers of some roof-garden I saw the sharp, hooked profile of an old woman watering her nasturtiums. Silhouetted in the crumbling frame of an attic window a young girl at her toilet thought that she was unobserved. I could only see her handsome brow and the long plaits that she was lifting into the light with graceful white arms. I gazed with pleasure at the ephemeral vegetations in the gutters of the roofs, pitiful weeds that some gust of wind had perhaps carried up such a height.

I studied the mosses and their colors vivified by the rain, which turned to brown velvet in the sun, brown with whimsical shadings. Finally the poetic and fleeting impressions of the day, the sadness of the mist, the sudden emergence of the sun, the silent magic of the night, the mysteries of sunrise, the smoke of the chimneys—all these happenings in the queer domain of nature became familiar to me and kept me amused. I loved my prison cell. I stayed there because I wanted to. These savannahs of Paris, formed out of the monotonous roofs that stretched like a vast plain above the abyss of life below, entered into my soul and mingled with my fantasies.

Books helped him to pass his lonely hours, too, and his reading became more intense than it had been in his student days. There were no public libraries in Paris, the wealthy kept their own volumes locked behind metal grills, and he was too poor to buy books. But he was a graduate in good standing of the University of Paris, and therefore was entitled to borrow whatever he pleased from the vast libraries the school maintained. He utilized the privilege to the utmost, and said in *La Peau de chagrin* that he read an average of six to ten books every week, their subjects covering "every phase of human endeavor."

An author who hopes to win success as a novelist must be an astute observer of the humankind, and Balzac took a graduate course in observation without quite realizing what he was doing, or why. Seeking relief from the monotony of working and sleeping, reading and eating in his tiny garret, he allowed himself the luxury of going out each day for a walk that lasted from one to two hours. It was the only diversion he could afford, and his route usually took him down the Boulevard Bourdon to the Faubourg

St. Antoine. He described the experience in another of his major works, *Facino Cane.*

He began to observe the activity of the Faubourg, its inhabitants, its characters. As badly dressed as the workers of the quarter, and indifferent to outward appearances, he mixed among them without their showing any reserve toward him. He could join their groups, watch them shopping, and listen to their discussions on their way home from work.

Observation soon became a matter of intuition with me; I looked into their souls without failing to notice externals, or rather I grasped these external features so completely that I straightway saw beyond them. My method of observation endowed me with the capacity to share in the life of the individual in question just as he lived it; it permitted me to put myself in his place in the same way that the dervish in the Arabian Nights *assumed the form and the soul of the people over whom he uttered his magic incantation.*

I understood these people's ways, I espoused their way of life, I felt their rags on my shoulders, I walked with my feet in their tattered shoes; their desires and their distress penetrated my soul, or my soul passed into theirs. It was like a waking dream.

With them I flew into a passion at the employers who tyrannized over them, or at the malicious trickery which compelled them to return many times before they were paid their wages. I entertained myself by giving up my own habits, by transmuting myself into somebody else in a kind of intoxication of my moral forces, and by playing this game as often as I liked. To whom do I owe this gift? Is it a kind of second sight? Is it a quality which by abuse can border on madness?

I have never explored the sources of this power. I possessed it and I used it—that was all.

It mattered only that since that time I was able to analyze into its component parts the elements of that compound mass we call "the people." I had analyzed them and was able to distinguish between their good and their bad qualities. I knew well the im-

portance to me of this Faubourg, this seminary of revolutions, with its heroes, its inventors, its men of practical wisdom, its rogues and criminals, its virtues and vices, all hemmed in by misery, subdued by poverty, steeped in wine and ruined by brandy.

You cannot possibly imagine what innumerable adventures unfold themselves unnoticed in this city of pain, what swiftly forgotten dramas! What terrible and yet what beautiful things one sees here! Imagination cannot hold a candle to the reality which lies hidden here and is never discovered. One has to dive down too deeply in order to find these remarkable dramas, these tragedies or comedies, these masterpieces born of chance.

Balzac's great works of fiction demonstrate that he learned his lessons of observation as few men have ever learned them, but his remark to the effect that he knew well the importance to him of this Faubourg seems to be hindsight imposed by success on an early period of floundering misery.

For two or three months after he moved into the garret he tried his hand at various forms, of which scraps and fragments remain. He tried to write lyric poetry and an epic, but had the good sense to realize his efforts were amateurish and crude, a critical opinion he wisely maintained to the end of his days. He started a tragedy, which was hopeless, then attempted to write a comedy, which was worse. He finished several chapters of a novel, but it had to be discarded.

He was gloomy, sometimes desperate and always desolate during these early months, and his letters to his sister, Laure, indicate that he sometimes thought of abandoning his venture. Freedom was very sweet, but he was accomplishing nothing. Then, suddenly, inspiration struck. He would write a tragedy in blank verse on the English puritanical tyrant Oliver Cromwell!

It is interesting to observe that the dour Cromwell, whose life is so difficult to translate into a play, fascinated the French dramatists of the nineteenth century. Even Hugo could not resist writing a play about the Lord Protector of England, and he failed as badly as all the rest.

Honoré de Balzac could not have made a worse choice. He could not have attended the theatre more than a half-dozen times in his life, having lacked the funds to buy a seat for himself, so he knew virtually nothing about the medium or its mechanics. He was equally ignorant of the English background, and knew only a few scattered facts about Cromwell. In addition, his decision to write in blank verse when he knew his poetry was inadequate was a mistake in judgment.

Nevertheless, having made up his mind, he plunged into the project with a fury that became his trademark. First he spent days reading every book translated into French on Cromwell that he could find, his command of English being inadequate for the task. Then, and only then, did he begin to write. He worked day and night.

Even this first effort displayed the compulsive writing habits that would become characteristic, and would enable him to produce vast numbers of books throughout the rest of his career. Frequently he did not leave his garret for days at a time, going out only to replenish the supplies of the water, bread, milk and coffee on which he subsisted. He wrote so steadily for so many hours on end that his fingers became cramped, yet he refused to call a halt, even though the pains in his hands were so intense he sometimes wept.

He wrote for as long as eighteen to twenty hours at a stretch, leaving his table momentarily to relieve himself, and when he became so exhausted that he began to nod over his manuscript, he drank more coffee. Eventually he became so weary that the coffee was no longer effective, so he forced himself to fall into bed, where he snatched three or four hours of sleep before returning to his labor.

The coming of winter added to his problems. The garret became bitterly cold. Balzac wrapped his legs in an old rug that had belonged to his father and swathed the upper part of his body in a heavy woolen scarf that his sister Laure had given him. But the chill numbed his fingers, and he became alarmed when he discovered his writing was becoming illegible. For the sake of greater warmth he took to his bed, writing while propped up on his only pillow.

He labored for month after month. He gave up his walks, and lived what was tantamount to a hermit's existence. He was too shy to make friends. In spite of the lessons his mother had forced him to take, he had never learned to dance, and he was too poor to dine at a restaurant or even spend an hour sitting at a coffee-house table. Only his own inner sense of discipline compelled him to adhere to his rigorous schedule under such adverse circumstances. He had never before displayed such strength. But his will proved equal to the challenge he had set himself. And he did not falter.

Only one person intruded on his solitude and gave him a small measure of the relief he craved. Theodore Dablin, a middle-aged wholesale ironmonger, was an old friend of the Balzac family, and was concerned about the young man's welfare. How he knew where to find Balzac is something of a mystery, inasmuch as his parents took great pains to conceal both his whereabouts and his ambitions from their circle. They suggested that Balzac was in Normandy, or on the Mediterranean coast—anywhere their fancy of the moment dictated. They told no one he wanted to be a writer; their bourgeois feelings shrank from the concept.

But Dablin learned about Balzac's hideout, and visited him at regular but infrequent intervals, perhaps twice each month. He realized the youth was ruining his health, and insisted on taking him to a restaurant for a nourishing dinner. Dablin had to expend great effort in his attempts to cajole Balzac to accompany him, but when they reached the restaurant, Balzac ate ravenously. It was not unusual for him to consume two or three bowls of soup, several portions of fish and three or four orders of a main course. Unable to decide between several desserts, he ordered and ate all of them.

These acts of kindness resulted in a lifelong friendship. Dablin was unassuming and gentle, modest to a fault and scrupulously honest, qualities which his young friend soon recognized. Years later Dablin achieved his own measure of immortality when Balzac used him as the model for the notary, Pillerault, in *César Birotteau.*

As *Cromwell* began to take shape Balzac suffered the self-doubts that assail authors when they survey their work. He wrote agonized letters to Laure. She, alone in the family, continued to have faith in him, and her replies always were the same. "*Write!*"

Oddly enough, Balzac did not lose his sense of humor. In one note to Laure he said:

"Fire broke out in this quarter, at 9 Rue des Lesdiguières, in the head of a young man on the fifth floor. The fire brigades have been working on it for months, but cannot put it out. The young man is consumed with a passion for a beautiful woman whom he has not met. She is called Fame."

Other letters to his sister indicate the same goal. Riches, he told her sententiously, did not bring happiness, but renown was "the queen, the Strumpet, the great lady to whom I plight my troth."

While Balzac pursued his dream, Laure became involved in a very real romance with Eugène de Surville, a brilliant young civil engineer who, according to the girl's parents, was of noble birth. Other, more prosaic sources indicated he was the illegitimate son of a provincial actress who had used De Surville as her stage name. Whatever his antecedents, he was vigorous, ambitious and handsome, and Laure, who had been indifferent to him when he had started to court her, soon fell in love with him.

Balzac took the news badly. Every girl, he wrote his sister, should have many suitors, and the larger their company the more attractive she became to yet more men. A flirtation was one of the more pleasant of a woman's prerogatives, but marriage was quite another matter, and he urged her not to succumb to persuasion that might lead her to the altar.

Laure cheerfully ignored her brother's advice, and in April 1820, she was betrothed.

Meanwhile *Cromwell* was nearing completion. One of the bizarre aspects of the entire enterprise was Balzac's utilization of Corneille, the greatest of French dramatists, as his model and inspiration. He had read and studied all of the tragedies Corneille had written, yet he confessed in a pathetic letter to Dablin that he had never seen one performed on the stage.

The good Dablin was so distressed he offered to buy seats at the Théâtre Français the very next time something by Corneille was offered. But Balzac refused the kindness, explaining he was afraid he might be overpowered, and that Corneille would influence him unduly.

In May the play was finished, and Bernard-François summoned his son to Villeparisis. There the work would be read in the Balzac parlor, by an audience consisting of relatives and friends, and due judgment would be rendered.

Balzac protested, but if he thought that the prospective audience was unfit to judge his work, he was discreet enough to keep his opinion to himself. Since his father insisted on the reading, Balzac suggested that Dablin, who had encouraged him through the long and difficult months, be included. Bernard-François agreed.

The reading took place one day in late May, with a group of about twenty persons solemnly gathered in the Balzac parlor. Mama served refreshments consisting of tea and a light wine, probably watered so no one's senses would be dulled. Laure sat with De Surville in a corner, whispering, and the giggling Laurence joined them. Papa shared his son's nervousness, and was so irritable that everyone took pains to avoid him. Only Grandmama Sallambier was cheerful, and offered to bet as much as twenty francs that the play would be a spectacular success. No one cared to accept a wager.

Balzac, who had vanished while the guests sipped their wine and drank their tea, came back into the room looking very pale. When he tried to smile it was obvious that his teeth had suffered from decay and discoloration during the months he had neglected them. Those bad teeth would remain prominent for many years, until one of his mistresses finally persuaded him to have them extracted and to substitute false teeth that would improve his appearance.

Now his labor of many months was to be weighed by an audience of middle-class provincials who knew nothing about the theatre, nothing about blank verse and nothing about literature.

Years later Laure described the occasion in a letter:

"The ordeal began. The reader's enthusiasm steadily diminished as he felt how little impression he was making and saw the frozen or disconsolate faces of those who sat listening."

There was a hush when Balzac came to the end of his manuscript. Then the candid Dablin broke the silence. He delivered the opinion that *Cromwell* was totally lacking in merit. It was dull, it did not tug at one's heart, and none of the characters seemed real.

Balzac, deeply wounded, tried to counter his friend's arguments, but Dablin was supported by the rest of the audience. Although they spoke less bluntly, their message was the same. The play was filled with imperfections.

Papa was overcome by his son's distress, and wept. Laure and Laurence, who loved their brother, also wept. Mama's pride was hurt, and she withdrew from the room. Grandmama Sallambier poured herself a stiff drink of unwatered wine.

Eugène de Surville proved he was a diplomat, as well as a future member of the family in good standing, when he suggested there might be an expert who could render a more professional opinion. Providentially, he was acquainted with just such a person, his former professor of literature at the Collège de France, a Dr. Andrieux. It so happened that Andrieux was not only a minor poet of some distinction, but a member of the Académie. He was also the author of two professionally produced plays, albeit failures. De Surville offered to get in touch with his former teacher.

Professor Andrieux, all but forgotten for years, was flattered, and offered his services. Mme. Balzac, who used the "de" in her correspondence with him, took the manuscript to him personally. The mission was apparently too important to be left to Balzac.

Andrieux proved to be both a competent literary critic and a man of common sense. He found the manuscript sadly wanting, yet saw no reason why Balzac shouldn't be encouraged, and he wrote to Mme. Balzac accordingly:

It is far from my desire to wish to discourage your son, but I am of the opinion that he could employ his time better than in writing tragedies and comedies. If he will give me the pleasure of paying me a visit I shall be happy to explain to him how, in my view, belles-lettres should be studied and the benefits that can be derived from it without necessarily adopting poetry as a profession.

Balzac did as he was bidden. He called upon Professor Andrieux and let the words of advice flow in one ear and out of the other. Laure wrote:

My brother received the body blow without wincing or turning a hair, because he did not admit defeat. "Verse tragedies aren't my line, that's all," he said, and began to plan new works he would write.

A full-scale family crisis erupted. The elder Balzacs felt, with considerable justification, that Dr. Andrieux's advice was excellent and that it should be followed. If their son wanted to write immortal words, he could do it in his spare time. But he had been trained as a lawyer, a junior partnership awaited him in an established firm. They felt it was his duty to resume his career in the law.

Yet Balzac showed the same stubborn streak that had first manifested itself when he had resolved to become a writer. He had concluded a two-year contract with his parents, and the agreement still had a year to run. He was determined to keep his end of the bargain, and expected them to live up to theirs. As for returning to the law or taking up a career in some other business, the prospect sickened him. He wrote:

If I take a position I am lost. I should become a machine, a circus horse with prescribed hours for doing my thirty or forty laps in the ring, drinking, eating and sleeping. I should become merely a man intent on doing his daily round. And this is what people call living—this rotating like a millstone, this eternal recurrence of the eternally selfsame things.

By mutual consent of the combatants, the battle was postponed for Laure's wedding and the attendant festivities. Papa bored everyone with his prediction that anyone who followed his regimen would live to the age of one hundred and would never see the inside of a physician's office. Mama played the *grande dame*, while Laurence and little Henry devoured all the sweetmeats in sight.

Although Balzac was present in body, he continued to daydream, and wrote, "*Shall I ever fulfill my only but immense desires, to be famous and to be loved?*"

He hadn't quite given up hope for the future of *Cromwell*. Dablin had a friend who was a prominent actor in the Comédie Française, and, at Balzac's insistence, agreed to show the script to the man, who, in turn, swore that the management of the theatre would also read it. Whether anyone but the actor, one Lafon, ever saw the play script is unknown. But Lafon returned it to Dablin with the comment that it was not only a very bad play, but had been written by someone who knew nothing about the stage. Thus, from a mechanical aspect alone, it was unplayable.

Balzac responded by calling Lafon an idiot, incompetent to judge a work of art. Yet he himself must have realized he had failed: he put away the script and never attempted to salvage it.

The family fight over Balzac's career was resumed after Laure and De Surville went off on their honeymoon. Balzac was determined to hew to the agreement, but Mama was adamant. Finally a compromise was reached. Balzac was to have his second year of trial, as promised, but the family could save money while he was doing it. Now that Laure was married, her room was vacant, and her brother would live there, thus saving rent and other expenses. What was more, the family still kept a tiny flat in Paris, and he could stay there anytime he found it necessary to visit that city.

Balzac capitulated, writing Laure of his reasons. He hadn't enjoyed privation and physical discomfort, and would be in far better physical circumstances at home. He and Papa had at last achieved a true understanding, and even enjoyed spending their leisure hours together. As for Mama, she was a trial beyond comparison, but he thought he could manage her. He would lock himself in his room when he was working and would refuse to answer when she wanted to send him on errands. And he would adopt Papa's technique when forced to spend time in her company: he would neither listen nor reply when she addressed him.

The novel was becoming increasingly popular as a medium of entertainment, and readers were displaying a lively, continuing interest in fiction. The peace imposed on Europe at the end of the Napoleonic era had resulted in a dull, drab world, and the literate were turning to the imaginary worlds of the novel for excitement.

The knights of Sir Walter Scott's historical romances were successful everywhere, and on a lower level the so-called Gothic novel, a blending of horror, suspense and sentiment, was attracting a wide audience. A number of French authors were achieving financial success and a measure of respectable fame in both fields, and Balzac decided, with the same impetuosity that had caused him to write *Cromwell*, to try his hand at the historical novel.

He called his book *Falthurne*, and his setting was medieval Italy, about which he knew literally nothing. He wrote a complete draft, finishing it in five months in spite of his mother's innumerable interruptions. But when it was done he needed no committee of relatives and friends to tell him he had failed again. He knew himself that he had written an inferior, adolescent work that was false in both tone and characterization from the first page to the last.

Time was passing. In six months his two years would end and he would be forced to return to the law. In desperation Balzac started a second novel. He thought of writing it in the form of correspondence between major characters, and he thought of it as a romance in which he would also examine man's relationship with God. He called it *Sténie ou les erreurs philosophiques*, and closely modeled his heroine on Laure.

Twenty-two years old in 1821, Balzac deemed this work second-rate, and his margins are filled with notes to himself, most of them demanding that long passages be rewritten. Although he didn't realize it at the time, he was showing his first real progress as an author. Perhaps he had exhausted his youthful enthusiasms. Whatever the reason, he was employing the critical faculty that every first-rate author requires.

Yet he was in no position to develop these qualities and his other skills at his leisure. As his mother reminded him every day, when the two-year contract expired, he was honor-bound to return to work in the law office of Maître Passez. Fame, which Balzac was courting so assiduously, would have to wait. He realized that independence and money were closely interrelated.

III

For hundreds of years, prior to the restoration of the Bourbons, authors had held a unique place in French society. Never considered the social equals of aristocrats, they had nevertheless been respected, and the nation's leaders had been shrewd enough to recognize the power of the written word. François Villon, the fifteenth-century poet, had been a pickpocket, thief and procurer, yet his talents had earned him the right to dine with royalty. Three hundred years later Voltaire had won even greater standing for his profession. He had become the intimate of kings and princes.

In the early 1820s, a quiet revolution was taking place. As noted previously, the spread of literacy and the increasing demand for novels were creating new markets which authors of stature could not and would not fill. People wanted inexpensive novels, written in language they could understand without straining. The demand was creating a supply, and the age of the hack writer dawned.

A number of publishers, eager to earn money in the new market, offered small sums to writers who would give them books of romance and adventure in quantity. These books were printed on cheap paper, inexpensively bound, and were rushed to the bookstores, where women who had just learned to read snatched them from the shelves.

The authors of these less than immortal works were, in the main, clever and cynical young men who had mastered the required formula needed, and were able to turn out third-rate fiction quickly and painlessly. Perhaps the most envied of the group was an elegant youth of approximately Honoré de Balzac's age who called himself Auguste le Poitevin de l'Egreville. His father was a well-known actor named Lepoitevin, and the son inherited not only his dashing style but a shrewd business sense.

The market for his work was greater than his own ability to turn out cheap fiction rapidly, so he formed a syndicate with a number of his colleagues, among them Étienne Arago, the younger brother of the country's most distinguished astronomer. Auguste was always on the watch for newcomers he could add to his stable.

In 1821 Balzac made a number of brief journeys to Paris, staying at his parents' tiny apartment there, and on one of these trips his path crossed that of Auguste. It has been said they met in either a library or a brothel, but each version is probably apocryphal. It is far more likely that they fell into conversation at one of the cafés frequented by writers and would-be writers. When in Paris Balzac liked to visit such establishments, linger over a cup of coffee purchased with money he won at cards from his grandmother, and eavesdrop on the professionals he so badly wanted to emulate.

No details are available regarding the friendship of Balzac and Auguste, and it is not known whether the latter ever saw any of his abortive literary efforts. For whatever his reasons, however,

Auguste offered the desperate Balzac an opportunity to earn money as a writer.

Auguste had already signed a contract to write a short, melodramatic novel to be called *Charles Pointel ou mon cousin de la main gauche.* Aside from the title, there existed nothing but a brief sketch of the plot. If Balzac would write the book, Auguste would split the eight hundred franc author's fee with him.

The young man who had referred to himself in his correspondence with Laure as the new Corneille, the successor to Voltaire, had a brief and bitter fight with his conscience. If he accepted, he would be forced to cast aside his literary aspirations and worship at the altar of the golden calf. Anything was better than the law offices of Maître Passez, however, so Balzac accepted.

He returned to Villeparisis, and in four weeks of furious day-and-night writing that caused his mother to criticize him mercilessly, he finished the book. It was no better and no worse than dozens of similar works that appeared each month, and the publishers accepted it without change. Overnight Honoré de Balzac became a professional writer.

The happy Auguste visited him at Villeparisis, and they struck a bargain. Henceforth they would write in partnership, with Auguste attending to the business details and originating the ideas, while Balzac, hidden away in the sleepy country town, would turn out the required manuscripts. Both would use pseudonyms based on anagrams of their names, Auguste calling himself A. de Villerglé, while Balzac was to be known as Lord R'hoone. It should be noted here that Balzac suffered no false illusions about the career on which he was embarking, and always, without exception, used a pseudonym when turning out cheap fiction to order. At no time did his own name appear on any of these books, and he sometimes went to great lengths to conceal his real identity from the public. No matter how much he debased his talent, he remained determined to win fame, power and respect as Honoré de Balzac.

Seen in perspective, the next few years of Balzac's life were beneficial. He not only became self-supporting but also permanently erased the threat of being compelled to spend his life as a lawyer. It can also be argued that, in churning out vast quantities of Gothic novels, adventure stories, romances, fantasies, mock-historicals and even pseudo-religious tales, he learned his craft. He gained an astonishing facility, and could create any mood on demand. He poured thousands of words on paper, and learned how to use them. In later years he told Dumas, "Very often, when scribbling trash, I would tell myself that if I were writing this book under my own name, I would cut this entire paragraph and word the next sentence in such-and-such way. I was no longer afraid of words, and stopped holding them in awe. In brief, I became a writer."

The first effort by the two young men was called *L'Héritière de Birague*. Contracts were signed in July 1821, with a publisher named Hubert. Balzac produced the completed manuscript in less than a month, and the book was published at the end of September. Pocketing his four hundred francs, Balzac wrote to Laure that the book was "a piece of literary offal."

It is significant that, from the very beginnings of his career as a novelist, regardless of whether he was working under a pseudonym or his own name, Balzac wrote with blinding speed, suffering none of the "writer's blocks" that have been the despair of so many of his colleagues through the centuries. He wrote as he read, in great gulps, or as he spoke in his maturity, pouring out words, ideas, philosophical concepts in deluges. This talent was neither acquired nor developed, and Balzac did nothing to nurture it. Aside from the painful, childishly inept *Cromwell*, he found he could write as fast as he could move his pen on the paper before him, and even then he could not keep up with his mind, which raced even farther ahead.

No one has ever been able to explain how Balzac turned out such prodigious quantities of work. His pace was always the same, regardless of whether he was writing a hack novel or a masterpiece. The only difference, as will be seen later, was the technique of rewriting he used in books under his own name. When spilling out trash under a pseudonym, he did not bother to rewrite.

His efforts during the summer and early autumn of 1821 are even more remarkable than appears on the surface: Balzac's labors were interrupted by a new round of family festivities. A marriage was arranged for Laurence with Armand-Désiré de Saint-Pierre de Montzaigle, an undisputed member of the aristocracy who held a minor civil service post in the government. All that mattered to the family was that he was an aristocrat, and Laurence resigned herself to her fate.

Balzac found his prospective new brother-in-law impossibly overbearing, privately nicknamed him "Il Troubadouro," and wrote to Laure:

He writes verse; he's such a superb marksman that when he goes shooting he brings down twenty-six birds with twenty shots; he's an expert at billiards; he does gymnastics—magnificently; he is an expert rider; he is a hunter extraordinary and a fisherman without peer. He . . . he . . . he . . .

Had the Balzac family taken the pains to look into the background of the aggressive braggart, they would have learned he had long been a gambler, and since his mid-teens had consorted with prostitutes and their procurers, many of whom had criminal police records. Laurence's marriage promised to be difficult, and Balzac's intense dislike of his newest brother-in-law was justified.

But the young author was far too busy to worry for long about anyone else. His newest venture with Auguste was a book the pair called *Jean-Louis, or La Fille trouvée*, and Balzac wrote it in eight weeks, completing it before the end of 1821. Auguste secured them a better contract, based on the success of their previous work, and each received six hundred francs. Balzac thought he had written rubbish, but the work was memorable in one sense: it consisted of four volumes, and in writing it he had averaged forty to fifty pages of manuscript per day, an incredible performance.

It is easy to agree with Balzac that this novel and all of his other early books were garbage, worth no more than the paper on which they were printed. But there were flashes of the developing talent that would make the author a master of the novel. Long descriptive passages were sometimes accurate and colorful. Occasionally characters were true to life, and now and then the plots became gripping. There could be no doubt that Balzac was learning his craft.

He was also earning a real living for the first time in his life. A third book written in toto in 1821 was *Charles Pointel*, which bore only the pseudonym of Auguste, although it was written by Balzac. The reasons for this failure to give credit where it was due are difficult to fathom, since the two young men rarely corresponded, but it appears that Auguste managed to obtain a fee of two thousand francs for the work, and therefore felt he alone should receive a byline. Balzac was willing enough, since his own fee amounted to one thousand francs.

But this project marked a sharp turning point in the career of Honoré de Balzac as a literary hack. He gradually realized that he was doing virtually all of the work while he received only half of the fee. The publishers knew him now, and he no longer needed Auguste to handle the business arrangements. As for ideas, he himself had enough to burn.

The parting of the two young men was surprisingly amicable. Auguste must have known he had fared well at another's expense, and the life of a writer was beginning to pall on him. He was developing ambitions to follow his father onto the stage, and needed no persuasion to end the partnership. Balzac stood on his own.

Making a quick trip to Paris late in 1821, Balzac first visited his sister, Laurence, and found her in a sorry situation. Her husband had spent her entire dowry of thirty thousand francs and was hopelessly in debt. But he refused to work, and had become abusive to his bride of a few months.

Already despising his brother-in-law, Balzac persuaded Laurence to go home to their parents in Villeparisis. He himself remained behind to confront Montzaigle, and although the young man-about-town was reputedly a crack pistol shot and an excellent swordsman, he offered no rebuttal and made no attempt to challenge the plump, dowdy Balzac to a duel. He allowed himself to be called a scoundrel, and went off to get drunk.

Family honor satisfied, Balzac went calling on the publishers of cheap fiction, and was elated to discover he had achieved a measure of renown. Those who had already bought his work wanted more, and the others were willing to accept as many books as he cared to send them. He was regarded as an established professional now, and therefore would receive the standard rate of two thousand francs per book. He dared to ask for three thousand, and several publishers indicated they might pay him an extra thousand as a bonus if a book earned back the initial sum.

Balzac immediately sat down with paper and pencil in his parents' tiny Paris apartment and did some figuring. Suppose he wrote a total of four books per year. Suppose two of them earned him three thousand francs each, while the other two earned only two thousand each. In all he would bring in an annual income of ten thousand francs, a dazzling sum.

He wrote an ecstatic letter to Laure, explaining the situation to her, and then went a step farther. By exerting greater self-discipline, he declared, he well might be able to write an additional two books per year, making a total of six in all. Even if each of the "extra" books earned him only two thousand francs, his total annual income would be fourteen thousand. It should be remembered that, before his parents moved to Villeparisis, the entire family was able to live in comfort on about ten thousand francs per year. So it is small wonder that Balzac ended his letter with an enthralled, *"I shall soon be rich!"*

Returning to the home of his family, he locked himself into his room and began to write with a frenzy that has seldom been equaled. His contemporary, Alexandre Dumas the elder, is believed to have written approximately three hundred books in his lifetime, but he was assisted by a stable of at least four or five writers who did the actual work on manuscripts and turned them over to him for a final polishing job. Balzac, writing alone, achieved a record of more than one hundred long works of fiction, many of them running two to four volumes. This total excludes his plays, the magazines he edited and wrote, innumerable newspaper articles and many hundreds of critical essays.

It is literally impossible to make a catalogue of the novels Balzac wrote during his hack days because, in his enthusiasm, he developed a number of new pseudonyms, keeping each of them a secret from the publishers other than the one who was purchasing that specific work. Some of his biographers estimate that he wrote as many as ten to twelve books per year, spewing out complete manuscripts at a rate of one per month. Even the most assiduous literary detective work has failed to reveal the entire list.

The books he wrote under the name of Lord R'hoone alone indicate his industry and zeal. He returned to Villeparisis shortly before Christmas, 1821, with contracts bulging in his pockets. He was already at work on a novel called *Le Tartare*, and he wrote to Laure that he was about to begin writing no less than four others: *Le Vicaire des Ardennes*, *Le Savant*, *Odette de Champdivers* and *La Famille R'hoon*. The schedule was staggering, but he regarded it with equanimity, and actually dared to tell Laure that, in his spare time, he intended to write some "theatrical pieces."

Balzac was still courting fame, but was deliberately sidetracking himself for what he considered a relatively short period of time. He mapped out his future with great care, and on the surface, at least, his goals sounded sensible. For a few years he would earn as much money as he could by spewing out hack novels at a furious rate. Occasionally he would write a play. These efforts would bring him large sums of money which he would set aside, and then, when he had accumulated enough, he would give up the cheap novels and would turn to the serious fiction he believed he could and would write. If he set a figure in his own mind for the savings he wanted to pile up, he revealed it to no one.

Almost overnight he had become the biggest earner in the history of the Balzac family, in itself a feat not too difficult to achieve, yet one which should have caused satisfaction within the clan. Laure was delighted, as she always was with her brother's accomplishments, and began to press her husband, trying to nudge him toward greater success. Although she didn't realize it, she was beginning to emulate her mother. Laurence, the bride of only a few months, was so miserable when she surveyed the shambles of her marriage that she may not have been aware of what Balzac was or wasn't doing. If Henry had any feelings on the subject of his brother's expanding vocation, no one bothered to record them.

Papa was pleased, and enjoyed telling his neighbors, the local shopkeepers and the attractive young women of Villeparisis that he was responsible for his son's rise in the world. His own mind was filled with ideas for books, many of them based on his observations of a long lifetime, and he passed these along to his son. It so happens that he actually did contribute some thoughts to the word factory, and Balzac, being a dutiful son, listened respectfully. Whether he actually utilized any of his father's ideas, however, is a matter of conjecture. The young author revealed in letters to Laure and Dr. Nacquart that Papa was bombarding him with plots and characters, but he neglected to mention whether he found these contributions useful.

To the surprise of no one, Mama's tender heart was broken, and she made no secret of her reaction to friends, relatives and neighbors. In order to make certain that the eldest of her children was aware of the sorrow he was causing her, she pounded at him unmercifully, too. Balzac was required to join his parents each day at breakfast, and Mama complained. If he failed to appear at dinner or supper, she went to his room and repeated her tale of woe. He tried to escape by barricading his door, but her voice was so shrill that he didn't miss a syllable, and sometimes, when he was particularly rushed in trying to maintain his impossible schedule, he was forced to take refuge in the homes of neighbors so he could work on his manuscripts.

He had dishonored the fair name of *de* Balzac, Mama said. He could have been a lawyer, and by applying himself to his calling —something he had never done—he might have become a distingished member of the bar. Instead he had adopted a profession little better than that of a procurer, and her only consolation was that he didn't put the trash he wrote under his own name.

What made matters still worse was that writing did not really interest him, and he had become an author for only one reason: he had no regard for his mother's sensitivities, and was deliberately trying to hurt her.

But Mama managed to bear up under the situation. In fact, she charged Balzac for room and board, and when he protested mildly, saying her fee was so high that he could live far more cheaply elsewhere, she wept.

If Mme. Balzac failed to appreciate her son's efforts, the general reading public did not follow her example. It is significant that, even at this early stage of his career, when his talent was still raw and undeveloped, Balzac established a rapport with his audience. It may be true, as some of his biographers have declared, that he scarcely knew what he was doing and was too busy to write anything worth reading, but his sales indicate that he could tell a story about characters who caught and held the reader's imagination. He may have been scribbling rubbish, but his books sold so well that several publishers began to pay him the unprecedented sum of four thousand francs for a single work.

But the reputation he acquired on the fringes of the literary world did not disturb him, and his correspondence with Laure indicates that, if he could not laugh at himself, at least he could smile. He was bolstered by the ever-present thought that his situation was temporary. It wouldn't be too long before he acquired a small fortune, which would make him independent, and then he would write classics that would endure for centuries. In letter after letter he referred to himself as the future new Corneille or Voltaire, and in one note he said he was the "French Shakespeare of tomorrow."

Yet even the most compulsive worker needs occasional diversions other than those afforded by the company of a mother who was a termagent, a father who was a bore, a sister who had become a semi-recluse because her marriage was ruined, and a brother best described as a clod. Some neighbors, who had known the Balzac family in Paris, gave the young author the friendship he needed.

The head of this household was Gabriel de Berny, a wealthy minor aristocrat in his fifties who, because of ill health, allowed his wife to supervise the management of their finances. Louise-Antoinette-Laure de Berny was a true member of the nobility. Born at Versailles in 1777, she was highly regarded by the restored Bourbons because the "martyred monarchs," Louis XVI and Marie Antoinette, had been her godparents. She was the mother of nine legitimate children, seven of them living, and several of her daughters were close friends of Laure and Laurence Balzac.

There was one skeleton in Mme. de Berny's closet, and she made no attempt to hide it, so the Balzac family undoubtedly knew the details. At the turn of the century she and her husband had lived apart for several years, and she had given birth to an illegitimate daughter. The child's father had vanished into the Sicilian mists from which he had emerged, and the girl, Julie Campi, lived with the De Berny family. The Balzacs referred to her in correspondence as a great beauty.

It was difficult to find suitable tutors in a town the size of Villeparisis, and Balzac, aware of the problems the De Bernys faced in trying to educate their younger children, offered his part-time services on a volunteer basis. Laure felt certain her brother was merely utilizing an excuse to see something of the ravishing Julie, and Mme. Balzac was afraid her son would heap fresh disgrace on her already bowed shoulders by becoming involved in a romance with the illegitimate offspring of an aristocrat.

Balzac was too busy to listen to his mother's scoldings. A new market was opening for his writing, and he signed a number of contracts for a series of non-fiction books. Called *Codes,* these volumes contained advice, presumably witty, on a variety of specific subjects, among them marriage, social conduct and fashion. Turning to this specialized brand of non-fiction with his accustomed vengeance, the shy, inexperienced young semi-recluse enlightened his middle-class reading public with streams of supposedly witty advice on how to dress, how to behave at the theatre or in a salon, and how to make love to one's marital partner.

The success of the *Codes* was remarkable. Balzac, whose authorship was kept a strict secret, was paid three to four thousand francs per book, while the publisher, Horace Raisson, earned at least twelve thousand on each. Inasmuch as these figures did not come to light for many years, it must be presumed that Balzac himself had no idea his popularity had increased dramatically.

By the time he celebrated his twenty-third birthday in 1822, however, work was no longer his sole reason for existence, and he found something to think about other than accumulating a nest egg. As his mother and sister so shrewdly guessed, he fell in love, but not with Julie Campi.

The object of his ardor was her mother, Mme. de Berny, a grandmother whose age was almost double his own. No member of either family guessed his secret, and some months passed before Mme. de Berny herself realized that Balzac was smitten.

Several generations of amateur psychiatrists have examined this romance and then proclaimed the obvious: Balzac was seeking a substitute for the mother who, ever since his birth, had been repeatedly rejecting, abusing and humiliating him. Although it is true that Laure de Berny provided him with a highly satisfactory mother substitute, she was far more than that to him.

Her portraits made during this period and in later years reveal that she was an exceptionally handsome woman who looked much younger than her years, and whose supple, slender figure certainly was not that of a woman who had brought ten children into the world. She had masses of dark hair, brown eyes emphasized by long lashes, and an almost perfectly formed, oval face. Her complexion was clear, and her skin was surprisingly free of wrinkles.

Mme. de Berny's own unhappy life with a crochety semi-invalid had given her a compassionate understanding of the problems of others, and she happened to be endowed with common-sense attitudes that were rare in the aristocrats of her era. An omnivorous reader, she had developed an unusual talent for literary criticism, and the trials she had undergone in rearing seven legitimate children and one illegitimate daughter had made her unusually tolerant. Although she herself may not have known it, she was also an exceptionally passionate woman; as she would discover, no man had ever aroused her.

No one knows when Balzac first became interested in her or recognized the extent of his own emotional involvement. In later years he disclosed that he had wanted to declare himself on a number of occasions, but shyness and the absurdity of the situation had forced him to remain silent. He tried to convey his sentiments with his eyes, but the unsuspecting Mme. de Berny failed to recognize the signs.

So, in the spring of 1822, possibly within a week one way or the other of his twenty-third birthday, Balzac took the plunge in a way that best suited his author's temperament: he wrote Mme. de Berny a letter, which still exists a century and a half later. Exercising great preliminary care, he told her, "*At first you will think this is one of the best jokes ever invented, a fitting subject for your own type of humor.*" Then, gradually, his nuances balanced and calculated, he warmed to his theme:

Think, madame, that far from you there exists a being whose spirit, greatly privileged, covers all distances, flies to you through the air and is constantly near you; who delights to share in your life and your sentiments; who now pities you, now desires you, but always loves you with that ardor and freshness of love which flowers only in youth. A being to whom you are more than a friend, more than a sister, almost a mother but still more than all this; a kind of visible divinity to whom his every action is referred. Indeed, if I dream of grandeur and fame it is that I may use them as a steppingstone to bring me nearer to you; if I attempt great things it is in your name.

To me, though you do not know it, you are truly a protectress. Think finally of everything that is tender, loving, delicate and glowing in the human heart. I believe these things to be in my heart when I think of you.

When Mme. de Berny recovered from her initial shock, she laughed at him. Balzac had anticipated just such a reaction, and wrote her another letter. She became concerned, and tried to reason with him, pointing out that one of her sons, who had died several years earlier, had been almost precisely his own age.

The undismayed Balzac replied promptly: "*Think of me as your son, then, but as far more than your son, madame!*"

Alarmed by his persistence and not wanting to appear ridiculous, Mme. de Berny reminded him that she was his mother's age. In fact, she said, she was forty-five, a year older than her friend, Mme. de Balzac.

His reply was ready: "*If I were a woman, even of forty-five, and still pretty, I would behave very differently from you! I would surrender to love and seek to rediscover the delights of youth, its innocent illusions, its simplicities and exquisite privileges.*"

The battle raged unabated. Occasionally Mme. de Berny replied to Balzac's arguments in writing, but more often she told him in person that he sought the impossible. He refused to become discouraged, however, and remained unmoved by her arguments. His letters became longer, more demanding, more passionate. Already certain in his own mind that he would be of interest to posterity, he took pains to preserve his side of the correspondence. After writing each of his letters he copied it in a bold hand and then carefully filed the original.

Neither then nor later did Mme. de Berny know there were copies of his correspondence in his possession. Many years later, on her deathbed, she destroyed his letters by throwing them into a burning hearth, and died falsely believing that the story would never become known.

In the spring and summer of 1822, however, she was thinking only in terms of the immediate present, and was annoyed. She sent her young suitor an ultimatum, informing him that the door of her house would be closed to him and would remain closed unless he desisted.

Instantly responsive to her moods, Balzac capitulated. He was heartbroken, he declared in a short note, but rather than be deprived of the sight of her, he would do as she directed.

There the matter seemed to rest. But Mme. de Berny's stand

was not as rigid as it appeared on the surface, as Balzac well knew. Had she been completely sincere in her desire to be rid of him, she would have ordered him not to return to her house under any circumstances. The two young daughters he was tutoring could have been sent off to the boarding school she could well afford. Or, for that matter, a full-time tutor could have been hired in Paris and brought to Villeparisis.

But Balzac continued to go each day for an hour to the De Berny house, and each day he sighed, stared pensively at his love and otherwise made certain she was aware of his persisting, deep regard for her.

Laure de Berny was flattered. She and her eldest daughters frequently were believed to be sisters, and she was proud of her ability to dress as a young woman. Unlike Mme. de Balzac and others of her own age she did not hide her figure beneath drab, voluminous dresses and thick shawls. Now she had proof that she not only looked young, but that a man the age of her late son found her desirable.

Recognizing the chink in her armor, Balzac waited a few weeks, and then, finding her depressed one day, renewed his campaign by letter. A few evenings later she walked through the garden with him, presumably seeing him to the front gate, and permitted him to kiss her.

Thereafter Mme. de Berny's defenses crumbled, and in mid-summer, 1822, she became Balzac's mistress. All thoughts of the differences in their ages vanished from her mind when he aroused her to greater depths of passion than she had ever known, and she soon discovered that she reciprocated his love. Within a short time it was she who became the aggressor, and casting aside all discretion, made no secret of her feelings.

It was Balzac's turn to become embarrassed, and the tone of his correspondence changed. Now he begged her to exercise greater caution in front of her family, not to mention in the presence of outsiders. While it was true that her relationship with her husband had deteriorated to the point that he no longer cared what she did, or with whom, even the most indifferent of spouses would be forced to take a stand if an open scandal threatened to make him a laughingstock.

The affair was not kept a secret from either family. The married daughters of the middle-aged, smitten woman were horrified, and openly snubbed Balzac. His sisters, Laure in particular, recovered their equanimity after their initial surprise, and having already realized he was no ordinary person to whom the usual rules and restrictions of the middle class applied, they accepted the affair with resignation, if not with approval.

Mama Balzac was kept in the dark by everyone concerned for as long as possible. But Balzac visited the De Berny house daily, and she knew his volunteer tutoring could not be responsible for his devotion. Julie, Mme. de Berny's illegitimate daughter, was still the principal object of Mama's suspicions for a time, but the girl went off to visit friends in Switzerland—and Balzac's daily visits continued. So his mother finally pieced together the truth.

At first she held both of the culprits responsible, and for a time stopped speaking to Mme. de Berny. But this attitude wasn't practical, since there were no more than three or four women in the little town of Villeparisis whom Mme. Balzac considered her equals, and she well knew that Mme. de Berny stood a notch above her on the social ladder. So, inevitably, she concentrated her fire on her son, who became the sole villain. She had cause to berate him now, she felt, and insisted that his immorality was driving her to a premature grave. Most of her diatribes were delivered at the breakfast table, in the presence of her own illegitimate younger son, but Mama was not one to be deterred by the incongruity of her own position.

Balzac shut out the sound of her voice, accepted the quiet congratulations of his father, who was immersed in affairs of his own, and concentrated on the mountains of work that would have inundated a lesser man. His romance did not interfere with his writing, and actually appeared to increase his already gargantuan capacities for work. He began to accept assignments for the writing of newspaper and magazine articles which were, in the main, short versions of the *Codes*. These pieces were done under a variety of pseudonyms, and as he neither kept records nor filed copies for posterity, no one has ever known just how much of this sort of writing he actually did. For more than one hundred years a favorite sport of literary detectives was the tracing of articles published during this period to Balzac, but even today, a century and a half after the work first saw the light of print, the list is admittedly incomplete.

Before long everyone in Villeparisis was whispering about the May-November affair, and Mama Balzac could no longer tolerate the humiliation. If distance separated the lovers, she reasoned, they would soon recover from their infatuation. So she sent Balzac off to visit his sister, Laure de Surville, in the little Norman town of Bayeux. He agreed with such alacrity that some biographers believe that, as in the past, Mama cowed him. But that appears to be too pat an explanation.

By accepting the order and leaving Villeparisis, Balzac was killing several birds with one stone. He was escaping from his mother's incessant scoldings. He could discuss his work with the sympathetic Laure, who always encouraged him, and he could work without interruption in her house. As for Mme. de Berny, he could meet her in Paris whenever they wished, as both had legitimate reasons to go to the city, and there they would be far removed from the eyes of the small-town gossips. The solution was perfect.

The relationship with his mistress may have been the best thing that had ever happened to Balzac. He was maturing rapidly, thanks to her interest in his work, her correction of his gauche appearance and, above all, her ability to give him a confidence in himself that he had never before felt. He himself best describes, in the pages of his *Madame Firmiani*, what happened to him:

Have you ever the good fortune to meet a woman whose melodious voice lends her words an enchantment which equally invests her whole bearing? A woman who knows when to speak and when to be silent, who claims one's attention with a perfect sense of delicacy, who chooses her words with felicity and speaks a lan-

guage that is remarkable for its purity? Her teasings are like caresses, her criticism does not wound; she does not handle things in a quarrelsome spirit, but is content to guide a conversation and to bring it to a close at the right moment. She behaves with smiling charm, her courtesy is not forced, and she can make an effort without becoming overanxious. The respect one renders her is never more than a sweet shadow; she never tires you, but when you leave her you are satisfied both with her and with yourself. And you find all the things with which she surrounds herself stamped with the same pleasing grace. Everything in her house flatters the eye, and the air you breathe is like the air of home. This woman is natural. All she does is effortless, she does not show off, she expresses her feelings simply because she feels sincerely.

She is both tender and cheerful, and her sympathy is displayed in a way that is particularly agreeable. You will love this angel so ardently that even if she were to make a mistake you would be ready to admit that she is right.

The true miracle of the relationship is that Mme. de Berny allowed herself to be swept off her feet by a clumsy, badly dressed young man who had no interest in personal cleanliness, by an oaf with the braying laugh of a butcher's assistant, by a clod who picked his nose in public and sometimes ate with his knife when he was particularly hungry, in short, by a man whose physical appearance was unprepossessing, if not somewhat revolting, and who lacked all the social graces.

It is even more miraculous to peer ahead into Balzac's future and discover that many women reacted as Mme. de Berny did. When he wanted a woman, she became his, and only rarely did he fail. Almost without exception the women whose path crossed his, including many with whom he did not have affairs, found him fascinating.

George Sand, who became his friend but had no real romantic interest in him, may have best described the phenomenon. Honoré de Balzac displayed, in person, the same deep understanding

1. Balzac's father, Bernard-François Balzac, 1745-1829. (Musée Balzac; Photographie Bulloz)

2. Balzac's mother, Laure Sallambier Balzac, 1778-1854, as a young woman. (Musée Balzac; Photographie Bulloz)

3. Pastel of Balzac's sister Laure as a child. (Roger Viollet)

4. View of the Collège of Vendôme in Balzac's time. (Musée Balzac; Photographie Bulloz)

5. Madame Laure de Berny, Balzac's first mistress and long-time confidante. (Roger Viollet)

6. The house in which Balzac installed his first printing shop, 17 Rue Visconti. (Roger Viollet)

7. Madame Zulma Carraud, Balzac's lifelong friend. (Musée Balzac; Photographie Bulloz)

3. Balzac's house on the Rue Nationale in Tours. (Roger Viollet)

9. Presumed to be a portrait of Balzac's mother. (Maison de Balzac; Lauros-Giraudon)

and sympathy for women that appeared in the pages of his great novels, she said. His ability to *know* how a woman felt or reacted in any given situation was unerring and often uncanny. It may be that, wanting love so desperately, he was capable of comprehending the nature of those who might give him that love.

The correspondence of a score of women, Mme. de Berny among them, is filled with references to his hypnotic voice and eyes. Men found his voice rasping and a trifle uncouth, but he communicated his own excitement, his own genuine intensity of feeling when dealing with a woman. Balzac, the author, concentrated on a book to the exclusion of everything else around him, and that book, while he was writing it, became his whole world. Balzac, the man, concentrated equally hard on the objects of his romantic and sexual desires, and a woman felt, quite rightly, that she was his whole world. What she was unable to guess was that he could switch from one of his worlds to another instantly, at will, and after adoring a woman one moment, could completely forget her the next. As Mme. de Berny and all the others would learn, his was an exceptionally complicated personality.

IV

Thanks to the influence of Mme. de Berny, Mme. Balzac lost her influence over her son. Soon after Balzac went to Laure de Surville's house in Bayeux, in the summer of 1822, Mama wrote a letter to her daughter in which her despair is evident:

I asked Honoré to give me his word that he would revise his manuscripts carefully. I told him to submit them to somebody with more experience in writing than he had himself. Honoré acted as if nothing I said to him was of the slightest importance. He did not listen to me. Honoré is so sure of himself that he refuses to submit his manuscripts to anyone.

The older woman who had become his surrogate mother, his friend, his adviser, and who would be his active mistress for a decade, effectively cut his apron strings and brought to an end the harm his mother was doing. He had gained the courage to lead his own life as he himself saw fit, and no longer cared what his mother thought. Many years later, when he was middle-aged, he paid a moving tribute to Mme. de Berny in a letter to Laure:

She was my mother, friend, family, companion and adviser. She made me a writer, she gave me the sympathy I needed when I was young, she guided my taste, she wept and laughed with me like a sister, she came to me every day like a healing sleep that allays one's pain. Without her I doubtless would have died.

When great storms threatened to submerge me, she kept my head above water by her encouragement and acts of sacrifice. She stimulated in me the pride which protects a man against all the baseness of the world. If I survive, I owe it to her. She was everything to me.

Independent, busier than ever, Balzac worked from dawn until dinner in his sister's house, then returned to his manuscripts after eating. Frequently he went off to Paris on business, and Laure refrained from mentioning to him her suspicion that he was holding secret meetings with Mme. de Berny.

In the autumn of 1822 the Balzac family's situation changed rather dramatically. A nephew whom Mama had befriended and taken into the house to occupy Balzac's room, in return for a small weekly stipend, died unexpectedly and named her as his principal heir. She had almost one hundred thousand unexpected gold francs in her purse now, and she quickly found a way to solve the problem that had been causing her so much pain. The family would give up the house in Villeparisis and return to Paris.

The new apartment, located on the Rue de Roi Doré, was large, comfortable and included a suite for Balzac that consisted of a fair-sized bedchamber and a tiny sitting room in which he could work. Mama was determined to woo him back to the family hearth.

Balzac outsmarted her, or so he thought. Quarters in the family apartment were less expensive than a place of his own, there were servants to wait on him and cook nourishing meals, and when he wanted conversation, Papa was always close at hand. Now that he was free of Mama, it wouldn't matter what she said or did.

So he not only moved into the apartment, but, on November 1, 1822, he signed a formal agreement with his father, not only writing the contract himself but insisting that Bernard-François sign it. Balzac obligated himself to pay one hundred francs per month for his room and board, and either party could terminate the contract on one month's notice. He would be charged separately for his laundry, light and firewood, and he agreed to pay the full price for his meals even on those occasions when he dined elsewhere.

He wrote happily to Laure that his position would be that of a lodger in their parents' home. He had insulated himself, and would be impervious to Mama's attempts to interfere. Not for the first time in his life, and not for the last, either, he seriously underestimated Mama.

A few weeks after the reunited Balzac family returned to Paris, in January 1823, tragedy struck suddenly. Grandma Sallambier suffered a stroke and died, and Balzac lost his most devoted supporter. His parents determined to maintain prestige, gave the old lady an elaborate, expensive funeral. Many years later Balzac observed, "Of all the dozens who attended my beloved grandmother's funeral, I alone shed tears. My mother was too busy counting the francs in her estate. My father had always hated her, and was privately relieved. My sisters were engrossed in their own problems, and my brother, as always, was incapable of feeling anything for anyone other than himself."

Yet he was too busy to grieve. Life in Paris was far more hectic than the bucolic existence he had enjoyed in a remote country village, and he soon found himself caught up in a variety of new projects. He became a major contributor to two notorious magazines, *Le Corsaire* and *Le Pilote*, which specialized in salacious gossip about prominent persons. Libel laws were loosely defined, and if one wrote under ever-changing pseudonyms, he was likely to escape trouble. Besides, the pay was good, the accuracy of what one wrote was never questioned, and the editors did not insist that a writer check the sources of his stories. A young man endowed with a vivid imagination could add appreciably to his income.

In the early months of 1823 Balzac had his first brush with the censors and lost the battle. A new novel, *Le Vicaire des Ardennes*, was banned as immoral, and Balzac was pained because he would not receive two thousand francs due under the terms of his contract. The story was simple—and shocking. The heroine of the book was a middle-aged noblewoman who more or less fell in love with a young vicar, but believed her feelings toward him were strictly maternal. At the climax of the book she discovered he was her illegitimate son who had disappeared in childhood, having been removed from her sphere of influence by his father, a bishop.

This novel has sometimes been cited as proof of Balzac's contempt for the Church, but the argument may not be valid. It is possible, even probable, that he wrote another of his many cheap, melodramatic books for only one reason, to make money quickly. Women of the French middle class were always eager to buy novels about the sexual misdeeds of the clergy.

Authors whose works were banned by the censors had the right of appeal, but the board of censorship rarely reversed its findings, and Balzac did not bother. It was far simpler to put aside *Le Vicaire*, and by increasing his already frenzied writing schedule, he made up the difference in income.

Perhaps the greatest benefit Balzac derived from the family's move to Paris was the ending of his hermitlike existence. In spite of the long hours he spent at his writing desk he was forced to go out into the world, and he soon discovered there were other young men with whom he shared a point of view as well as a vocation. These authors, almost all of them cynics who turned out books under pseudonyms, were accustomed to observing life and exchanging opinions on the passing scene from a small bistro, the Café Voltaire, which was located a short distance from the Théâtre de l'Odéon.

A publisher invited Balzac to meet him there one day, and it wasn't long before the young author became a regular patron. He arranged his writing schedule so he could reach the Voltaire by mid-afternoon, and he spent two or three hours there, chatting with colleagues. There were others, attracted by the presence of writers, who came to the Voltaire too, and Balzac soon struck up friendships with young professors from the Sorbonne, idealistic politicians and progressive clergymen who wanted to reform the Church.

This period marked Balzac's first encounters in depth with his intellectual peers, and the experience was the equivalent of a post-graduate course in human nature. Always affable, always grateful to be accepted, he watched and listened, he stored away fragments that would emerge years later in some of his rich characters, and he expanded his own limited concepts.

For the first time, he began to think in adult terms, and his lifelong cynical convictions were reinforced. He held a low opinion of the restored Bourbon monarchy, but he could not believe that the quality of life would be improved under a republican form of government. He no longer attended church services, although he still believed in God, but he held nothing against those who supported the Church. People needed aspirations and goals, ideals and crutches, and organized religion was the answer for many, just as his own search for love and fame supported and sustained him.

There were only two men in all French history whom he admired. One was Napoleon Bonaparte, for whom he felt a blind hero worship, in part because he saw their situations as similar. Napoleon had been short, homely, rejected and poor, too, but had conquered a world. What he had done, Honoré Balzac—who still rarely signed his name with a *de*—also could do. His other god was Voltaire, whom he wanted to emulate for two reasons. Financially, the great eighteenth-century author had been the most successful man of letters of all time in his profession, and only Balzac's contemporary, Victor Hugo, would better his record. Even more important, Balzac was developing a conscious appreciation of Voltaire's contempt for the sham in human nature, the dishonesty and double-dealing that marked human relations.

Oddly, Balzac formed no lasting associations with any of the colleagues he met at the Café Voltaire. He was still too unsure of himself to feel he was the equal of the others, too shy to either accept dinner invitations or extend invitations to others. He knew he was writing trash, and therefore could not think of himself as a respectable author; apparently it did not occur to him that his stories were no worse than the published efforts of the others.

Nevertheless such minor figures as Victor Ducange and Henri Monnier left their mark on him. They were instrumental in broadening his world, forcing him to spend at least a portion of his waking hours outside of the dream world he created in his own mind.

In the summer of 1824 the Balzac family situation changed again. Mama's cousin owned the house in which they had lived in Villeparisis, and as he was having some financial problems, he offered to sell it for a bargain price of ten thousand francs. Papa, who was approaching his eightieth year, was sick of city living, and felt he would survive longer if he could take long walks in the country—and renew his virility with country girls. Mama, always one to snatch at a bargain, could not refuse the offer.

The entire family took it for granted that Balzac would return to Villeparisis, too. But he refused to contemplate the idea, and not only insisted he would remain in Paris, but abruptly ended the discussion by renting a small apartment on the top floor of a building on the unfashionable Rue de Tournon. He wanted to work, he said, and could accomplish far more by living alone. In addition he had no desire to be cut off from the literary world, in which he was beginning to be accepted.

Mama was convinced he was merely making excuses, and wrote long letters of complaint to Laure. Honoré, she said, wanted to stay in Paris for just one reason: it would be far more convenient for him to entertain "the lady from the other end of town" if he lived alone in the city.

Mme. Balzac's suspicions were grounded in some truth, to be

sure. It had been difficult for Balzac and Mme. de Berny to meet in private; the only place available to them had been the small De Berny town house in the city, which various members of the family used, and there was always the risk they would be surprised during a rendezvous by one of Mme. de Berny's children.

So the convenience of an apartment of his own as a place of assignation undoubtedly appealed to him. But far more was at stake, and he needed to live alone in order to get his work done. He had learned in recent months that it was no longer possible for him to dwell under his mother's roof, even though he was now twenty-five years of age. Mama was unrelenting in her efforts to bind him to her; she needed a whipping boy, and would be lost without him to abuse.

Always careless with money, he had bought some new clothes, and also had purchased some expensive gifts for Mme. de Berny. As a result he had gone into debt, but Mama had offered to advance him enough to pay off all of his obligations. Her reason, she wrote sententiously to Laure, was her desire to "allow his talents free play, so that he may at last write something we can all acknowledge."

Recognizing the trap his mother had set for him, Balzac evaded it. He, too, was confiding in Laure, and wrote to her that he had done the whole family a favor by taking his apartment. Now Mama would have so much bile to release from her system that, by the time she was done complaining about him, she would have no energy to attack her husband or her other children.

Balzac settled into the apartment in late summer, 1824, and Mme. de Berny soon visited him there. She was ambitious for him, and recognizing his latent talent, wanted him to write works more lasting than the melodramatic novels he turned out under a pseudonym. Goaded by the mistress who believed in him, but still finding it necessary to earn his living, Balzac wrote several more *Codes*. They were still crude, but his satiric observations on the failures and pretensions of mankind were somewhat reminiscent of Voltaire and Dean Swift.

Provincials, he wrote, complained that Paris was filled with pickpockets, thieves and robbers. These good people failed to realize that French society would collapse if there were no criminals. Thousands of policemen would be thrown out of work. Lawyers would starve, and there would be no need for judges. To be sure, he added, lawyers could perform many sly, underhanded tricks without the knowledge of their clients, and thus perpetuate the true Parisian criminal tradition. Drawing on his own knowledge of the law and law offices, he went on at some length mocking the profession that his family had wanted him to make his own.

One brief quotation will suffice to indicate flavor of the *Codes* Balzac wrote during this time. Lawyers, he declared, were so expensive that few clients could afford their services. But there was a way to take care of one's legal needs, provided one understood the system. Lawyers were wealthy because their clerks, who did all the work, were so badly underpaid they were near starvation. So he advised:

Take the lawyer's clerk to dinner without bothering to see his employer. Lavish truffles, rare dishes and rich wines on him, observing that three hundred francs spent in this way will save you three thousand. The clerk will give you the same advice he would have put on paper for his employer, and you will win your suit at a relatively small cost.

The writing of humorous material required enormous research, and Balzac found himself busy day and night. He felt increasingly ashamed of the novels he was writing under a pseudonym, and felt that the *Codes,* including a *Physiologie du mariage* he could not complete, came closer to what he wanted to achieve. He was a philosopher, he wrote Mme. de Berny, a man whose deep thinking was a natural outgrowth of the philosophical concepts propounded by that original thinker, his own aged father, whom he admired so much.

This period was one of the loneliest periods Balzac ever endured. His small apartment was plainly furnished, and he enjoyed few luxuries. He was earning enough to indulge himself in an occasional feast, but he was far too busy to dine in splendor, and he discovered he had little appetite when he ate alone.

The highspots of his life were Mme. de Berny's visits, but she came to Paris infrequently, spending two days there every three weeks, and the rest of his time he spent by himself. He was in love with her, to be sure, but he wasn't necessarily devoted to the principle that he couldn't make love to other women in her absence. Unfortunately, he was too shy, too conscious of his ugly face and thick body, his bad manners and his uneasiness in the presence of ladies. So he sat for an hour or two at the Café Voltaire each day and watched the procession of untouchables, the lovely women of Paris.

Overwork made Balzac ill, but he was afraid his mother would insist on returning to Paris to take care of him if she learned of his condition, so he mentioned his ailment to no one, and for two weeks remained in bed, so weak he could not go out for fresh supplies when the food in his larder was exhausted.

His illness increased his feeling of despair, and he could not shake it off after he recovered. The cheap novels that were his principal source of income were ephemeral, and he was building nothing for a long-range future.

His self-disgust was so great that, according to accounts written years later by several acquaintances, he seriously contemplated suicide. In justice to Balzac, his correspondence makes no mention of a possible suicide attempt.

He was in such a melancholy state, however, that Mme. de Berny came to Paris late in 1824, taking up more or less permanent lodging in her small town house, which was located only a few blocks from Balzac's apartment. His mood improved accordingly, but he remained dissatisfied. Not even the proximity of the woman who meant so much to him could disguise the truth that he was acquiring no standing in his profession and that the renown he sought was still remote.

His faith in his own ability to write great masterpieces remained undiminished, although he was thinking in terms of philosophical treatises, metaphysical studies and other serious works. The possibility that he might become a major novelist did not cross his mind.

But he knew he could not write good and bad books simultaneously, and as long as he had to earn his living with his pen he had no opportunity to concentrate on what he wanted to do. Perhaps, if he found some way to earn large sums of money, he could give up the cheap novels and begin his writing career in earnest.

Mme. de Berny's influence on him at this critical juncture was vital. She urged him to think in terms of giving up his writing for something more solid. He would be twenty-six years old soon, and the world of business might be more lasting than the hand-to-mouth existence he had been leading. Balzac brooded and was ripe for something new.

At just this time fate seemed to beckon. One of his publishers was an ambitious bookseller, Urbain Canel, who took the young author into his confidence. Canel had conceived of a business venture that was certain to make him wealthy within a very short time. There was a steady, ever-increasing market for the great works of French literature, but most people could not afford to buy more than a volume or two at a time. Now the importation from the Orient of a new, very thin rice paper could create a revolution. Canel proposed to print the complete works of a great master in a single volume, using small but legible type. The first would be La Fontaine, to be followed by Molière.

Honoré de Balzac was endowed with more than a gifted imagination. As he proved repeatedly throughout his life, he had the ability to grasp the essentials of a sound business proposition, the instinct to recognize the commercial value of a promising idea. Any one of a half-dozen ventures might have made him a multimillionaire, but there was one flaw in his character that repeatedly thwarted him. Like all compulsives he was impatient, and expected every enterprise to pay handsome dividends overnight.

In any event, his enthusiasm for Canel's venture was overwhelming. It was apparent to him that there would be a tremendous market for single-volume works of the masters, and he asked, rather diffidently, whether he might have a share in the plan.

Canel, who had no funds and no hope of acquiring any, was delighted to take in a partner, provided Balzac could supply the capital.

Twenty thousand francs was needed, and Balzac had only two thousand. He borrowed nine thousand from two other publishers, agreeing to pay them exorbitant interest, and at Mme. de Berny's insistence, she loaned him the remaining nine thousand.

The Balzac family was delighted. Papa, who always liked new adventures, applauded heartily. Mama said she was relieved, because any vocation was better than the flimsy profession that had occupied him. Laure, who was becoming more like her mother, thought that Balzac would become respectable at last. If Henry had any opinions in the matter, they have been lost to posterity. Only Laurence, sorely beset by her own problems, urged her brother to be cautious, to devote all of his efforts to the world of business and to let nothing dissuade him.

Balzac threw himself into the enterprise with all of the enormous enthusiasm he was capable of mustering. He hired an engraver, he bought paper, he conferred with printers and he dined with the literary critics who would give the books the publicity they would need to achieve sales. He also wrote introductions for both the La Fontaine and the Molière volumes.

By this time he had become the sole owner of the enterprise, which had frightened Canel, who no longer saw it as a profitable enterprise. The costs were too high to sell the books at a reasonable price, and he was afraid the public would not respond to a high-priced book. Balzac suffered no such qualms, and arranged to have the Molière printed as soon as the La Fontaine was off the presses. In that way he would save money because the printers would quote him a special fee for the double job. Unfortunately, he needed another five thousand francs in a hurry, and began to look around for it.

Laure de Surville and her husband had moved to Versailles, and through their friend Mme. Delannoy they had met a fascinating lady. The widow of one of Napoleon's generals, Junot, who had been created Duke d'Abrantès by the Emperor, the wealthy Laure d'Abrantès was notorious for her many love affairs, among them one with Prince Metternich, the Austrian Chancellor, who was the principal architect of the post-Napoleonic world. Her hair was somewhat darker than it had been in her younger days, but she still called herself a blonde. No one knew her real age, but in 1825 she liked to tell people she was in her early forties.

The duchess was still attractive as well as wealthy, and the combination of her beauty, her aristocratic position in society and her money fascinated Balzac, who met her through his sister. Perhaps he could obtain a loan from her and make her his mistress, too! It would be a real accomplishment to sleep with the woman who had slept with Metternich.

The Duchess d'Abrantès was no fool. The intense young man amused her, and she agreed to become his friend. But she would not go to bed with him, and she refused to make him the loan. So Balzac, in order to keep his venture afloat, had to obtain the five thousand francs from a friend of the Balzac family named Assonvillez.

In August 1825, there was a brief, tragic diversion. Balzac's younger sister, Laurence, died in childbirth at the home of her parents. She had made the mistake of going back to her husband for a short time, but had become convinced he could not change his habits, and had left him for a second time. Balzac was convinced she had died of a broken heart, and had seen her early death as inevitable. He went home for the funeral, and when he returned to Paris he became more active than ever.

Showing the same furious drives as a businessman that he had displayed as the author of cheap novels, the *Codes* and numerous articles, he worked from early morning until late at night. He supervised the work of the printers and engravers, he visited the warehouses where the paper for his books was stored, and he assiduously cultivated the all-important literary critics.

He also made the time to see Mme. de Berny regularly, and in spare moments he dashed off long, impassioned love letters to the Duchess d'Abrantès, whom he continued to pursue. Often on

Sundays he went out to Versailles to see her, and he was relieved when she moved into her Paris town house. Now he would be forced to spend less time in travel when he wanted to woo her.

In September the duchess finally capitulated and became his mistress. But his relationship with Mme. de Berny did not diminish in any way, and she remained his emotional support. Certainly he was not the first or the last to enjoy the favors of two women during the same period, but what made his situation remarkable was the intensity of both affairs. No matter what Balzac did, he threw himself into the enterprise with an all-consuming zeal, and he actually managed to persuade himself that he was totally committed to each of these older women. When he wrote to Mme. de Berny, when he conversed with her and when he went to bed with her he believed she was the only woman in his life. He felt precisely the same way in his dealings with the duchess, and convinced himself that she alone was important to him.

But there are complications when a man is writing love letters to two women at the same time. Both of these ladies were named Laure, which also happened to be the name of Balzac's mother and of his sister. He addressed Mme. de Berny by her Christian name in his impassioned notes to her, but his delicacy of feeling did not permit him to do the same when he wrote to the duchess. He solved the problem by finding new salutations for his second mistress, and called her by pet names he invented for the purpose.

Late in 1825 the first printing of the La Fontaine book appeared, and the literary critics co-operated by proclaiming it a triumph for French literature. But Balzac now made a major mistake. He was sorely in need of cash to repay the loans made to him by his publishers, so he priced the book at twenty francs.

The booksellers of Paris refused to buy the volume outright at three quarters of the retail price, as was the custom of the time, so Balzac was forced to let them take copies on consignment. In all, three thousand copies had been printed, and he wrote to Mme. de Berny, who had gone to Villeparisis for a visit, that he expected the entire edition to sell out by Christmas. He was so certain he would be out of debt that he began to discuss a second printing.

By January 1826, a total of fifty copies of the La Fontaine had been sold. The public obviously could not afford to buy the book at such a high price. Balzac became desperate, and reduced the retail price to fourteen francs, then twelve and finally ten. He would lose money if the book sold for ten francs, but he needed cash to make at least partial payments to his creditors. The printers, the engravers, the paper sellers all were beginning to hound him for money.

Balzac's financial situation was complicated by additional factors. When he had received his initial loans he hadn't paid out all of the money for paper and printing, but had kept a portion of it for his own living expenses. Balzac was totally incompetent in money matters, and when he had one thousand francs in his pocket, he invariably spent at least two thousand.

A man of business needed appropriate clothing in order to make the right impression, and Balzac purchased a complete wardrobe, specializing in the somber attire that wealthy middle-class men were wearing. The entertainment of literary critics cost money, and as he frequently brought these men to his apartment for an evening of talk and wine, he needed the right setting. So he threw out the simple furnishings that had served him when he had been a mere hack writer, and bought quantities of expensive furniture.

Balzac needed cash so desperately that he finally sold the better part of three thousand volumes for the remainder price of five francs per book. He used this money to pay off the most demanding of his creditors, but he was still in debt in the amount of fifteen thousand francs.

Had he returned to his writing at this point he might have been able to pay off his obligations over the period of two or three years. Instead, he had a new idea. Since his troubles had been caused by the high costs of printing, he could solve the problem boldly by becoming a printer himself. Captivated by the notion, he planned to start his newest venture by printing Molière in a single volume, then doing the works of Corneille and Racine.

There were a number of hurdles to be overcome. He needed presses, he must hire competent help, and, above all, he required a small fortune to launch his new business. Undaunted by obstacles that would have discouraged a more sensible man, Balzac launched his campaign. Through publishers with whom he had done business as an author, he met a master foreman named Barbier, whom he immediately made his partner, and Barbier, in turn, took him to a printing shop in the Rue de Marais, near the Faubourg Saint Germain, which was for sale. The price was sixty thousand francs.

Instead of declaring himself bankrupt, which would have been a far more sensible course of action, Balzac sought a backer. At this point, his private indiscretions suddenly brought new complications that interfered with his work: Mme. de Berny discovered he was also involved with another woman. She complained bitterly to Balzac's mother.

Mama was duly shocked and took the part of her old friend. Both ladies wrote the culprit long, reproachful letters, and, aware of his precarious financial position, they impolitely applied pressure. Mama was pleased that her son wanted to go into a bourgeois business of which she approved, and wrote to Laure de Berny that she might soon be able to stop crying herself to sleep over him. It so happened that she and Papa had thirty thousand francs to invest in a sound enterprise, and would be willing to advance Balzac the money. But they placed a condition on the loan: he had to give up the duchess.

Balzac weighed his mother's terms and weakened. Additional pressure was now applied. Mme. Delannoy would advance him an additional twenty thousand francs. With his goal in sight, Mme. de Berny promised its fulfillment: she would give him the rest of what he needed, provided he vowed he would never again see or communicate with the duchess.

Unable to resist the bait, Balzac capitulated, and wrote a sad farewell to the Duchess d'Abrantès. She replied bitterly and at length, having no idea he had every intention of violating his pledge at the first opportunity.

The money for the new business having been duly raised, Balzac was ready for the next step. The government of the restored Bourbons regarded printing as a vital industry, as the ministers of Louis XVIII realized that men's minds were influenced by books, magazines and newspapers. All printers were therefore required to obtain government licenses, and the first requisite was a police investigation.

Balzac passed the examination without difficulty. He had been faithful to the Crown, and although as a writer he was suspect, he had never joined his colleagues in secret machinations against the Bourbons. Balzac was also required to present a letter of sponsorship from a member of the nobility.

Mme. de Berny promptly obtained one from her husband, who had no idea she was having an affair with the son of old friends. M. de Berny was pleased to write:

This young man has been known to me for a long time. The correctness of his convictions and his knowledge of literature are in my view a guarantee that he is fully aware of the obligations which will be imposed on him by the profession of a printer.

The President of the Royal Police Board was pleased to issue a license as a printer to one H. Balzac.

The house in the ancient Rue de Marais was more than two hundred years old and consisted of a printing shop on the ground floor and a gloomy, four-room apartment on the second. Balzac had to buy new presses and other equipment to replace antiquated machinery that would not function, and, with the help of the loyal Mme. de Berny he bought new furnishings for the apartment.

His ambitions still soaring, Balzac decided he needed typesetting equipment, but he had exhausted the funds he had borrowed. He conceived the idea of taking in a new partner, someone who would not only supply funds in order to buy into the enterprise, but would act as a salesman for the job printing contracts that would be needed to pay for the typesetting machines. It did not occur to him that he was drifting into deep waters.

Barbier brought in the third partner, a man named Jean-François Laurent, and the ever-enthusiastic Balzac hired a staff of twenty-four printers, binders and cutters. In his own mind, at least, he was already the proprietor of the most thriving printing business in Paris, although in reality he had yet to bring in one sou of outside business.

The first task was the printing of the one-volume Molière, and while the printers went to work, he assisted Laurent in bringing in new business. True to his compulsive nature, Balzac worked from dawn until midnight. He haggled with the sellers of ink and paper. He called on scores of potential customers, occasionally bringing in a few small jobs. He worked with the printers in the shop, energetically smearing his hands, face and clothes with ink. No task was too menial for him to perform, no detail was too small to escape his attention.

This devotion to duty should have resulted in a resounding financial success, but Balzac knew nothing about the printing business, and was too eager for his own good. He signed contracts with two publishers, but instead of insisting on receiving cash for the books he was printing, he agreed to accept a percentage of their future income. Both books failed, and he was left holding worthless certificates. Meanwhile the sellers of ink and paper took advantage of his lack of experience and sold him inferior stock. Bales of paper crumbled in the cellar of the plant, and barrels of printers' ink dried and hardened.

By the summer of 1827 the situation had become so intolerable that a sensible man would have called a halt. The one-volume edition of Molière had been printed on paper that smudged, and the ink was of such a poor quality that it blurred, so this effort was a dismal failure. A bookseller from Rheims came in with a large order, but was short of cash; Balzac, who seemed incapable of learning a lesson, agreed to accept the man's splendid library of eight thousand volumes as security. The book was printed on schedule, but the bookseller went bankrupt before the order could be delivered to him, so Balzac not only had several thousand volumes of a useless treatise on his hands, but took possession of a library that would bring him almost nothing if he tried to sell it in the secondhand market. He chose to keep the library, and these books remained in his possession for the rest of his life.

Barbier, sensing disaster, pulled out. Laurent soon followed his example. Once again Balzac stood with his back pressed against a financial wall, and once again familiar creditors came to his assistance. In spite of his mother's hesitation, his father elected to dream Balzac's dreams and advanced him an additional twenty thousand francs. The long-suffering Mme. de Berny gave him another twenty thousand, and Mme. Delannoy was persuaded to protect her investment by parting with ten thousand more.

The windmill turned still more rapidly, and by the early spring of 1828 Balzac had allowed the new capital of fifty thousand francs to sift through his fingers. Almost twenty-nine years of age, he faced almost certain bankruptcy and had accomplished literally nothing. Even worse, he had not written one line for three years.

Mme. Balzac and Mme. de Berny joined forces to prevent Balzac from suffering the almost certain fate of languishing in debtors' prison. Mme. de Berny's son, Alexandre, took Balzac's place as president of the printing company, while Mama, acting without the knowledge of her eighty-three-year-old husband, called in a cousin, Charles Sedillot, a highly successful businessman, to act as financial manager of the enterprise. Mme. de Berny canceled her loan in return for her son's participation in the company. Sedillot sold type foundries and other expensive equipment that Balzac had purchased. Outside creditors, including Mme. Delannoy, were paid off in full, more than ninety thousand francs pouring out for the purpose.

When the smoke lifted, Balzac was in the clear, except for the better part of fifty thousand francs he still owed his parents. He had no position, no future in business, and even had to give up the apartment over the printing shop, along with the furniture it contained, although he stubbornly refused to part with the books he had accumulated. Most of his clothes had been soiled beyond repair because of his carelessness in the vicinity of the presses, so that even his wardrobe was inadequate.

He could no longer turn to his family for help, because Mama and Papa were having problems of their own. Bernard-François, in spite of his advanced age, had made a teen-aged girl pregnant. Mama paid off the family, but could no longer hold up her head in Villeparisis, so she sold the house there, and she and Papa went to live near Laure in Versailles. Henry, who was not working for a living, although now in his twenties, accompanied them.

Pride prevented Balzac from asking Mme. de Berny to help him again, so, until he could find himself, he went to live with his old friend, Dablin, who offered him refuge for as many weeks or months as he found necessary. The crates containing Balzac's books filled the cellar of the Dablin town house in Paris, but his other belongings, including his entire wardrobe, were packed in two small valises.

On a warm morning in June 1828, twenty-four hours after Balzac moved into Dablin's house, the two men went out on an errand, and Dablin reported the incident in a prosaic letter to his old friends, M. and Mme. Balzac. When they reached the Place Vendôme, Balzac paused abruptly and stood for a long time gazing up at Napoleon's column.

Dablin spoke to him, but he was lost in a world of his own. Finally Balzac turned, his eyes clear, his disgrace and failure already forgotten. "Some day soon," he said in a loud, firm voice, "I, too, will conquer the world."

V

After spending a few days with Dablin, Balzac moved into the house of a new friend, Henri de Latouche, who in some ways was one of the most remarkable men in nineteenth-century Paris. A wealthy newspaper publisher and would-be literary and art critic, De Latouche was singularly lacking in every talent except one: he had an almost infallible ability to recognize genius in others, and to encourage the development of their gifts. Within a very short time, perhaps a week or two, Balzac completely recovered his equilibrium.

His first task was that of finding a place to live, and he discovered a little house on the outskirts of Paris that suited both his mood and his needs. It was located near the Observatory, on a little street off the Boulevard Montparnasse called the Rue Cassini. The place was within the physical boundaries of Paris, but for all practical purposes it was a rural retreat. On one side stood the Luxembourg, which was still a thick forest. The Boulevard Montparnasse ran through open fields, and the nearest sign of civilization was a fairground, open twelve months of the year. Yet the heart of the city was within a half hour's walk.

There were two tiny villas located on the lane known as the Rue Cassini, and Balzac rented the five-room apartment on the second floor of one of these. He had no money at all, so his brother-in-law, De Surville, paid the first quarterly installment of his modest rent. Then, encouraged by De Latouche, Balzac decided to furnish the place in a style befitting a man of distinction. He bought draperies of pure silk, antique furniture for his sitting room, a four-poster bed and a magnificent chest of drawers for his bedroom. A clock that stood on a marble pedestal was a real bargain for fifty francs, and some secondhand oriental rugs were cheap at forty francs each, so he bought three of them. The walls of his sitting room were covered with a material that looked like silk, but actually was calico, so he saved money. He needed bookcases for his library, and could not resist buying several hundred francs' worth of new books, handsomely bound in leather.

A gentleman could not live in these surroundings unless he was dressed accordingly, so Balzac went to a tailor and ordered several pairs of trousers, a blue dress coat, a black dress coat and a number of waistcoats, one embroidered and another made of fine chamois leather. Laure and her husband were the only members of the family who were aware of his vast expenditures, and they were convinced he had gone mad.

But De Latouche had faith in him, and so did Mme. de Berny; their confidence was all that Balzac needed to launch a new career on the ruins of the old. He intended to resume his writing, but now he planned to become a serious author.

His reversion to this aim was the result of no sudden decision. Although he had allowed himself to be lured into business by the middle-class thinking instilled in him by his parents, he had also long realized that success as a printer was eluding him, and the desire to write had been growing stronger.

The years Balzac had spent in the world of commerce had not

been wasted. He had matured, and his understanding of the bourgeois mind had deepened. Although he had put no words on paper, he had observed and remembered countless details of Parisian life. These observations, combined with the technical skills he had acquired in the years he had been writing potboilers, readied him for the challenge of serious work.

The enormous success of Sir Walter Scott's works, in France as well as in England, had created an almost insatiable demand for historical novels, and Balzac made up his mind to launch his new career in this field. He insisted that his background material be accurate, and after selecting as his subject a fairly recent event —the Royalist insurrection of 1800 in Brittany—he started to work by doing intensive, meticulous research. He already owned some of the books he needed, and he obtained the others from the National Library. Four weeks thereafter he steeped himself in the period, reading from early morning until late at night, interrupting his labors only when Mme. de Berny paid him a visit.

While still engaged in research on the work that would become *Le Dernier Chouan ou la Bretagne en 1800*, he already knew precisely what he wanted to achieve. As a guide for himself he wrote the introduction to the novel, and succeeded so well that he made no change in the wording when it appeared in the volume:

It is not the author's intention to limit himself to a narrative style in which facts are tediously paraded and the action revealed step by step as one demonstrates a skeleton whose bones have been carefully numbered. The great lessons which speak to us from the open book of history must, in our present time, be depicted in a way that everyone can understand. This method has been followed for a number of years by authors of talent, and the author of this book wishes to join their ranks. He has attempted in the present book to reproduce the spirit of an age and to bring to life an historical episode. He prefers to offer living speech rather than a documentary record, the battle itself rather than a report of the battle, and instead of epic narrative he has chosen dramatic action.

A writer must be supremely confident of his own ability to prepare such a statement long before one word of a book is written. Balzac possessed such self-confidence. Also, it now appeared that he no longer needed the reassuring ministrations of Mme. de Berny, De Latouche or his sister.

Balzac discovered he needed more information on the Royalist insurrection than he could obtain from books. He wanted to explore the countryside in which the revolt had taken place, familiarize himself with the people of the area and, if possible, talk with survivors of the insurrection. One day he remembered that a good friend of his parents, the retired General Gilbert de Pommereul, lived in that region, so he wrote a letter to the general and his wife, asking if he could visit them. They replied at once, graciously inviting him to visit them as their house guest for as long as he cared to stay.

Carrying only one suitcase, Balzac set out on his journey, sitting in the cheapest seat on the public coach, and he was so poor that he had to cover the last thirty miles on foot. Perspiring and covered with dust, he made such a disreputable appearance that the butler at the De Pommereul home thought he was a vagrant. Mme. de Pommereul, in a letter written some years later, described the impression Balzac created:

He was a short young man with a thickset figure that was emphasized by his badly cut suit. His hat was deplorable, but as soon as he removed it and one saw the expressiveness of his face, everything else was forgotten. After that it was his face alone that I saw. Anyone who has not seen him can have no conception of what a forehead he has, and what eyes! An expansive brow, which had a luminous look; golden-brown eyes, as full of expression as what he said. His nose was thick and square, his mouth enormous and always twisted in a laugh in spite of his defective teeth. He wore a heavy mustache and very long hair thrown back over his shoulders. At that time, and particularly when he first arrived, he had on the whole a rather lean look, as though he had not had enough to eat . . .

In his whole manner, his movements, his bearing, and the way he spoke, there was so much good nature, naïveté, and frankness that one could not help liking him as soon as one saw him. But his most prominent characteristic was his constant good humor, which was so exuberant that it became infectious.

The life in the De Pommereul household was luxurious. Balzac slept and made his notes in a large, handsomely furnished bedroom, and ate several very hearty meals each day. The general reminisced at great length about the 1800 revolt against Napoleon Bonaparte, and brought in various friends and neighbors who had participated in the insurrection and were willing to talk about it. Balzac enjoyed himself so thoroughly and acquired so much information that his visit of one week stretched to more than six, and De Latouche wrote him irritable notes from Paris, urging him to come home.

At last he returned to the house on the Rue Cassini, and began writing, employing work habits and laboring in an atmosphere that remained unchanged for the rest of his life. Although the rest of his house was garishly furnished, his study was as somber as a medieval monk's cell. The only items of furniture were his small, plain desk, a straight chair and a large, unpainted table on which he kept his supplies and notes. His quill pens were ravens' feathers, which were pliable but strong, and he kept at least twenty of them in a jar. His manuscript paper was an off shade of white, to reduce glare, as he was already beginning to encounter difficulty with his eyes. He used an expensive brand of smoothly flowing ink, and always kept two extra jars on hand for use in case he ran out. His lamp was tall but lacked ornamentation, and in the corner stood a tiny stove on which he brewed the endless cups of coffee that he drank day and night. On the floor was a solid-colored rug, and the drapes were a solid, monotonous gray. He permitted nothing in the room that might distract him from the task of writing.

His work schedule was staggering. He was awake by eight o'clock in the morning, and after a quick toilet sat down at his desk. He had no breakfast other than coffee, and wrote without interruption until two in the afternoon, when he paused long enough for a light meal that usually consisted of cold meats or cheese, and a little fruit. Returning to his labors, he did not halt again until eight or nine at night, when he ate his one substantial meal of the day, which he cooked for himself in his kitchen. Under no circumstances did he allow himself a respite of more than an hour for the repast; what the dishes lacked in quality they made up in quantity. Later he would acquire a reputation as something of a gourmet, but he was already a gourmand, and could devour enormous amounts of food at a single sitting. Until this meal he had consumed no liquids except coffee, but now he permitted himself a half bottle of a rough, inexpensive wine. Refreshed after his meal, he went back to his desk again, and stayed there until at least four o'clock in the morning.

When the words were flowing, Balzac stretched his schedule still more and worked until five or six. He never required more than four hours of sleep, he said, and frequently managed on no more than two or three. He was convinced he did his best work at night, when other people were asleep, but his imagination was partly responsible for his belief that the world around him was quieter then. His apartment on the Rue Cassini was so isolated that no one was close enough in the immediate neighborhood to disturb him, and at this time he had no neighbors, either in his own house or the adjoining villa.

He discouraged the visits of friends and made it plain to De Latouche and others that he did not welcome their interruptions. Only Mme. de Berny was permitted to remain for more than a few minutes, and she limited herself to two visits per week.

Le Dernier Chouans, later to be known as *Les Chouans*, was completed in January 1829, and the author made the deliberate decision to publish it under his own name. He signed it Honoré Balzac, not yet having added the *de*. It was published in March and filled four fat volumes.

De Latouche made certain it got off to a good start, giving it a superlative review in *Le Figaro*. But the public failed to respond, and only 450 copies of the book were sold. The friendship of the two men cooled, Balzac blaming De Latouche for the failure of the novel; a few months later a novel by De Latouche himself appeared under the title *Fragoletta*, and Balzac wrote a review for the *Mercure* that strained the relationship of the two men to its limits.

It appeared as though the new career of Balzac was ended almost before it began, and other troubles made life miserable for the young author. Bernard-François Balzac was seriously ill for the first time in his long life, and required medical help that drained the family's resources. This situation impelled Mme. Balzac, who needed little encouragement, to write long letters to her son, upbraiding him for his many extravagances.

Discouraged and beset by problems, Balzac secretly broke his pledge to Mme. de Berny and resumed his affair with the Duchess d'Abrantès. There were two kinds of love, he wrote at this time, the true love which was a combination of the physical, the sentimental and the intellectual, a blending of passion and tenderness, while the other was exclusively physical. He had sorted out his own thinking, and believed that Mme. de Berny represented the first, and was the great love of his life, while the duchess was a representation of the second.

His frustrations were so great that Balzac used sex as an outlet, and for the first time began to frequent the prostitutes of the city. He was willing to be taught all their tricks, and they were first-rate teachers. He acquired a knowledge of sexual relations that he found helpful for the rest of his life. Without exception his mistresses said he was an exceptionally able and virile lover who could please them—and himself—by utilizing a variety of techniques.

In June 1829, Bernard-François Balzac died at the age of eighty-three. Mme. Balzac fainted at the funeral, but came to her senses in time to scold Balzac when he was about to throw water on her. The eldest of her children was relieved to escape to Paris.

Balzac was living on borrowed money, and although he was planning a number of new books, his heart wasn't in his work.

The miserable failure of *Les Chouans* had disappointed him grievously, and he discussed with Mme. de Berny the idea of taking up some other profession. At this juncture luck played a role in his destiny.

Several years earlier he had received a small advance royalty of two hundred francs from a publisher named Levasseur for one of the *Codes*, a light and witty book that was to have been a manual for "a man of affairs." Balzac had completely forgotten the debt, but Levasseur had remembered it and tracked him to the Rue Cassini. Unable to repay the money, Balzac burrowed through his old manuscripts, and found one of the unpublished *Codes*, the manuscript he had called *Physiologie du mariage*.

The publisher took it, but wanting to capitalize on what little prestige the author had acquired through *Les Chouans*, he insisted on bringing it out under Balzac's own name. In no position to argue, Balzac was forced to agree.

Physiologie du mariage appeared in midsummer of 1829, and to the astonishment of the entire book world, it was an overnight success. No worse and possibly no better than the many *Codes* Balzac had written under pseudonyms, this volume appeared at a time when the intellectuals of Paris were bored with the dull life they were leading under the Bourbon restoration, bored with censorship and bored with the unwritten rules that required authors of stature to cast their works in a classical mold.

In two weeks the *Physiologie* sold ten thousand copies, and in the next fortnight another fifteen thousand were purchased. The intellectuals and aristocrats were as eager to read the book as were the housewives of the middle class. Even more important, authors and publishers of stature wanted to meet the man who had been sufficiently versatile to write both *Les Chouans* and the *Physiologie*.

Overnight Balzac found himself not only solvent, earning more money each month than he had ever made in a year, but famous too. Even *Les Chouans* began to sell at a steady pace, thanks to his unexpected renown. Suddenly everybody who was anybody wanted to meet him, and every important door in Paris was opened to him.

Mme. Récamier, whose salon was visited daily by publishers, editors and authors, insisted that the Duchess d'Abrantès bring the new sensation to her house. Balzac attended the reading of a new work by Victor Hugo, already the idol of the younger generation of authors and artists, and established a friendship that would last until the end of his days.

Delacroix, the painter, noted in his diary that he had met Balzac and was charmed by him. Balzac dined with Alfred de Musset, Jules Janin, Alfred de Vigny and Prosper Mérimée. He became friendly with Lamartine, the author-politician who would become one of a triumvirate heading the short-lived Republican government in 1848. He met Sainte-Beuve, the most formidable literary critic of the day, and secretly disliked him. He became acquainted with the gigantic Alexandre Dumas, who invited him to a party at which everyone present, Balzac included, drank far too much.

But the intoxication of overnight fame was far greater than that caused by wine. The works of the hitherto unknown writer were in sudden demand, and Balzac raced back to his pen and paper. His accomplishments in the next two years beggar description, particularly when it is remembered that he led a very active social life between the autumn of 1829 and that of 1831. He wrote several novels under his own name, and an undetermined number under pseudonyms. He wrote newspaper articles, literary reviews, social commentaries for magazines and even a number of bland political articles. He produced a *Philosophie de la toilette* and a *Physiologie gastronomique*. He turned out at least one piece for literally every newspaper, magazine, literary journal and other periodical in Paris. In 1831 alone, at least seventy-six pieces are directly traced to his pen. He wrote a minimum of sixteen printed pages per day, and this total does not include his revisions, which entailed far more labor than his first drafts. Now that he was writing under his own name he refused to permit trash to appear under his byline, and using an extraordinary system he devised for himself, which will be discussed in detail subsequently, he revised incessantly. Word by word, sentence by sentence and paragraph by paragraph he altered everything he put onto paper, sometimes turning out as many as twelve to sixteen drafts of a single work.

His subject matter was as broad as his total output was stunning. He proved himself a master of fiction, and his new *Codes* established him as a wit. A thinly disguised eulogy of Napoleon caused the censors to regard him with suspicion, and he joined the ranks of the philosophers with two short, pungent works on the trends of philosophical writing in seventeenth- and eighteenth-century France. He became an expert of stature on food, women, men's fashions, morals and mores. It is difficult to find any subject in his contemporary scene on which he did not comment.

With the appearance of each new piece his renown increased. It is even more significant that he won the respect of the literary community when it was discovered that, although some of his articles and longer pieces contained ordinary writing, others proved to be polished gems. The literary world was stunned, and saluted the versatile genius who had been living unknown and unpublished. At the age of thirty Honoré de Balzac—who began to use the *de* more or less regularly now—came into his own.

Lovely ladies, among them the most important in France, actually listened to him when he spoke and sometimes flattered him. Fortunée Hamelin, soon to become a short-term mistress of Hugo, spent an entire evening chatting with him at a party. He met Sophie Gay, who could tell him stories about the Emperor Napoleon, and the haughty Duchess du Faubourg Saint-Germain, who giggled like a schoolgirl when he regaled her with the plots of his forthcoming books.

The ladies of the aristocracy enchanted him, and whenever the opportunity presented itself, Balzac made another conquest. By now he had become promiscuous in the extreme, as greedy for affairs as he was for fame and money. The faithful Mme. de Berny remained his emotional anchor, and he continued to sleep with the Duchess d'Abrantès, too, but they were merely the foundation on which he based his sex life. He slept with aristocrats, courtesans and trollops indiscriminately, displaying in his love life the same dazzling diversification that appeared in his writing. His yearning for romance, like all of his other appetites, was insatiable.

Just as Balzac's newly acquired stature brought hitherto untouchable women within his grasp, so his increased literary reputation enabled him to begin writing the books for which his talents and temperament were best suited. Once again he was fortunate, because French literary tastes were in a process of change. Even the conservative critics were no longer inexorable in their demands that every work of value be written in the old classical forms. Victor Hugo stood at the head of a band that had turned to romanticism, which in turn would lead to realism, but Balzac marched a long step ahead of the procession.

His novels of middle-class life reflected a world he knew and thoroughly understood, and he turned to them when his work became in demand. He did not intend, at the outset, to become the great explicator of the bourgeoisie.

Balzac's plots, as he himself often admitted, were second-rate, at times unbelievable. They occasionally reflected the pseudonymous melodramas he had produced in his youth. Yet his characters were genuine, three-dimensional, and he bolstered them with the idiosyncratic detail that brought them to life. It was not enough for him to mention a chair; he described it physically, told how it had evolved from earlier types of chairs and even discussed its manufacture. In fact, he sometimes elected to describe the history of a *particular* chair, weaving its story into the background of his characters.

Balzac had no precedents for this sort of writing. He developed an approach and style that grew from his own observations and experience of life. His genius appealed to an audience who thirsted for realism. Thus Balzac appeared in the right place at the right time, armed with the right talents.

By the end of 1829 the market was glutted with historical novels, biographical novels, historical romances and other fiction that looked toward the past. Hugo and his cohorts were breaking away, and publishers, sensing the growth of a substantial middle-class market, were asking for short novels on subjects with which these readers could identify.

Honoré de Balzac obliged the trend. In 1830 and 1831 he wrote an astonishing number and variety of novels. *La Vendetta* concerned a painting school attended by the daughters of the middle class, while *Une Double Famille* had a bourgeois setting in Bayeux. *Le Bal de Sceaux* concerned a dancing school similar to that which Laure and Laurence Balzac had attended in the years when their mother had seen to it that they received the polish required of middle-class girls. *La Maison du chat qui pelote* lay still closer to home, and was centered on the drygoods shop operated for many years by the Sallambier family.

Some of his works were actually long versions of the short story, and were equally as pungent. *El Verdugo, Sarrasine* and *Une Épisode sous la terreur*, were hailed as masterpieces, and are still read today.

It was in still another realm that Balzac achieved his greatest success. He delved into the world of the Parisian woman who was more than thirty years of age, the woman whose arranged marriage left her cold and who was slowly dying of lethargy and hostility. This woman, Balzac declared, had a right to live—and to love. The theme appeared repeatedly, first in *La Femme de trente ans*, which gave its name to the genre, and then in *La Paix du ménage*, *Étude de femme*, and in *Scènes de la vie privée*, which not only scored a triumph in France, but was equally successful when translated into English, Russian, Italian and Polish. Women of many nations, it appeared, responded to his sympathetic treatment of their problems.

Balzac's understanding of the mind, temperament and moods of the middle-class woman, and often of the aristocratic woman, proved to be uncanny. No other French author had demonstrated such insight, and he quickly developed a huge, adoring feminine readership. It is small wonder that thousands of women virtually worshiped him, or that he encountered few problems when, after meeting a breathless reader, he suggested opportunities to become far better acquainted.

Balzac's versatility did not stop with his books about women. Two of his most effective novels were *L'Auberge rouge* and *Le Chef-d'oeuvre inconnu,* and in them he revealed the basic philosophy of life that his years of privation and disappointment had created in him. Man, he declared, was weak, fallible and a conniver, friendships were meaningless, and one was more often betrayed by his friends than by his foes.

Vanity was the curse of the aristocracy, weakening and destroying it, whereas the lust for money rotted the very heart of the bourgeoisie. In fact, the love of money—which Balzac called "the modern god"—was the root of all modern evil. The upper classes needed money to maintain their luxurious way of life and to sustain their place in society. The middle classes gathered money for its own sake, and could not relinquish the habit, even when they had insured their own security. They were so anxious to acquire more, more and still more money that they were unable to enjoy the benefits and pleasures of the things money could buy. The masses suffered more than did the rest, their lack of money condemning them to lives of squalor, to a hopeless inability to raise themselves any higher in the world, and their poverty was directly responsible for their crimes and their escape into liquor.

None of these views seem new a century and a half after Honoré de Balzac first put them on paper, but his approach was shockingly candid in his own time. He was the innovator, the literary clinician who first turned the harsh light of realism on the world in which he lived. In *La Peau de chagrin,* more than in any other work, he tore off the polite masks of romanticism and sentimentalism to reveal the world as it was. On the surface this book was romantic in the extreme, a turning of the *Arabian Nights* into a series of interrelated stories about the Paris of 1830. But he cut to the heart of that Paris.

Part of the story was autobiographical, and his descriptions of his own poverty, loneliness and despair were gripping. He spared no one in his descriptions of lower-class squalor, of middle-class pretensions and aristocratic indifference to the fate of others. Unlike his contemporaries, he approached sex realistically and succeeded in shocking countless thousands of readers. Judged by the standards of a later, more explicit age, he did not write in clinical detail on the subject, and handled his sex scenes with great delicacy. But he was blunt in relating the consequences of sexual encounters, and did not spare his readers' feelings in his descriptions of the guilts, the despair, the hopeless yearnings for something more than meaningless affairs of all sorts.

Certainly it can be said that Balzac found himself in 1830 and 1831. He had long known he possessed a talent that was unique, an ability to write enormous masses of material at a speed that no other writer could hope to match. But it was not until the success of the *Physiologie du mariage* brought him forcefully to the attention of Paris publishers that the demands of the market brought him to his vocation.

Probing like a surgeon, he searched for motive. It was not enough to describe the actions of a character, but he felt compelled to discover and tell his readers *why* a character had behaved in a certain way. Rarely were these causes simple; Balzac had learned enough of life to realize that man's motivations are complex, varied and often contradictory, and it was his genius to examine them in such great realistic detail that his readers came to know his characters even better than they knew themselves.

Balzac still lacked self-recognition, however, and in spite of the furor he created and the comfortable living he was now earning, his years of failure made him wonder whether the bubble might burst. Nowhere are his self-doubts more clearly illustrated than in a letter he wrote to his mother early in 1832, saying, "*Sooner or later I shall make a fortune, either as a writer, or in politics, or in journalism, either by a wealthy marriage or by some big business coup.*"

He was daydreaming. The abortive Revolution of 1830 scarcely touched him, and in no way changed his own mode of life or his ideas. The insensitive Charles X, the successor to Louis XVIII, had been responsible for a series of repressive measures that had deprived the middle and lower classes of the personal liberties they had won in the great Revolution of 1789 and had secured under Napoleon. The king had been forced to flee into ignominious exile, but a more agile member of the Bourbon clan, Louis Philippe, had seized the throne.

There was a subtle difference in the new monarch's status, which few foreigners comprehended. He was king of the French, not king of France, and it was tacitly understood on all sides that he sat on a probationer's throne of sorts. Thoroughly bourgeois in his own attitudes, Louis Philippe gave up the trappings of royalty, wore a plain businessman's suit and even traveled about Paris on foot in order to win the support of his subjects.

Balzac, believing that the lot of the people did not improve when there were government upheavals, flirted briefly with the notion of entering politics only because a young man who became a member of the National Chamber could make himself a multimillionaire in a few years. It was far better, as Balzac revealed in correspondence, to dream of marrying a wealthy widow, retiring to a life of luxury in the country and, when the spirit moved him, writing an occasional book.

Until one of these near-miracles occurred, however, he found it necessary to earn a living. Publishers were clamoring for his long fiction, short fiction, new *Codes*, and articles on any subject that interested him. A number of his books were being translated into foreign languages, and even though publishers abroad sometimes neglected to pay him for the rights, his renown was spreading rapidly in Europe and was even reaching across the Atlantic to the young United States, where he was acquiring a small but enthusiastic following in the larger cities. As he well knew from bitter experience, there were far worse lives than that which he was leading.

It was an unsettling experience to become prominent overnight, but Balzac was fortunate, and found a new counterweight, a friend who, along with Mme. de Berny, helped him achieve stability. His relationship with Mme. Zulma Carraud, which lasted for the rest of his life, was unique: they were intimate friends but never became lovers, and the idea of having an affair did not seriously occur to either. Major Carraud, Zulma's husband, was a professional army officer whose advancement was hampered by the strong Republican beliefs that he and his wife held. He, too, became Balzac's good friend, and although his wife handled their correspondence, he offered his aid on many occasions when Balzac was in need.

Mme. Carraud was not only lovely by the standards of her own day, but would have been considered a beauty one hundred and fifty years later. She had masses of black hair, violet eyes and an unusually fair complexion; her figure was slender, and she did not look like a woman who had borne her husband several children.

For more than a century many of Balzac's French biographers have speculated on the possibility that Balzac and Zulma might have loved each other, but were unwilling to express that love because of their mutual regard for the major. But it is useless to conjecture whether they might have had an affair or married had Zulma been a widow. She was an intellectual who found army life stultifying, and in her correspondence with Balzac she found a natural outlet for her thoughts. She was fond of him, certainly, but above all she felt sorry for him, realizing he was his own worst enemy, and although she was a member of his own generation, her relationship with him was, in the main, maternal.

As for Balzac, he would have violated his own code of ethics had he tried to make love to her. With all his faults he tried to avoid affairs with married women. In addition, Zulma Carraud filled a great void in his life and became his confidante. He could tell her all his problems, regardless of whether they were professional, financial or romantic, and he knew he had an understanding audience. He liked to tell her he relied on her advice, but his record over the years proves otherwise. She was far too sensible, gently condemning the innumerable excesses in which he indulged.

Yet the fact remains that, after Balzac achieved sudden fame, he needed good friends as never before.

VI

The Duchess d'Abrantès taught Balzac that he was correct when he wrote that anyone who trusted another member of the human race was a fool. She was preparing her memoirs, which were certain to have a wide sale because of her candid revelations concerning her relationships with her many celebrated lovers. Balzac accepted the challenge with his usual vigor, and not only reorganized the book, but actually rewrote the better part of it for his number two mistress.

When he was finished the duchess calmly informed him that she had no intention of publicly acknowledging his assistance or giving him a share of the book's earnings. Balzac fumed, but she said she would deny his participation in the venture, and he would only succeed in making himself appear ridiculous. Balzac realized she was telling the truth, and had the good sense not to press his claims against her. It would be absurd if "the man who understood women" became involved in a legal brawl over a literary property with a woman known to be his mistress.

So, in the autumn of 1830, he licked his wounds by renting a cottage in Touraine for a number of weeks and going there with Mme. de Berny. He worked, they went on long walks, she admired his writing and he doted on being mothered. This was the last idyll of its sort the couple enjoyed, as the physical side of their relationship was declining. Mme. de Berny was now in her late fifties, while Balzac was still a young man, and he no longer found her physically attractive.

Her sense of dignity impelled her to begin a gradual physical withdrawal from him, and if her own desires remained strong, she managed to conquer them. There was nothing more pathetic, she wrote him after their return to Paris, than the attempts of an old woman to cling to a young lover.

Balzac became panicky when he thought he might lose her, but his fears were groundless. Laure de Berny remained his intimate friend for the rest of her life, and continued to cherish, succor and bolster him. He was grateful for her generosity, and his association with her remained tender. To the extent that he was capable of expressing loyalty, he demonstrated that trait in his dealings with her.

By the end of 1830 there were many changes in the Balzac family's way of life. Laure de Surville and her husband moved to Paris, where he intended to obtain the financing for a new canal he wanted to build. Mme. Balzac discovered that her nest egg had shrunk, and knew it was unlikely she would ever recover the fifty thousand francs Balzac owed her so she cut her expenses by moving in with her daughter, her son-in-law and their children. Half brother Henry's life also took on a new direction. Unable to hold any position for more than a few months, he left France early in 1831, intending to make a fortune for himself in the colonies. When the ship, aptly named the *Magellan*, reached the little British island of Mauritius in the Indian Ocean, Henry promptly fell in love with the place and stayed there.

Balzac dealt with these various family disruptions by doing his best to ignore them. He had started a novel called *Les Adventures administratives d'une idée heureuse,* when the idea of *La Peau de chagrin* occurred to him, and he knew that, if he could bring it off, he would write a major work. It would be an allegory, a fable told in the manner of Rabelais, and would be based on the theme that "human society is the road to death."

Canel paid him an advance royalty of two thousand francs for the work, and Balzac blithely signed contracts for other novels, among them one to be called *Scènes de la vie militaire,* which he based on his observations when visiting Zulma Carraud and her husband. He had more than enough to keep him busy.

But his social life was expanding, in spite of his sporadic attempts to curb it, and he discovered that most of his evenings were occupied. He became friendly with Eugène Sue, a fellow novelist who was a dashing man about town, and soon found himself copying Sue's elegant clothes style, although the new attire looked outlandish on his short, plump figure.

Through Sue he met one of the most fascinating women of the century, Olympe Pélissier, a ravishingly beautiful and highly intelligent courtesan. She conducted a brilliant salon, where such men as Rossini, the composer, and the Duke de Fitz-James spent hours in conversation. Not all of her guests were her lovers, and she granted her favors only to those whom she found attractive.

Her independence challenged Balzac, who began a campaign to lure her into bed. Olympe enjoyed his company and considered him a stimulating conversationalist, but she made it plain she had no interest in him as a lover. Besides, she was already involved with Sue, and she made it a rule never to have affairs simultaneously with two or more members of a single profession. The others in her circle watched Balzac's efforts with amused tolerance.

Neither they nor the alluring Olympe was aware of Honoré de Balzac's determination when he set out to reach a goal. His dogged persistence finally wore Olympe down, and she consented to go to bed with him in the hope that, thereafter, she could be rid of him. To her surprise she found he was as adept in the art of love-making as she herself was reputed to be, and she enjoyed the experience so much that he became a regular visitor to her bedchamber.

Their relationship was far more significant than it would at first appear. In Olympe's drawing room Balzac met men of a caliber he had never before known. Brilliant, witty and sophisticated, they represented the quintessence of all that was cosmopolitan, and by observing them he added new characters to the vast portrait gallery that would make him immortal. He was also able to persuade Olympe to chat with him about various men she had known, and by drawing her out he obtained the plots for a half dozen of his novels.

She was helpful to him in yet another way: she bolstered his ego. Balzac had never allowed himself to be seen in public with Mme. de Berny, and only on rare occasions did he visit someone's house in the company of the Duchess d'Abrantès. The prostitutes he frequented were low women, and no self-respecting man could be seen in public with them. But the beautiful, handsomely gowned Olympe Pélissier caused every man who saw her to be jealous of her escort, and the good-natured Olympe, who was aware of his emotional needs, allowed herself to be seen with him at the theatre, the opera and in restaurants.

Sometimes Eugène Sue, who cut a fine figure, was also present, and Balzac looked like someone who had joined the party by accident.

"I feel sorry for Balzac," Alexandre Dumas is alleged to have said. "He presents such a sorry spectacle that he ought to stay at home behind a closed door."

"You're mistaken," the great Victor Hugo supposedly replied. "It is Balzac who feels pity for all the rest of us, and he'll be remembered long after those who mock him are forgotten."

An unorthodox young couple living in a garret on the Quai Saint-Michel also became Balzac's good friends at this time. The man, Jules Sandeau, had aspirations to become a writer, and was also considering a career on the stage. His fiery mistress, Aurore Dudevant, was unique. Although feminine in appearance she had many masculine traits, and adopted a man's attitude in her scorn for conventions. She was a writer, too, as yet scarcely recognized, and because the market for works by women was limited, she wrote under the name of George Sand.

She and Sandeau were so poor at this time that, when Balzac went calling on them, he always brought the evening meal with him, and was breathless by the time he carried a bag of groceries and several bottles of wine to their attic room. But the trips were worth the effort. He and George Sand were intellectual catalysts. A decade later George Sand rather wistfully said she wished she had made a record of their conversations, which she called the most stimulating and provocative she had ever known.

She, too, became Balzac's lifelong friend, although they eventually saw each other infrequently because of the demands of their work and their very active private lives. According to a story that may or may not be true, but certainly should be granted a raised eyebrow, George Sand supposedly offered herself to Balzac at a time when both had reached the apex of their fame and influence. According to this tale he refused politely, later explaining, "I didn't want to become her fifteenth lover, or victim, if you prefer, depending on how one views the matter."

Even if they didn't become intimate, George Sand was another member of the illustrious company of women who understood Balzac. His emotional demands were insatiable, and he needed all the help he could get. George Sand stood apart from the others because, being a professional writer herself, she achieved a detachment, an objectivity that was lacking in those who became involved with him.

She was the first to read *La Peau de chagrin*, which he gave her in unfinished manuscript form in the late spring of 1831. She predicted it would be an enormous success, and she was right. Balzac combined harsh realism and a fairy-tale quality, and the literary critics accepted him as one of the foremost authors of the day. The publication of the book forced those who saw him as no more than a versatile freak to revise their opinions, and he permanently established himself as a major figure.

Thereafter no one denigrated him as an author, regardless of one's opinion of him as a person. There were many who disliked him intensely because of his coarseness and negative appearance, but his circle of real friends continued to grow, and he no longer led the life of a hermit. Sycophants would have surrounded him had he permitted them to draw near him, but Balzac knew they were insincere opportunists, and he was at his boorish worst in dealing with them.

Certainly fame did not improve his manners. Unkempt and frequently dirty, dousing himself with scent instead of bathing, he looked like a butcher who had dressed in garish clothes that didn't quite fit his bulging frame. Every author of the period who wrote about him mentioned his vitality, and it appeared that his energy was boundless. Even when he was working sixteen hours per day, seven days each week, he showed no signs of fatigue when he went out to spend an hour or two with colleagues and other friends at dinner. He told innumerable stories, embellishing wildly in order to make a point or entertain his listeners. His raw, booming laugh drowned the voices of others, and made it easier for him to monopolize a conversation.

His table manners were atrocious. He waved his knife or fork, using one or the other like a musical conductor's baton to illustrate his remarks. He gorged his food, frequently ate with his fingers and thought nothing of wiping his mouth on his sleeve, even when wearing an expensive new coat. Unlike Victor Hugo, who maintained a strict regimen in order to keep his weight down, Balzac loathed physical exercise, and became so gross that the slightest exertion caused him to perspire and pant for breath.

Only on the most formal occasions did he refrain from removing his cravat and unbuttoning his collar, and he usually found it more convenient to leave his vest open. Instead of sitting politely, as other people did, he hurled himself at a chair, and if it was in the least delicate, it groaned beneath his assault. He continually interrupted the conversations of others, and if someone else stole and held the spotlight he was inclined to sulk.

But his charm was undeniable, and even those who despised

him were forced to admit it. He could capture and hold the attention of any audience, and people who enjoyed his company relished an evening with him. Eugène Sue wrote of a night when he went into the Grand Véfour, the favorite restaurant of both Balzac and Hugo, and found his two noted colleagues dining together at a corner table. They were so engrossed in their conversation they failed to notice him, so he sat at another table and watched them. Soon they were laughing so hard they began to weep, and Sue, unable to stand the suspense any longer, went to them and asked why they were laughing. Balzac and Hugo looked at him blankly, and neither was able to answer the question. There had been no remark or series of remarks that had caused them to laugh; instead, they were simply relaxing in a convivial atmosphere.

Most of the established writers of the day were inclined to shun Balzac. He was too crude, too overbearing for their taste. Hugo was the exception, not only recognizing the true worth of Balzac's books, but learning to appreciate him as a human being. Hugo's attitude caused other members of the literary fraternity to have second thoughts. Nevertheless, there were few who shared Hugo's personal admiration for Balzac.

The first two years of his success convinced Balzac that he was wasting his energies by writing so many books on diverse subjects. Gradually he realized that he needed to establish goals and strive toward them.

Unable to resist spending his money faster than he earned it, Balzac still owed his mother fifty thousand francs, but apparently had no intention of repaying her. In 1831 he earned about twenty-two thousand francs, a sum which would have permitted a bachelor with no obligations to live in great comfort. But he demanded so many luxuries that he managed to incur debts to various tradespeople, and by the end of the year found he owed them fifteen thousand francs.

The reasons are not difficult to find. He bought two horses and a carriage on which he had his crest painted. Since the Balzac family had never possessed a crest, Balzac invented one for himself, then made sure it was executed to his satisfaction by standing over the artist who painted it on the carriage door. He found a tailor named Buisson who not only did competent work, but was a good dinner companion, and they soon became friends. Balzac promptly placed a strain on the relationship by his failure to pay Buisson's bill of seven hundred and fifty francs. The apartment on the Rue Cassini had become too small for a renowned author who felt it necessary to entertain at dinner parties in style, so he took over the first floor of the villa, too, and furnished it sumptuously.

The art and bric-a-brac dealers of Paris soon came to know him. He prowled through their shops, searching for bargains, and inevitably found many. A marble-topped table at one hundred francs was a marvelous buy because the table was of the type that Napoleon's sister Pauline had favored. By the following day the giddy author was boasting that the table had been Pauline's, and that he knew he could dispose of it for five hundred francs. Scores of useless items found their way into his house, which soon was crammed with candlesticks, clocks, porcelain figures, tapestries and odds and ends.

A compulsive fever kept Balzac at his desk when he was working, and a similar obsessive spirit gripped him when he went shopping. Once started, he could not stop. His greatest extravagances were gloves and books. Urbain Canel, his publisher, revealed that Balzac requested a dozen pairs of lemon-colored kid gloves, a pair of deerskin gloves and two heavy pairs of goatskin gloves as payment for a short story. George Sand, who spent an evening marveling at the wonders of his expanded house, wrote that she counted forty-three pairs of expensive gloves in a new chest of drawers, most of them unused.

Balzac had valid reasons to buy books, of course, but even here he went too far. He reasoned that a distinguished author needed a library that would match his reputation, so he went to various booksellers and ordered sets of the classics bound in leather. These hand-tooled, gilded volumes were very handsome, but it was discovered after his death more than two decades later that the pages in at least half of the books of the various sets had remained uncut.

Laure de Surville urged her brother to be more thrifty, and Zulma Carraud, who had moved to Angoulême, where her husband had been made commandant of a gunpowder factory, wrote him several long letters on the subject. But Balzac refused to heed anyone's advice. It was far more important that he had been invited to dinner at the home of Émile de Girardin, Paris' most important newspaper and magazine publisher, and that Girardin's bride, Delphine, the daughter of Sophie Gay, had found the uncouth author enchanting. Balzac did no business with De Girardin, but his social conquest of Delphine meant as much to him as the financial and critical success of a new, major book. He had starved too long in anonymity and poverty, and was making up for lost time. He thought of himself as the toast of Paris, and to an extent he was right, even though many people ridiculed the idea behind his back.

It was difficult to blame those who laughed at him. He kept finding new ways to put on airs, and one of these proved to be shockingly expensive. He developed a fondness for walking sticks, and after some ladies were impressed when he appeared at a dinner one evening carrying a stick with a silver handle, he immediately ordered another with a much larger handle of gold. The most famous of his walking sticks was a cane of his own invention. It was studded with turquoises, and an enormous stone was set in the knob at the top. It cost him seven hundred francs, and he never paid the bill. But the stick acquired a fame of its own, and virtually every gossip writer in Paris devoted at least one or two paragraphs to it.

Aware of its value as a conversation piece, Balzac went to great pains to keep the talk alive. He told the gullible that the cane possessed magical properties, and a few foolish women believed him. The most widespread of his stories was a tale to the effect that he kept a portrait of a secret mistress inside the knob. She had been painted in the nude, he declared, and was a member of the very highest aristocracy. So many people swallowed this fancy that

Balzac deliberately permitted no one else to touch the knob of the stick, and it amused him to see how many people made the attempt to find new ways to open the lid. By thwarting them, he declared, he was able to maintain a degree of fame greater than any he could achieve through his books.

In literary circles Balzac was fast acquiring a reputation for arrogance, and few of his colleagues realized he was merely trying to win acceptance by emphasizing his new-found importance. All they knew was that he was overbearing. He offended Dumas and Jules Janin by boasting to them that he was paid advance royalties far greater than any that either of them had ever received. Eugène Sue was his friend for a time, but eventually Sue became weary of his bragging.

Balzac was equally inept in his handling of the press. He played the role of the great man when dealing with the literary critics and other journalists, and treated them with such condescension that some of them loathed him. Many went out of their way to ridicule him in print, and there were some critics who tore all of his books apart, regardless of their worth. Sainte-Beuve and the other important critics were even more cruel. They ignored most of his work.

His friends tried to persuade him to change his ways. Dr. Nacquart, who loaned him one thousand francs late in 1831, told him he would become the greatest author in all of French history if he acquired the habit of displaying the deep, hidden humility that was always a part of him. Mme. de Berny wrote him, in vain, urging him to curb his excesses. Zulma Carraud was even more blunt, and wrote:

Honoré, you are now a celebrated author, but you are destined for something higher. Mere fame should mean nothing to a man of your stature. You should set yourself a far higher goal! If I had the courage I would say to you, "Why are you, out of pure vanity, wasting your unusual intelligence in such a foolish manner?" Give up this life of meaningless elegance! You will never find a statue by Cellini that will cost you a mere eleven sous, or eleven francs, or eleven hundred francs. I beg you, apply to your daily life the discipline that enables you to work so hard and to such good effect. You are no longer a boy, and it is time you begin to behave like a man!

But Balzac was not yet capable of listening to such sound advice. Even Olympe Pélissier was startled one night when, escorting her to dinner, he ate three dozen oysters and a lobster, two large bowls of soup, a great slab of beef and a whole stuffed chicken, followed by a rich chocolate dessert, several kinds of cheese, and a large bowl of fruit. Such gluttony was unsettling, even though he excused it on the grounds that he ate only one meal a day.

Balzac's increased income permitted him to make some changes in his style of living that added to his comfort and convenience, too. Now he had a manservant who prepared his meals, including his frugal lunch. When he worked he disliked being encumbered by too much clothing, which distracted him, so he designed a floor-length garment that looked like a monk's robe. It was loose enough for him to forget what he was wearing, and it provided him with the warmth required during the long hours he spent at his desk.

The new Honoré de Balzac could not be satisfied with an ordinary robe, however, and Buisson made a number for him in white wool, with corded belts of gold ornamented with fringed gold tassels. The few people who saw him wearing this garment reacted in the same way: without exception they said he looked grotesque.

What Balzac's critics forgot or did not realize was the fact that even though he was leading an active, flamboyant social life, he was still working furiously. When he returned to the elegantly furnished house on the Rue Cassini after an evening on the town, he invariably retired to his drab study and spent the rest of the night writing. After snatching a few hours of sleep he returned to his labors, and refused to permit any distractions until long after sundown. Although he was enjoying the fruits of those labors for the first time in his life, his work remained his principal preoccupation.

Over the years that quota gradually increased, and, until ill health forced him to moderation, he continued to increase his daily output. At the beginning of his career, he had forced himself to turn out fifteen closely written pages per day. By the early 1830s the total rose to twenty, together with the equivalent of twenty pages of revisions. A decade later, he was writing twenty-five and rewriting twenty-five. By 1850, he produced the staggering total of thirty written pages and thirty more that were rewritten.

The system of correcting printed proofs that he invented for himself was as tortuous as it was complicated. He was a perfectionist who demanded that every page, every paragraph, every sentence and every word express the precise shade of meaning and mood he wanted to convey. Therefore the first proofs, which were prepared from his handwritten manuscripts, were just the beginning. A printer's messenger picked up the latter from him each day.

The proofs were printed on the same off-white shade of paper on which he did his original writing, and he refused to accept the rough, yellow paper on which proofs were usually printed. Each printed page was set up on paper with exceptionally wide margins; in fact, the printed material occupied approximately one fifth or one sixth of the space on the page.

Balzac was never satisfied with his work of the previous day. Cutting, changing, adding, often revising completely, he filled the margins, and frequently the blank back of the proof sheet as well. The usual printer's symbols were insufficient for his purposes, so he invented scores of new symbols, which he expected the compositors to follow to the last comma. Any deviation drove him into a frenzy.

The corrected pages were returned to the printers, and the compositors set the new copy in type, returning the newly printed pages to Balzac the following day. It was so difficult to decipher his tiny, scrawled handwriting, much less make out his intricate changes within changes, that compositors often felt they were losing their sanity. A new printer sometimes needed months of training to be able to set Balzac's words in type, and the task was so difficult that the owners of printing plants were forced to offer their men double wages in order to persuade them to undertake the job. Yet the extra money was frequently an insufficient inducement, and in some printing shops it became customary for a compositor to turn—with relief—to other work after putting in a stint of one to two hours on a Balzac manuscript in a single day. The plants in which most of the books were printed finally designated a master printer to supervise the work and, when necessary, decipher words, phrases and sentences that were unintelligible.

When Balzac received the second set of proofs he felt that his own work was just beginning. He repeated the entire process of changing and revising, adding and expunging, and again the product of these labors was returned to the printers. A third set of proofs came back to him, then a fourth, a fifth, and so on. As a rule he made fewer corrections on each set, and by the time he finished working on the sixth or seventh set he was changing only sentences, then individual words.

An examination of his seventy-four novels, his short stories and his many articles, reviews and miscellaneous words indicates that he rewrote each of them on an average of seven to eight times. Occasionally he demanded and received as many as fourteen or fifteen sets of proofs.

What called a halt to this endless process was the pressure of a final printing deadline. At times even the entreaties of publishers could not stop his rewriting. As a last resort the harried publisher threatened to bring a lawsuit against him. On a number of occasions suits were actually begun. The printing process was expensive, obviously, so that some of Balzac's publishers inserted clauses in his contracts requiring him to bear the financial burden after the customary three or four sets of proofs had been printed at the publisher's expense.

What enabled him to perform this Herculean task, he told his good friends on many occasions, was coffee. He lived on it, consuming dozens of cups each day, countless thousands in his lifetime. He permitted no one else to make his coffee for him, even when he was working in his own house, with a staff of several servants available. No mistress could make coffee to his liking, and no hostess was allowed to perform or even supervise the task.

A glass or two of wine aided digestion, Balzac wrote, and could be an aid to conviviality. He did not object to the drinking of alcoholic spirits by others, but admitted that he was not particularly fond of even the mildest wines. As for cognac, the Dutch gin that the lower classes consumed in order to induce forgetfulness, or the foul-tasting whiskey that the English and Americans drank, he refused to touch any of them. "These beverages," he told Dr. Nacquart, "reduce one's ability to control his thoughts and actions. If he drinks more than a small amount he behaves foolishly, often ignoring his own best interests."

Tobacco, taken in any form, be it snuff, a cigar or in a pipe, was equally repellent. "The fumes cloud the mind," he said, "and injure the body. The use of tobacco on a broad scale can dull the wits of entire nations."

But coffee was a blessing, a boon to mankind, and he suggested that a contented world express its gratitude to the Ottoman Empire for its innovation and the Viennese for introducing it to Europe. Coffee enabled man to work at the peak of his efficiency, keeping his mind clear and his spirits untroubled. He wrote:

Coffee glides into one's stomach and sets all of one's mental processes in motion. One's ideas advance in column of route like battalions of the Grande Armée. Memories come up at the double, bearing the standards which will lead the troops into battle. The light cavalry deploys at the gallop. The artillery of logic thunders along with its supply wagons and shells. Brilliant notions join in the combat as sharpshooters. The characters don their costumes, the paper is covered with ink, the battle has started, and ends with an outpouring of black fluid like a real battlefield enveloped in swaths of black smoke from the expended gunpow-

der. Were it not for coffee one could not write, which is to say one could not live.

To the end of his days it did not cross Balzac's mind that the illnesses that plagued him in his last years were at least partly caused by the excessive quantities of coffee he consumed, that his weakened heart, shattered nerves and complicated digestive complaints could be traced to the coffee to which he had enslaved himself. Late in his life, when he complained to Dr. Nacquart about the pains in his stomach that were so intense they blotted everything else from his consciousness, the physician suggested that he had poisoned himself by drinking too much coffee, and that his only hope of obtaining relief would be by giving up the brew.

"Never!" Balzac replied. "I wouldn't be able to write a single word!"

After he became a successful author he allowed himself to indulge in other habits that, in the main, he acquired because of his desire to emulate Napoleon I. The great Emperor was still his idol, and Balzac allowed himself one luxury in his study. He placed a small marble bust of Napoleon on a pedestal near the windows, where he could see it, and he carried the little statue with him whenever he traveled.

Like Napoleon, he took hot baths to relax, and imitated the Emperor's habit of immersing himself in a tub before dining, whether it be at home or elsewhere. Yet Balzac could not permit himself to squander time, so he employed a board that rested on top of the tub so he could correct proofs of his books while taking a hot bath.

The Emperor had always signed his letters with the initial N. Balzac emulated him, signing most of his letters with the letter B. This initial also indicated final approval on manuscript corrections, proofs, contracts and written instructions to attorneys, tailors, mistresses and servants. Eventually he signed only the initial when writing to his publishers.

Napoleon was often portrayed in paintings and sculpture with one hand inserted inside his waistcoat, and it was generally believed he had formed the habit in an attempt to ease the pain caused by an ulcer. One day, in Balzac's later years, when he was trying to ignore, then deny the stomach pains that tormented him, Dr. Nacquart tried to force him to admit he was in distress. "Why do you stand there with your hand grasping your stomach?" he demanded.

"I didn't realize that's what I was doing," Balzac said. "It must be because I've so admired the Emperor that I've grown to resemble him."

VII

Honoré de Balzac always dreamed of an aristocratic lady of high station, wealthy and beautiful, who would fall in love with him and become his mistress, perhaps even his wife. She would be all things to him, just as Mme. de Berny had been: lover, confidante, adviser, helper, mother. The Duchess d'Abrantès had been a wealthy aristocrat, to be sure, but she had been somewhat shop-worn, and at best had met only a few of his qualifications. So his search continued.

The sympathy he expressed in his books for women over thirty, his sensitive understanding of their moods and problems, brought him great quantities of complimentary letters, most of which he answered with one of several forms of short, form replies. But in late October 1831, he received a letter from a reader that piqued his interest. The lady's handwriting was not only unusual, but indicated she was exceptionally well bred, perhaps highly educated.

Her language was becoming to a woman of high station. Having been in the printing business he knew fine paper. Her stationery was the most expensive made in France.

She signed the letter with an English name, but he suspected a pseudonym, and surmised that she was French. She used colloquial expressions difficult for a foreigner to manage. And it was obvious she wanted to hear from him because the letter contained a return address.

What interested him more than anything else was her direct challenge to him. He pretended to admire and understand women, she said, but in reality he hated them and wanted to denigrate them. His *Physiologie* was not only written from a lofty male point of view at the expense of the female, but he also dealt frivolously with women, thus proving that he had no genuine respect for them.

Although Balzac was working furiously to fulfill his many obligations, he paused in his labors long enough to write an impassioned defense of himself to his unknown correspondent. With the same concentrated energy he gave to his books, he sent her a letter of five closely written pages, treating her with calculated shrewdness. He opened the letter by thanking her for her criticism, remarking that it proved she was interested in him. Then he said:

For a woman who has known the tempests of life, the sense of my book is that it attributes the faults committed by married women wholly to their husbands. You must suppose that your letter, filled with the touching expression of feelings natural to a woman's heart, has left me indifferent. Such sympathy inspired at a distance is my most cherished possession, my whole fortune, my most pure delight.

Five long pages written in this vein were enough to dispel the mists of anonymity surrounding any woman sufficiently interested in Honoré de Balzac to have taken the initiative, and the lady revealed her identity to him in a second letter. She was the Marquise de Castries, who would become the Duchess de Castries when her estranged husband came into the higher title. The former Claire-Clemence-Henriette de Maillé was a blueblood of bluebloods, a bona fide member of a very small group of France's ultra-aristocrats.

Balzac, like every other literate Frenchman, was familiar with the lady's romantic story. A red-haired, green-eyed beauty, she had been married at a very early age to the Marquis de Castries, whose preference for handsome young men had caused her to leave him. In 1822, she and Victor von Metternich, the dashing son of the Austrian Chancellor had fallen in love, and five years later Claire had borne him a son. At the instigation of the Chancellor, the Austrian Emperor had given the baby the title of Baron von Aldenburg.

In 1828, the lovely Claire had suffered a broken leg when she had fallen from her horse, and since that time had walked with a decided limp. The following year young Metternich had died, and she had returned to France from Vienna. Her scarlet past had made it difficult for her to take her place at the court of Charles X, much less that of the self-righteous, moralistic Louis Philippe, so she had spent most of her time either at the country estate of her father, the Duke de Maillé, or that of her uncle, the Duke de Fitz-James, who was a great-grandson of King James II of England.

Balzac had come to know the Duke de Fitz-James at the home of Olympe Pélissier, and Claire had questioned her uncle at some length about the author, so she already knew a great deal about him. Balzac, on the other hand, knew only that his correspondent was a wealthy aristocrat with a romantically scandalous past, and that she was alleged to be one of the most beautiful women in France. That was all Balzac needed to know.

After an agonizing wait he received another communication from her late in February 1832, suggesting that he call on her at her father's Paris town house. Balzac replied with indecent haste:

It is rare to encounter noble hearts and true friendships. I, more than anyone, am so lacking in disinterested support on which I can rely that, at the risk of losing a great deal by making myself known to you in person, I accept your generous offer. If I were not engaged in an urgent task I should have called upon you already to pay my respects with that openness of heart which you value. But after many struggles and honorable misfortunes—calamities of which one is proud—I have still some work to do before gaining a few hours of leisure during which I need be neither author nor artist but myself alone. It is those hours which, with your permission, I hope to devote to you.

Balzac made it appear he was unhurried, yet the next ten days became a torment, and he summoned all his powers of concentration to keep at work. Finally, during the second week of March, his coachman maneuvered his carriage through the narrow entrance of the Maillé inner courtyard. Never had he visited such a magnificent house.

And never had he encountered such a lovely woman. Claire was thirty-five, three years his senior, but she resembled a girl in her early twenties. There was no blemish or wrinkle that marred her skin, her green eyes were luminous and she wore her dark red hair loose, letting it cascade over her bare shoulders. Although her limp was barely perceptible, it obviously made her painfully self-conscious. Her gown was of the purest silk, and her charm was so infectious that Balzac could scarcely believe she was real.

He wrote to Zulma Carraud that he had been tempted instantly to declare his undying love for her. Yet he later revealed to George Sand that he knew all would be lost if he moved too quickly. He spent a dignified hour with the marquise, discussing literature, and then he retreated. He hoped he could see her again, but since he was extremely busy, perhaps they could correspond.

For the next eight weeks he absented himself from the De Maillé home and contented himself with a measured, almost impersonal correspondence, although he confided to Zulma Carraud that he was madly in love. By May, he decided the time had come to step up the pace of his campaign. He wrote to the marquise again:

The author's business has been concluded. Will you now permit me to express my gratitude to you, a profound gratitude for the hours you have spent in writing to me. They are imprinted on my memory like unwritten poems, like dreams born of an arrangement of clouds in the sky, like the sound of beautiful music. I would tell you that I begin to fear such sweet enchantments, did I not feel that you are above foolish talk of that kind. For you there must be no flattery; you require nothing but the truth and, above all, the most affectionate respect.

He called on her again, thereafter leaving nothing to chance. Afraid that he might see the Duke de Fitz-James at Olympe's salon, and that Claire might learn of his relationship with the notorious courtesan, he not only broke with Olympe, but he also made it clear that he had no intention of seeing her again. Never one to burn his bridges, however, he secretly informed Olympe that he would resume their relationship in a few months, after he attended to a matter of pressing business. He was as good as his word.

Balzac's siege became intense. He escorted the marquise to dinner. He took her to the theatre, then returned to the handsome De Maillé house to chat with her, often until long after midnight. Meanwhile he drove himself to maintain his work schedule.

Claire de Castries was flattered by the attentions of a man whose work was being hailed in some quarters as that of a genius. She had been neglected for several years by her fellow members of high society, her limp had made her shy, and life in the country homes of her father and uncle had been lonely. But it did not cross her mind to become romantically involved with the homely little man who looked like a tradesman and whose manners were reprehensible, no matter how great his charm or how stimulating his conversation. She enjoyed his company, but she may have been stunned when he declared himself in an impassioned letter:

You have received me so kindly, the hours I have spent in your company have been so delightful, that I am firmly convinced that in you alone shall I find happiness. I am equally convinced I can offer you a full share of happiness.

Balzac presented her with gifts that were the most precious of his possessions, the manuscript of three books, *La Femme de trente ans, Le Colonel Chabert* and *Le Message*. His narcissism was so great that, for the rest of his life, he always presented an original manuscript to someone he wanted to overwhelm.

Claire stubbornly resisted his pressure, making it plain she had no intention of engaging in an affair with him. If he wanted her friendship, she was willing to give it. If he demanded something more, she was drawing a firm line.

Balzac was miserable. His love for her was genuine, or so he believed, and he convinced himself she enjoyed his suffering. Whether she actually encouraged his romantic interest up to a point, then called a halt when he pressed too hard, is impossible to determine. He himself went to great lengths to leave that portrait of the marquise, and later in his novel, *La Duchesse de Langeais*, he cruelly spelled out what he claimed was her attitude:

This woman not only received me kindly, but also displayed for my benefit all the arts of her very considerable powers of coquetry. She desired to please me and exerted herself to the utmost to keep me in my state of intoxication and to spur me on. She did all she could to force a quiet and timorous lover to declare himself.

It was true that Claire made a number of thoughtful gestures, such as sending him a bouquet of flowers on his name day, the feast of St. Honoré. Whether she intended such a gift as a friendly way of thanking him for his attention to her, or whether she was leading him on, as he later believed, is still a matter of conjecture.

In an effort to impress the lady, who was a firm Bourbon adherent, Balzac wrote an article for a Royalist magazine in which he strongly supported the Throne. The Republican friends who had considered him a liberal were deeply disappointed, and Zulma Carraud wrote him an anguished letter in which she asked, "Are you never going to abandon this empty, tempestuous life that leads you nowhere?"

To be sure, Balzac climbed out of the political arena as quickly as he entered it, and showed no more interest in the subject. He hated censorship, and to that extent was opposed to any repressive measures practiced by the regime, but otherwise he remained convinced all political systems were evil and corrupt, and that the individual was ill-served by all of them.

Balzac was seeing Claire one evening during the week and on Sunday afternoons. He permitted himself to be lured away from his desk one additional evening, perhaps to a dinner given by Delphine Girardin, perhaps to go to a restaurant with Victor Hugo. The rest of the time he felt he had to make up for lost time. He would sleep from eight o'clock in the evening until midnight, and write straight through until eight the following night. His schedule would have killed a man endowed with less will power and a weaker physical constitution, but Balzac survived his regimen, and actually appeared to flourish under a semi-monastic existence.

He could not resist Claire's summons, however, and he became concerned when she hinted that she might invite him to accompany her and her father on a trip to Switzerland in August. He told Mme. de Berny the tentative plans, and she urged him not to go since he would be wasting his time in the service of someone who had no intention of allowing him to draw closer. His first mistress was a far better judge of women than was Balzac himself, but he was incapable of accepting her advice. A letter he sent to Zulma in late July explained his predicament:

I must now go to Aix and climb up to Savoy, running after someone who is perhaps making sport of me—one of those aristocratic ladies who are no doubt an abomination in your eyes, one of those faces of angelic beauty behind which assumes there is a beautiful soul. She is a real duchess, very condescending, very amiable, sensitive, witty, a coquette, completely different from anyone I have ever before known. A woman who withdraws from every attempt at closer contact, who asserts that she loves me, yet if she had her way would keep me under supervision in the depths of a Venetian palace. She is a woman (you know I confess everything to you!) who wants me to write exclusively for her, one of those women whom one must worship without reserve and on one's knees if they ask for it, and whom it is such a pleasure to conquer—a woman such as one meets in one's dreams. She is jealous of everything!

Oh, it would be better for me if I were with you in Angoulême, near your powder factory, being sensible and having my peace of mind, listening to the windmills churning round, stuffing myself with truffles, laughing and gossiping in the company of you and your friends—instead of here, where I am wasting my time and my life!

In spite of his protests, there were reasons why Balzac wanted to absent himself from Paris. One was political and caused him to remove himself still farther from the problem of who should rule France and in what manner. The Duke de Fitz-James and a number of other prominent men were placed under arrest for conspiring against the Crown, and for a short time Balzac himself, to his amazement, was suspect. He was known to be friendly with Fitz-James's niece, and in the past year or so he had often spent an evening in the company of the duke and his friends. After lengthy questioning by the police Balzac was exonerated, but the fright he had suffered lingered on.

He was also beginning to find the Duchess d'Abrantès a nuisance. She used him as an errand boy, insisting that he take care of countless petty details connected with the publication of her memoirs. He not only lacked the strength to make a complete break with her, but repeatedly obligated himself to her by his inability to resist her summons to her bedchamber whenever she called him to her apartment. Had he closed her door firmly behind him, that would have ended the relationship, but he didn't know how to break off with her, and hoped that his absence from Paris for a few weeks would clear the air by helping her to forget him.

But Balzac had an even more important reason for wanting to leave Paris for a time. His extravagances were catching up with him, and he found himself unable to pay his innumerable bills. Bill collectors thronged to the house on the Rue Cassini, besieging him there, and refusing to depart when his servants insisted he was not at home. Whenever he looked out of a window, he could see creditors pacing up and down in the lane below.

A partial list of his debts, made in his own hand, indicates the precariousness of his financial position:

Hay for my horses	**900 francs**
Kidskin gloves	**378 francs**
My new enameled clock	**139 francs**
Back wages for servants (3)	**1,400 francs**
Carriage repairs	**97 francs**
Buisson (to whom I have already paid 400 francs in the past month for my new wardrobe, the wretch!)	**581 francs**
Wine delivered in April	**76 francs**
Shoes (4 pair)	**82 francs**
Perfumes	**40 francs**

It had become impossible for him to obtain additional funds. He had already received, and had spent the advance royalties paid to him by various publishers for three new novels, a novella, several short stories and a number of articles, none of which had yet been written. And no publisher would offer him a contract for still more work until he lived up to some of his present obligations. The royalties due to be paid him as they accrued on books already published had been attached by some of his larger creditors. He could not force himself to borrow from such wealthy new friends as the Girardins for fear of spoiling the relationship, and he had already borrowed to the limit from such old friends as Dablin and Dr. Nacquart.

To complicate his situation, his mother learned about his unhappy financial state, and not only wrote him scolding letters but came to the house on the Rue Cassini and followed him into his study, where she stood over him delivering long lectures.

Finally it dawned on Balzac that he could not afford to go to Switzerland until he produced more work, and the distractions of Paris were making life impossible for him there. He was seeing far too much of the marquise, too, and he estimated that during time already spent in her company, he could have written two short novels. Over the years he had remained friendly with his mother's onetime paramour, Jean de Margonne, who lived in a fine old château in Saché with his ugly wife. This was the time to accept their standing invitation to visit them. In the quiet of the country he would work more furiously than ever, and by producing more books would reduce his debts. Then he would join the elusive marquise and her father.

His finances were so chaotic that, before leaving Paris, Balzac had to subject himself to a final humiliation. The one person in whom he could place complete trust was his mother, and he knew it, so he humbled himself by asking her to restore order during his absence. A grimly triumphant Mme. *de* Balzac (she, too, had permanently ennobled herself) was happy to oblige.

Before his departure from Paris in mid-July, it occurred to Balzac that he needed pocket money for his sojourn in the country, so he persuaded a publisher to advance him fifteen hundred francs for two short stories he promised to write in the immediate future. Before he could leave town, however, several of his creditors pinioned him, and he was obliged to pay them fourteen hundred francs on account so he wouldn't be served with a restraining order that would have compelled him to remain. So the most discussed, most promising novelist of his age, a man already hailed as a genius, climbed onto a stagecoach for Saché with a total of only one hundred and twenty francs in his pocket.

Once he left Paris, his mother went to work. She immediately cut his overhead by discharging his three house servants and groom, and paid their wages by selling the horses and carriage. She disposed of every ornate piece of furniture and bric-a-brac that could be sold for an appreciable sum. She went to his principal publishers, who were relieved to find someone responsible in charge of his financial affairs, and they agreed to pay her a portion of the income accruing from his already published books.

Unable to pay off all of her son's creditors in full, Mme. de Balzac made payments on account to those who could afford to wait for the rest. But there were some, particularly small tradesmen, who were feeling a severe pinch themselves, so she tried to accommodate them.

It was difficult for Mama—as it has been to posterity—to believe the size of many of Balzac's bills. He owed a nearby butcher the sum of fifteen hundred francs and was indebted to a baker to the tune of another seven hundred. How it was possible for him to run up such enormous debts for food has always remained something of a mystery. He was a bachelor who lived alone, ate meat and bread no more than once a day, and frequently dined out. It is true that he gave occasional dinner parties, but it would have been necessary for him to hold a permanent open house to have plunged that far into debt. The butcher and baker were able to show Mme. de Balzac their books, and she was finally convinced that Balzac had not been fleeced by his servants. What may have happened, according to various French scholars who made a detailed study of his intricate, lifelong financial habits, is that Balzac borrowed relatively small sums from the tradesmen from time to time, and these debts mounted. He was habitually so careless about money that, when he found his pockets empty, he didn't care where he picked up twenty-five or fifty francs.

On the jolting stagecoach to Saché, Balzac had time to review his disgraceful situation, and he concluded that no matter how hard he worked, or how rapidly he completed manuscripts, it would be impossible for him to catch up. He would remain in debt forever unless he found a small fortune, and there was only one way he could get his hands on an appreciable lump sum: he must marry an heiress.

The Marquise de Castries, to whom he was still writing the most stirring of love letters, was too elusive, and he realized that, at best, he might be forced to pursue her for months, even years. He had to find someone else, and finally he thought of an eligible lady. One Baroness d'Urbroucq, who admired his work and with whom he had been maintaining a correspondence, owned a château not far from Saché. Unfortunately she was at present staying in another château which she owned at Jarzé, so he made up his mind to lure her to her nearer estate and then unleash an intensive campaign to persuade her to marry him.

Jean de Margonne and his wife were marvelously hospitable, life at their villa was serene, and Balzac went to work with a vengeance, taking time each day to write a love letter to Claire de Castries, and another, considerably more urgent, to the baroness. There were other distractions, not the least of them a series of exasperated communications from his harried mother.

Intolerant as always in his dealings with her, Balzac failed to take into consideration her own situation. She was nearing sixty, in poor health and had been saddled with an impossible problem that would have tried the courage of a martyr and the patience of a saint. Unwilling or unable to realize he had placed a crushing burden on her shoulders, or that she was under no obligation to help him, Balzac sent her a series of angry notes. In one of them he said:

I was just about to make a brave start on my work this morning when your letter arrived and jarred me so thoroughly that I wanted to weep. How can I possibly think in terms of my art when I am suddenly confronted with the ugly portrait of my dire poverty? What a mean and degrading picture you paint! Do you suppose that if I did not already feel crushed I would have fled from Paris to this remote haven? Do you suppose I should be working like this? If you are capable of expressing compassion for another human, even if he is your son, I beg you to be more considerate of my feelings!

His letters added to the load Mme. de Balzac was carrying, and Laure wrote a firm letter of remonstrance to her brother, telling him to treat Mama with the respect and honor due her for helping him.

This communication saddened Balzac, and he wept. He replied at length, telling Laure it was his mother's courage that enabled him to work, and he begged his sister to tell Mama it was difficult for him to write the letter because the tears in his eyes interfered. Then, having mailed the epistle, he promptly forgot all about Mama, who continued to wrestle with his problems in Paris.

The miracle of Balzac's stay at Saché is that, in the six weeks he spent there, he completed work on the book that he regarded as the great masterpiece of his life, a reply for all time to silence his critics. Posterity has been critical of the work, but, to an extent, has confirmed his purely intellectual judgment of *Notice biographique sur Louis Lambert.*

Balzac tried, consciously and deliberately, to cast *Louis Lambert* in the mold of Goethe's *Faust* and Byron's *Manfred.* Although he may not have equaled the former, most critics have felt that his work was on a par with the latter. Balzac wrote a tragedy, and ignoring his growing feminine audience, appealed exclusively to an intellectual readership. *Louis Lambert* well may have been the most cerebral of his novels.

Realizing there was a strong kinship between genius and madness, a notion that far outstripped the medical research of his day, Balzac made an intensive study of a concept that fascinated him. His protagonist was a genius who attempted, through leading a totally ascetic life, to perfect his powers of concentration. Unable to tolerate the strains of this existence in a world where the needs of the flesh and spirit are great and temptations are many, Louis Lambert loses his reason. The framework was simple, far less complex than most of Balzac's plots, but his psychological explorations into the human psyche were made in remarkable depth, and his handling of philosophical and theological themes showed that he had developed into a thinker of considerable powers, even though little of his rationale was original.

The childhood of Louis Lambert closely paralleled that of the author, as did the lonely poverty in which he lived as a very young man. But it would be a mistake to regard these portions of the book as completely autobiographical. Balzac availed himself of the author's prerogative to alter the material as he saw fit, and for the sake of improving a work of fiction he changed innumerable details. For example, his Louis Lambert read an astonishing number of books in early childhood, and while it is true that his creator also read them, he did not do so until late adolescence and early manhood.

There was a touch of the occult in Louis Lambert's philosophy, and here Balzac was expressing his own views. Every individual was made up of two distinct persons, the outer man and the inner man. The former was subject to all the laws of nature, to the processes of growth and decay, and his life could be ended by accident or war as well as by old age. The inner man, however, was inviolate, and was the possessor of an independent, vital power or force. A genius, and Louis Lambert had such a mind, was able to make a complete separation between the inner and outer selves, and could transport the inner man elsewhere. This phenomenon, Balzac declared, explained the ability of martyrs to suffer physical torments; they removed the inner man from his outer, physical shell and took it to a more salubrious, always cerebral climate.

The inner man was intuitive as well as intellectual. The ideas he formed were the outgrowth of an intellectual process, while the individual's desires, which also emanated from the inner man, were purely subjective in both their origin and their form of expression.

In order to achieve the ultimate plane of intellectual endeavor, the inner man must suppress his desires, an impossible goal in the material world, such as that exemplified by Parisian life. The individual's problem is that, in order to become more intellectual, he must renounce materialism. But the outer man needs the materialistic in order to survive, and this forces the inner man to practice guile, engage in chicanery, to lie, cheat and commit even more serious crimes if he wishes not only to survive, but to prosper as well.

A beautiful woman named Pauline de Villenoix loves Louis Lambert and tried to help him reconcile the forces that are warring within him. But Lambert tries to renounce her, too, in an attempt to subjugate the flesh to the mind. Eventually his efforts to rise to a totally intellectual level of existence drive him to madness, and he dies, cradled in Pauline's arms.

It might be noted here that Balzac made a daring innovation in his delineation of Pauline. The background he created for her was partly Jewish, and the nobility of her nature was the author's firm reply to the spirit of anti-Semitism that was rampant in French aristocratic, military and even intellectual circles. He was one of the first to attack the evil of anti-Semitism in his century, even though he must have known that he would receive additional critical abuse because of his stand.

Honoré de Balzac was a liberal without ever quite realizing it. He espoused all possible liberty for the individual, and his heroes and heroines repeatedly epitomized the spirit of free speech, a freedom to practice religion as one saw fit, or to turn away from faith in God altogether, freedom of the press and freedom of assemblage. His position was close to that of the men who were struggling to establish the new United States of America as a viable entity, both political and personal. But, whenever he had the opportunity to strike a blow for liberty in his own life, he stood aside, preferring not to take a position that might indicate he favored any cause.

Louis Lambert was a rich and sometimes unpalatable intellectual stew. In the course of numerous rewrites Balzac deliberately explicated all of his own metaphysical, social, philosophical and psychological thinking.

In many respects the book was a failure, and viewed exclusively as a work of fiction it is almost unutterably dull. Neither Louis nor Pauline comes to life, the plot drags, and the long digressions into the depths of the author's own thinking become irritating distractions that confuse the reader.

Nevertheless, the courage Balzac displayed in writing and publishing the book was great. Goethe, whom he held up as a model, spent a long lifetime in the preparation of *Faust*. Byron, the other model, worked for years on *Manfred*. But the peripatetic Honoré de Balzac completed *Louis Lambert* in six weeks of concentrated labor at the home of the Margonnes. His achievement, certainly his most strenuous and concerted effort to deal with exclusively intellectual themes, is at the very least almost beyond credence.

After sending the manuscript of the novel off to his publisher, Balzac realized he could not tarry at the Margonne villa without wearing his welcome thin. But he was not yet in a position to join Claire de Castries in Switzerland, and his scheme to lure the baroness to Saché had failed, so that he could not yet return to Paris with impunity. His affairs there were improved, but he still owed his creditors ten thousand francs, and knew he would be inundated with lawsuits if he set foot in the city.

So he found another refuge, this time in Angoulême, at the home of the Carrauds, where Zulma and her husband, both of whom had known dire poverty, welcomed him warmly. In this salubrious atmosphere he continued to work rapidly and well, and in a short time he turned out a novel, *La Femme abandonnée*, that would be particularly well received by his women readers, and several short stories that would be published by magazines and eventually would appear in his collection, the *Contes drolatiques*. Had he not been plagued by his debts, Balzac would have been a happy man.

Suddenly and without warning a guardian angel in the guise of his mother solved his problems. The exasperated Mme. de Balzac had been searching for a weapon, a lever she could use to curb her son's infantile extravagances without harming his new stature as a writer, and finally she found a way. She persuaded her generous and long-suffering friend, Mme. Delannoy, to loan Balzac the ten thousand francs he so badly needed. But this was not a free gift of the money. In return Balzac was required to swear a solemn oath, in identical letters to Mama and to Mme. Delannoy, that he would pay off all his debts, adding compound interest to the principal, and that hereafter he would live modestly, saving a minimum of twenty per cent of his income.

It was easy for a man who wrote thousands of words each day to scribble a few more on paper. Balzac solemnly gave the pledge his mother demanded, and then forgot the matter. He had been saved, he was free to return to Paris or travel anywhere else he wished, and nothing else mattered. In fact, it annoyed him that his mother elected to pay off his creditors herself, and used up all of the ten thousand francs. He would have found it convenient to take two or three thousand for his own purposes.

Balzac now shrugged off all sense of responsibility and made his immediate plans. Lord Byron had found contentment in Switzerland, he told Zulma and wrote Mme. de Berny, and he declared he would write another masterpiece in the Alps—a book even more profound than *Louis Lambert*.

He fooled neither his first mistress nor his good friend. Each knew he planned to visit the Marquise de Castries and accompany her on a tour of Italy. Mme. de Berny was positive that a great lady of Claire de Castries' standing, a woman descended from both French and English kings, would not contemplate a romantic involvement with a middle-class author, no matter how highly she regarded his work, and would laugh at him if he dared to ask for her hand in marriage. Only one recourse was left to the woman who was no longer sleeping with Balzac, but who knew he was still emotionally dependent on her. If he joined the marquise, Mme. de Berny wrote him, she would destroy his letters without reading them, and would forever close her door to him.

Zulma Carraud's stand was less drastic, and instead she tried reason. She and her husband sat up the better part of a night with their guest, arguing, begging, commanding, pleading. He would be chasing another of his phantoms if he pursued the marquise. She enjoyed the attentions of a man who had achieved recent intellectual renown, and his admiration softened the harshness which she herself was suffering, but under no circumstances could be serious about him, and common sense dictated that he abandon his foolish dream.

Balzac weighed the matter carefully, paying no attention to the good advice of the Carrauds. All that bothered him was the possibility that Mme. de Berny meant what she said, and the idea made him so panicky that he sent her several long letters, assuring her that no other woman meant anything to him. Analyzing her threat, he finally concluded that she was bluffing, so he would be taking only a slight risk by following his own inclinations. He could not banish his dream of making a lady of the highest caste his mistress, and he believed Mme. de Berny still cared too much about him to cut off all relations with him. Therefore, he resolved to follow his own inclinations.

It was necessary, however, to take care of a few practical details. He had spent the last of his one hundred and twenty francs on a stagecoach that had carried him only a part of the way from Saché to Angoulême, and had been forced to make the last part of his journey on foot. Right now he was literally penniless.

He assumed he would be the guest of the marquise, her father and her uncle, the Duke de Fitz-James, who had been released from prison, but he couldn't walk across the Alps to Aix. So he wrote his mother an imperious letter, directing her to send him three hundred francs to Lyon, where he would pick up the money. He also had to get to Lyon from Angoulême, so he borrowed an additional one hundred and fifty francs from the hard-pressed but generous Major Carraud.

Then, with coins once again jingling in his pocket, he set off on what he expected to be the great romantic adventure of his life.

10. Balzac's celebrated coffeepot. Note self-designed crest. (French Cultural Services)

11. George Sand with pipe. Drawn by Alfred de Musset, her lover. (Culver Pictures)

12. Alfred de Musset, Balzac's friend and George Sand's tempestuous lover. (The Bettmann Archive)

13. George Sand, Balzac's colleague and lifelong friend, by Delacroix. (Brown Brothers)

14. Jules Sandeau, George Sand's first lover, and Balzac's sometime friend. (Portrait painted in his mature years.) (The Bettmann Archive)

15. (Above right) The Paris Diligence of Balzac's time. After a contemporary copper engraving. (The Bettmann Archive)

16. (Right) Caricature of Balzac in the late 1830s to early 1840s, at the height of his powers. (French Cultural Services)

17. Balzac's house on the Rue Cassini. Note "secret" entrance on far left. (Photographie Bulloz)

18. Victor Hugo, Balzac's colleague and friend, in his own time regarded as the greatest French author of the age. (The Bettmann Archive)

19. (Below) Balzac with his colleagues and friends, Eugène Sue, Alexandre Dumas and Victor Hugo. Illustration from a book of the period. (Giraudon)

20. The Duchess d'Abrantès, one of Balzac's more illustrious mistresses. (Giraudon)

VIII

Honoré de Balzac was a great believer in omens and signs, and although there were no fortunetellers to consult in Angoulême, he received a letter the day prior to his departure for Aix that convinced him his journey held great promise. The publisher of the *Revue de Paris,* France's most successful magazine, unexpectedly offered him a contract: he would be paid the sum of five hundred francs per month in return for writing a short story each month.

So the journey began on an optimistic note. Yet within twenty-four hours the sky had been darkened by a bad omen. Balzac rode on the stagecoach box with the driver so he could observe the scenery, which he always found useful when writing descriptive passages. When the stage stopped at Thiers, en route to Lyon, for a change of horses, Balzac was thrown from his seat and suffered a severe injury. His leg was cut to the bone and he bled so profusely that other passengers urged him to see a physician in

Thiers and postpone the rest of his journey. But he was so anxious to reach the side of the Marquise de Castries that he ignored the pain and continued the journey. For the next four days he traveled in the open, stretched out on the roof of the stage.

There was a hint of autumn in the air when Balzac reached Aix, and more than a hint of disappointment. Claire de Castries had no intention of allowing the guest to live under the roof of her father's villa, so she had reserved a room for him at a small resort hotel. An additional indignity was a charge of two francs per day for his room, five sous for breakfast and another fifteen sous for lunch.

He saw the marquise every evening, joining her at the villa at six o'clock, and remaining through dinner until eleven. So, he wrote to both Zulma and his mother, he had ample time to write and was working hard on the manuscript of another new book, *La Bataille*. He and Claire dined alone every evening, an experience he enjoyed, but aside from a handshake when they met, she allowed him no intimacies and changed the subject whenever he tried to declare his love for her.

It was difficult to find compensatory pleasures he could mention in his correspondence, but he tried. Each day he gazed out across the mountains into Switzerland, and made an attempt to convince himself, along with his mother, Laure and Zulma, not to mention George Sand, in whom he was also confiding at this time, that the romantic atmosphere would improve as soon as the Duke de Maillé decided the time had come to travel. Then the entire party would be staying in hotels, and it would be impossible for Claire to avoid him.

Meanwhile he paid several visits to the thermal baths for which Aix had been famous since Roman days, and after only three treatments the deep gash on his leg was completely healed. It didn't matter that he would carry a scar for the rest of his days. He rejoiced because his work was proceeding without a hitch in an atmosphere where there were no interruptions. His hotel permitted him to make coffee for himself in his small room, and at noon his lunch, which usually consisted of a hard-boiled egg and a glass of milk, was brought to him on a tray. Aside from the hotel waiter and chambermaid, he saw no one but the withdrawn and elusive marquise.

Leaves were beginning to disappear from the trees, and the mistral, the wind that blows across southern France day and night in the late autumn and winter, began to howl outside the windows of Balzac's hotel room. His routine remained unchanged, and eventually the evasions of the marquise made him irritable. He wrote to Zulma:

I came here hoping for little and much. Much because I am afraid I shall never be loved by her. Why did you send me to Aix? Why did you not pull me from the stagecoach and either keep me in the snug warmth of your house or send me back to Paris?

She is a woman of the most fastidious kind. But are not her refinements acquired at the expense of the spirit? I, who supposedly know the soul of womankind, am unable to decipher her or gauge the sincerity of her moods.

Zulma replied with a long, wasted lecture, telling him to forget the marquise and concentrate exclusively on his work.

By that time Balzac's mood had changed. The publisher of the *Contes drolatiques* wrote him an enthusiastic letter about the book's prospects. The short stories not only dealt with the occult, which was a popular subject, but they had been written in a bawdy spirit that made him the direct descendant of Rabelais. It would be surprising if the book were not a great success.

The editor of the *Revue de Paris*, Pichot, wrote to ask whether he wanted his first month's payment sent to him. Balzac, flushed with the triumph that had not yet materialized, instructed him to send the five hundred francs to "my poor, dear mother, whom I am supporting." It did not occur to him that Mama, after receiving one such payment, would demand that all future payments be made to her as well, and would storm and rant until she got what she wanted.

One night, after returning from his evening with the marquise, an idea for a new book suddenly came to Balzac, and he put aside everything else to work on it. He called it *Le Médecin de campagne*, and in three days and three nights of grueling work he completed enough of it to assure himself a large advance royalty payment from even the most recalcitrant publisher.

To crown his improving situation, the marquise not only extended him a formal invitation to join her and her relatives on the journey to Switzerland and Italy, but she gave him permission to address her by her pet name, Marie. Balzac promptly read far more than she intended into these gestures, and was deliriously happy.

Wanting to make certain the omens were right for the trip, he wore a small piece of flannel next to his body for seventy-two hours, then carefully wrapped it in oiled paper and sent it to his mother. Mme. de Balzac was instructed not to unwrap the paper "so that the essence of my emanations will not be disturbed." Then she was to take the paper-wrapped flannel to her own fortuneteller, who would decide whether Balzac would fulfill his dearest wish on the journey. His letter also asked for a dozen pairs of yellow kidskin gloves, and he insisted she buy new gloves because "all" of his others were "soiled."

A book publisher in Paris sent him an advance payment of four thousand francs for *Le Médecin*, which gave him more than enough money to pay for his share of the coming trip. Still intimidated by his mother's response to his financial collapse, he sent her two thousand francs for the purpose of "disposing of any small debts that may remain." His euphoria, combined with the cash in his pocket, enabled him to make grand gestures.

The theme of *Le Médecin* was a typical Balzac inspiration, and it would become one of the books that would make him immortal. Like all of his great works, it had a basically simple core: a man who has suffered grievously at the hands of society retreats to a mountain village so he can nurse his wounds and recover his spiritual health. He is convinced he needs "silence and shadows" in order to survive. Gradually, against his will, he is drawn into the life of the community, and he persuades the people of the entire area to stop fighting one another, give up their materialistic approach to life and co-operate in a true spirit of brotherly love. The good deeds he performs are, in turn, responsible for his own spiritual regeneration.

It is odd that Balzac managed, once again at a time when he was distracted, to write a book of great power and nobility. Outside influences spurred him into doing his utmost, and he concentrated best when he was forced to put matters of serious personal concern out of his mind.

The Duke de Maillé was unable to make the projected journey, but the marquise and her uncle made no changes in their own plans, and Balzac regarded this as a good sign. The party set out late in the autumn of 1832, and stopped first in Geneva. There, the crisis that had been brewing in Balzac's relations with the marquise came to a boil.

The details of the encounter are unknown, although there are several accounts of what happened. According to one of the most popular stories, Balzac and the marquise paid a visit to the villa in which Byron had lived. The author was deeply moved by the experience, and his sentimental reaction touched Claire, too. For this reason she permitted him to embrace and kiss her for the first time. He leaped to conclusions—moving far too rapidly, apparently—and she felt compelled to tell him that under no circumstances and at no time would she become his mistress. He was forced to take her at her word, and after bidding her farewell he spent hours walking alone on the shores of Lake Geneva, unable to stem the tears that rolled down his face. Later that night he moved his luggage to another hotel, and did not see the Marquise de Castries again, or at least until much later.

A second version is also logical. According to this story Balzac had grown weary of Claire's elusive tactics, and forced a direct confrontation, telling her she had led him on and demanding that she submit to him, in accordance with the unspoken promise her attitude had indicated.

But she had no intention of sleeping with him, and made her position plain with such candor that she mortally insulted him.

He was too short, too fat and too sloppy for her to develop more than an impersonally friendly interest in him. She could not allow herself to be loved by a man whose hair was greasy, whose linen was dirty, who bathed infrequently and doused himself with evil-smelling perfume. In brief, she found him physically repulsive.

There may be more truth in the second story than in the first, if Balzac's reaction is any criterion. Immediately calling off his trip, he started to work on a novel he called *La Duchesse de Langeais*, in which he magnified all of Claire's faults and held her up to ridicule. And he wrote it at a rate even faster than his usual burning pace.

If that had been the end of the story of the Marquise de Castries and her bourgeois swain, it would have been a semi-tragedy with a wry ending. But the next chapter, which took place in Paris the following year, reduced their relationship to the level of comedy, if not of farce. After Balzac finished the final version of the book he took it to the De Maillé town house, and during the course of a visit that began soon after sundown and lasted until the small hours of the morning, he read every word to Claire.

She responded like a perfect lady. She recognized herself immediately, of course, but she made no complaint, and in a gracious gesture that has seen no equal in similar situations, she granted him her permission to publish the book without change, telling him she would not sue for libel.

The postscript is still more amusing. Enamored of literature and the literary world, Claire then formed a close friendship with Sainte-Beuve, the critic who loathed Balzac, who despised him in turn. The marquise's action solidified the friendship of Balzac and Victor Hugo, who had his own reasons for hating Sainte-Beuve. (The critic had seduced Mme. Hugo.) Few men needed friends who were his peers more than Honoré de Balzac, so, in the long run, he was well-served.

His immediate reaction to the dissolution of his abortive romance was significant. First he wrote to his mother that he could not tolerate a return to his Paris way of living for several months. Then he traveled straight to Nemours, where Mme. de Berny had bought a house, and submitted himself to her ego-soothing ministrations. They were no longer lovers, but that was not important at this critical juncture. His deflated soul needed restoration, and she could do more for him than anyone else.

His relationship with Mme. de Berny had become completely platonic by this time; she no longer attracted him physically, and was herself so sensitive to the differences in their ages that she made no physical demands on him. But she managed, as always, to restore his wounded vanity, and in gratitude he dedicated *Louis Lambert* to her, writing, "*To the woman I have chosen, now and forever.*"

The treatment he had received at the hands of the woman who had refused to become his mistress still smarted, however, and he fumed in his correspondence. "*I detest Mme. de Castries,*" he wrote to Zulma Carraud. "*She has shattered my life without giving me a new one in its place.*" And in a letter to Eugène Sue he declared, "*The relationship between us remained within entirely irreproachable bounds, precisely as Mme. de Castries wished. It was one of the most unfortunate strokes of ill fortune I have ever suffered, and my entire life has collapsed in ruins at my feet. I can no longer think! Alas, I can no longer concentrate, and hence am unable to write a word!*"

Balzac enjoyed the drama of strong letters, but his friends knew better than to take his exaggerated claims at face value. His work was going smoothly at Mme. de Berny's house, as it always had, and although his rejection by Mme. de Castries continued to annoy him, he slept soundly and ate heartily. In fact, he put on weight, and within a few weeks developed a pronounced potbelly that would grow larger over the years.

During his sojourn with his first mistress he made a careful evaluation of his personal and professional situation, dealing with the former in a comic-opera style that makes it difficult to regard him as a man of high purpose, much less talent, but also making a number of decisions regarding his work that were testimonials to his courage as well as his ambition. Mme. de Castries aside, no facet of his personal life was satisfactory. His debts stood at more than one hundred thousand francs, and while none of them were pressing, he despaired of being able to reduce them.

Mere money, of course, was never one of Balzac's major concerns. Regardless of whether his purse was full or empty, he spent vast sums with abandon, a process that accelerated as he grew older and more renowned. He acted as though he believed a man of his reputation deserved the best things in life, and whether he could afford them was irrelevant. In the autumn of 1832, however, he continued to suffer occasional pangs of middle-class conscience, and had not yet become inured to the idea of spending the rest of his life in debt.

What bothered him more than anything else was his lack of a satisfactory love life. Prostitutes gave him temporary physical satisfaction, but supplied none of his emotional needs, and he found himself unable to follow Sue's example and take a mistress. "One can buy love for an hour," he told his friend, "but I do not like the idea of buying it by the month."

A lady who would fulfill his needs was not easy to find, and he rationalized his reasons for not wanting to settle for less. "A woman of high standing simply will not make advances," he told Sue. "I, who find eighteen hours each day insufficient for the work I must do, cannot spare the time to prostitute my own nature by simpering and dressing up for the benefit of some easy woman whose company I am unable to enjoy except at odd moments."

He still dreamed of the ideal solution. He wanted to find a wealthy woman, preferably one of noble birth, who would not only marry him and make him financially solvent, but who would also fall madly in love with him. He wouldn't have believed it possible that no woman was rich enough or devoted enough to cater to his insatiable demands for both money and love.

His attitude toward his work was, in a sense, equally unrealistic. He knew he had acquired a large feminine following, and was as popular as his principal rivals, Sue and Dumas. By applying himself even more diligently, he could gain a still larger share of the women's market. But his ambition continued to gnaw at him, and he was more determined than ever to become the great historian of nineteenth-century French life, recording its morals, customs, mores and institutions.

How could he gain the higher ambition without losing any of his popularity? The deliberate decision he reached was typical of Honoré de Balzac: he would do both. He would continue to write books that would appeal to the ladies, and at the same time he would stretch his talents to their limits, and would experiment, try new forms, delve as deeply as possible into the complexities of human nature and relationships. On either level he would have won enduring fame, and the real miracle of Balzac, the author, is that he simultaneously achieved both goals.

Apparently he could think on several levels more or less simultaneously, and in the next four years his work was marked by a breathtaking variety. On the same day that he was engaged in making excruciatingly difficult revisions of a philosophical novel, *Séraphita,* he wrote a light, earthy story for the *Contes drolatiques.* Certainly it is a tribute to his genius that both have survived as literature. Rarely does his own basically exuberant nature, combined with his ability to tell a story for its own sake, appear more clearly than in the *Contes drolatiques,* and he not only cast these stories in a Rabelaisian mold, a gesture that in itself took courage, but he wrote in a mock-archaic French that he invented for his own purposes. It would have been too slow and painful a process to do the stories in genuine medieval French, so he preferred to develop a language of his own. In this way nothing was allowed to interfere with the easy flow of his storytelling.

By the autumn of 1832 Balzac knew he possessed the ability to make his feminine readers weep at will, but he decried this talent, and while not ashamed of it, made up his mind that he would be remembered for something more profound. Again and again, in what he himself considered his better works, he repeated the theme he had first stated in *Louis Lambert,* that of the genius who reaches for the stars and fails. The financial failure of these books, relatively speaking, convinced him that he was drawing a parallel to his own life in these works, but in spite of his increasing bitterness he battered at the door of immortality. Sometimes he believed he was incapable of opening that door, but on other occasions, and for brief periods, he was sufficiently objective in making his judgments to realize he had succeeded.

In *La Recherche de l'absolu* he wrote about a brilliant chemist who obsessively sought the primordial element, and was destroyed by that search. In *Le Chef-d'oeuvre inconnu* he dealt with a painter who sought perfection, went too far, and created a shambles. *Séraphita* and *Le Médecin de campagne* are considered "religious" novels because he made studies in depth of metaphysical themes, but in them, too, he sought to reduce the mystical to absolute terms.

Balzac has been criticized for his careless, sometimes slipshod writing in these major works, and even in his own day the more pedantic of the literary reviewers castigated him for allowing these books to appear first in popular novels as serials. No author, they said, could write cohesively for serialization, but what they failed to recognize was the grand sweep as well as the scope of Balzac's writing. His gusto was as great when he wrote in depth on philosophical subjects as it was when he was telling a story for its own sake.

To be sure, Honoré de Balzac has won his greatest renown as a "realist." He has been acclaimed for a century and a half as an author who wrote about real people living and reacting and interacting in real situations, feeling real emotions and suffering real personality defects as well as enjoying real triumphs. This also was the judgment of his contemporaries and the reading public.

His first overwhelming success was *Le Colonel Chabert*, and was followed by an even greater triumph, *Eugénie Grandet*. The pious and timid Eugénie was hailed as a real person, and so was the miserly father with whom she was in conflict. Within the limitations of the girl's own life her successes and failures were as important as the rise and fall of empires, and meant as much to her as the winning or losing of a throne meant to a monarch.

Many years passed, however, before posterity recognized what Balzac himself knew from the start. The characters who were the mosaics in the pattern that made up the *Comédie humaine* were not "real people." As Balzac told Victor Hugo on a number of occasions, and as Hugo then wrote, the characters created by Balzac were *enlarged* versions of reality. "Most people are trapped by the drabness of their surroundings and the mean nature of the lives they are forced to lead," Balzac said. "So, in order to capture the imagination and sympathy of the reader, I must exaggerate their real traits. It is this magnification that enables the reader to find parallels in his own life."

What is significant is that by the early 1830s, with the better part of his career still ahead of him, Balzac had mastered his craft. He knew precisely what he was doing. In spite of his bumbling personal life and its near-tragedies and near-farces, he was able to create, on paper, a world he could persuade his audience was genuine.

His stay with Mme. de Berny after the collapse of his serio-comic romance with Mme. de Castries created a number of profound changes in his own vocational life. None of these appeared overnight, and many had been developing for a long time, but now they jelled within him, and he made up his mind to go his own way, regardless of the consequences. This decision was foolhardy as well as audacious, and may have contributed materially to his subsequent financial problems. No man enjoys being snubbed, but Balzac deliberately determined to stop seeking the favor of literary critics. Other authors could wine and dine the critics, if they wished, but he would not. They could judge his work solely on merit, and if they refused, if they turned against him out of personal pique, his work would speak for itself, and would confound them.

Knowing what he wanted to do, he would no longer accept the advice of publishers. His mind was filled with a dozen or more projects that would make up a portion of the tapestry of the *Comédie humaine*, which he so clearly saw himself, but which he could expect no publisher to see, much less understand at this early stage. Therefore a publisher would be required to accept his work on faith, believing that in the long run the judgment of Balzac would prove itself right, and any publisher who refused to accept Balzac on this basis would be abandoned immediately for another.

Balzac knew his attitude was arrogant, yet by now he had acquired the confidence in himself as an author that he still lacked as a whole man. The newspapers were filled with malicious anecdotes about everyone in the public eye, but he did not care what was said about him, or how much the newspaper-reading public snickered. His work would be his reply, and by the autumn of 1833 he was so sure of himself that he wrote:

I shall rule unchallenged in the intellectual life of Europe! Another two years and patience is all I require, and then I shall stride on over the heads of all those who have wanted to fetter my hands and hinder my advance! Under persecution and injustice my courage has grown as hard as bronze.

The magnitude of the task he had set for himself had not yet occurred to him, and he believed he could accomplish the ultimate goals of the *Comédie humaine* within a relatively few years. Perhaps his arrogance was in part responsible for his shortsightedness, although it can be argued that even he did not fully realize quite how high he was aiming. By the autumn of 1834 he remained optimistic, and in a remarkable outline he exclaimed what still lay ahead:

By 1838 the three sections of the gigantic work will have been so far completed that one will at least be able to recognize the plan of the structure and arrive at some judgment of the conception as a whole. In the "Studies of Manners" are to be depicted all the repercussions of social conditions. I want to portray every situation in life, every type of physiognomy, every kind of male and female character, every way of living, every profession, every social stratum, every French province, childhood, the prime of life and old age, politics, law and war—nothing is to be omitted. When this has been done and the story of the human heart revealed thread by thread, social history displayed in all its branches, then the foundations will have been laid. I have no wish to describe episodes that have their springs in the imagination. My theme is that which actually happens everywhere.

Then comes the second stage—the "Philosophical Studies." The depiction of effects is to be followed by the depiction of causes. In the "Studies of Manners" I shall have shown the interplay of emotion, life and its consequences. In the "Philosophical Studies" I shall speak of the origins of the emotions and the motivating causes of life. I shall pose the question—"What are the operating forces, the conditions, without which neither society nor the life of the individual is possible?" And after I have dealt with society in this way, I shall examine it with a critical eye. In the "Studies of Manners" individuals will be depicted in types; in the "Philosophical Studies" the types will be depicted as individuals. I must make it very clear that it will always be life that I am portraying.

And finally, after the effects and causes, will come the "Analytical Studies," a part of which will be the Physiologie du mariage, *for after the effects and causes we must search for principles. The manners provide the drama, the causes represent the grooves in which life is conducted and the stage machinery. And finally the principles, in other words, the author of the play. In proportion, however, as the entire work gains height as though in a series of spirals, it narrows and becomes more concentrated.*

If I shall need twenty-four volumes for the "Studies of Manners," I shall require fifteen for the "Philosophical Studies," and only another nine for the "Analytical Studies." In this way I shall describe, criticize and analyze man himself, society, and humanity without indulging in repetitions in a work which is to be a kind of Arabian Nights *of the Occident.*

When all this is completed, when I have written the last word, then either I shall have been right or I shall have been wrong. But after this literary achievement, after this portrayal of a whole system, I shall apply myself to the scientific aspect, and write an Essay on the Forces by Which Man is Motivated. *And on the base of this great edifice I shall have traced, as a childlike and humorous decoration, the vast arabesque of the* Hundred Droll Stories.

The man's calm was as shocking as his effrontery was monumental, and a number of years would pass before the realization gradually dawned that he would require many more years than he had planned in order to complete his enormous project. What makes his grand scheme startling is not only his over-all conception of it, or even the self-assurance that led him to think he could do what he intended, but the staggering work load he set for himself. By 1834 only a few books that would be included in the *Comédie humaine* were either finished or had been reduced to some level of manuscript form. All of the others were still in his mind, yet he was casually planning to turn out forty-eight major works in a four-year period, or twelve per year. The man who had every intention of making himself the intellectual leader of Europe had set himself the seemingly impossible schedule of writing a major book every month of every year!

Even Balzac knew he could not achieve this seemingly impossible goal unless he could reorder his personal life. Creditors and bailiffs who pounded on his front door tried to set traps for him and loitered in the street outside his windows upset the rhythms of his work schedules and distracted him. Women who had to be wooed and pursued ate up his valuable time and made it necessary for him to write them letters when he could and should be devoting his entire attention to his newest manuscript. And the playing of the intimate, intricate game of love made it difficult for him to devote all of his energy to the creation of a masterpiece, much less a long series of masterpieces that would be unique in the history of literature.

Mistresses made demands on a man, just as the attempts to run a bachelor household were a time-consuming nuisance. Either one purchased food, wrangled with tradespeople and supervised the efforts of one's cook, or one was cheated. The world was filled with scoundrels who took advantage of the busy as well as of the unwary. When a man was married, however, all of these problems ceased. His wife gave him the love he needed, managed his household, and assuming she was wealthy—an assumption Balzac always made—his creditors would stop badgering him, too.

Common sense made it necessary for Balzac to find the wife who would fit his requirements. Then he could stop worrying about love, being distracted by money matters and becoming annoyed over the details of daily living.

He was the first to admit he would not be satisfied with an ordinary woman. Within a short time he would be recognized as the greatest European author of the century, so he needed a very special mate. She had to be rich, and as he had always dreamed of becoming an aristocrat, she had to be noble. Plain women not only bored him but depressed him sexually, so she had to be attractive, too.

In return he was prepared to give the full measure of his own life and love, and he did not discount the fact that she would be marrying a great and famous man. He was sensible enough, however, to realize it would not be easy to find a suitable mate. He knew that Parisian society laughed at his appearance, manners and pretensions, and he was homely, fat and in many ways thoroughly unattractive.

But the same logic, the same obsessive, inner drive that made him believe he could write the *Comédie humaine* convinced him he would find the right wife. He had already proved to his own satisfaction that Europe would accept him as a serious writer, and by the same token he had learned that many attractive women found him irresistible. Every day's mail brought him fresh proof: scores of women wrote to him, and he made it his business to answer the letters he found provocative. Several brief affairs had grown out of this correspondence with strangers.

Balzac's inexorable, peculiarly twisted logic therefore carried him to the conclusion that if he could have an affair with a correspondent, he could also find and marry the right woman through an exchange of letters.

Never was he more vulnerable than in 1832, when Mme. de Berny had grown too old to be his mistress, and when Mme. de

Castries first toyed with him, then rejected him. Then a correspondence began early in that year with a mysterious lady who called herself The Unknown, and out of her lighthearted, impulsive gesture there was destined to grow a relationship far more bizarre and complicated than any plot that Balzac ever wrote.

IX

Imperial Russia was remote from the rest of Europe in the nineteenth century, and few portions of that huge land had less contact with the civilized world than the Ukraine, itself as large as most nations on the Continent, a region of rolling hills and fertile farmlands, broad pastures and deep, brooding forests. Located in one of the most inaccessible portions of the Ukraine was a mammoth estate known as Volhynia, which was virtually a world unto itself. The property consisted of tens of thousands of acres, and the nearest community was a ride of a day and a half from its borders.

But Volhynia had its own town, populated exclusively by the thousands of serfs who lived and worked there under the rule of its master, a Russian-Polish nobleman, Baron Wenceslav Hanski. His domain was similar to that of other great Russian nobles, and he was the absolute master of the realm, with power of life and death over the serfs who labored unceasingly in the fields and lived in cramped cottages. His stables were overflowing with carriages, sleighs and riding horses. His wine cellar, as Honoré de Balzac subsequently noted, contained more than ten thousand bottles. It was possible to ride from dawn until sunset without leaving his property.

But Baron Hanski was atypical. He had added to his manor, and the new portion resembled a handsome French château. Unlike his fellow Russian nobles, he disapproved of hunting, and never went into the fields or forests carrying a gun. He disliked gambling, and having learned that quantities of liquor made him ill, he drank moderately. What set him even farther apart from his peers was his admiration of the West.

In his fifties and suffering from delicate health, the baron tried to make his home a haven of civilization and culture. His library of more than twenty-five thousand books contained many volumes in French, English, Italian and Spanish as well as in Russian and Polish. He had stocked the manor house with scores of expensive paintings purchased from galleries in London, Paris and Milan. His rugs were imported from the Ottoman Empire, his plates came from China and his silver had been wrought in England. It was one of his proudest boasts that there was no Russian furniture in the house; every table, chair, divan, bed and lamp had been carried all the way from Paris at staggering expense.

The baron's wife was also an extraordinary person. Born the Countess Eveline Rzewuska, she was a member of a distinguished Polish family that had espoused the Russian cause. A rare beauty with blond hair and blue eyes, she was in her mid-twenties, eight years younger than Balzac, and, like her husband, she fitted no stereotyped image. The ladies of the court at St. Petersburg disliked her because she was an intellectual who made no attempt to hide her erudition and wit.

The Baroness Hanska was also regarded with suspicion because she was the younger sister of the Countess Caroline Rzewuska, one of the most notorious women in Russia. Caroline, even more of an intellectual, had left her elderly husband and lived openly with the general who was the chief of the Imperial staff. After his death she had a brief affair with the romantic poet, Mickiewicz, and then became involved in a more scandalous liaison with the most celebrated of Russian poets, Alexander Pushkin. The Czar and his secret police considered Caroline dangerous, so a watch was kept on Eveline whenever she came to the capital.

But the Hanskis did not enjoy the barbarities of the St. Petersburg court and went there no more often than every three or four years to pay their token respects to the monarch. Eveline Hanska was bored when the nobles paid court to her, and found she had nothing in common with them.

Her own family background had been intensely cultural, and she could speak, read and write English, French and German, as well as Polish and Russian. She maintained a keen interest in the current literature being published in foreign tongues, and every month packages arrived from booksellers in Paris, London and Vienna. Like her husband, the Baroness Hanska was bored to distraction by the full life they were leading on their isolated estate. For six or seven dreary months of the year the great manor house was snowbound, and when spring came the couple relieved their tedium by attending a provincial ball in Kiev.

The Hanskis had virtually nothing in common with their nearest noble neighbors and rarely exchanged visits with them. And, as there was almost no one of their social station in Russia who shared their tastes, few guests were entertained at Volhynia.

In the years that had passed since her marriage as a young girl, Mme. Hanska had given birth to a number of children; the commonly accepted total is five, but according to some accounts there were six, and others say seven. In any event, all but one daughter had died as infants. That daughter was in the care of a Swiss governess, Mlle. Henriette Borel, a woman who had a good mind of her own but was inhibited by provincialism and her own strict, traditional Roman Catholic background.

There were two other adults at the estate, Denise and Séverine Wyleczinska, poor relations to whom the baroness had given a home. These sisters had resigned themselves to uneventful lives, and created their own enjoyment by reading the Paris and London newspapers and magazines that were sent regularly to the remote estate.

Baron Hanski was required by his physician to take extraordinary physical precautions in order to preserve his health, and habitually retired immediately after dinner every evening. This left his wife with nothing to do except chat with her cousins and Mlle. Borel. The good ladies felt a stronger emotional kinship with the French than with the English, so they read the Paris newspapers aloud to each other, and it was inevitable that they should discuss people surrounded by gossip, among them authors, actors and courtesans. Mlle. Borel was shocked by scandal, so the others amused themselves at her expense by discussing juicy tidbits at length, but even that pastime palled.

No name appeared in print more frequently than that of Honoré de Balzac in 1831, and the ladies of Vohynia were so intrigued by what they read that the baroness sent for copies of *Scènes de la vie privée*, *La Peau de chagrin* and the *Physiologie du mariage*. Somewhat to her own surprise, she was impressed and agreed with the critics who said a new, major star had appeared in the French literary sky.

Eveline Hanska found his work confusing, to say the least. He seemed to understand women so well, and he sometimes idolized them, but in the *Physiologie* he appeared to mock them. And his own life was obviously a disgrace. Scarcely a day passed without fresh gossip filling the newspapers of Paris!

Idling away the hours, the good ladies of Volhynia played a game in which they imagined the rehabilitation of M. de Balzac. He could be saved by a lady of high principle, who would help him to conquer the base elements in his nature, and with her to spur him, he would rise to new heights. For their own amusement the women began to compose a letter to the French author, and one night it occurred to them to play an infinitely more exciting game: they would actually send him a letter!

They went to work on it in earnest, ladling out quantities of saccharine admiration, using high-flown language studded with literary allusions and hinting at the possibility of a romantic, personal interest. They praised the *Scènes de la vie privée*, but chastised him for his abandonment of delicacy in *La Peau de chagrin*, which, they told him, was vulgar and beneath a man of his talents.

Mme. Hanska was the principal author of the letter, but she was a respectable matron, so she could not send it off in her own hand, and a protesting Mlle. Borel was persuaded to copy it. The paper was heavy, feminine and perfumed, and bore a crest too small to read. And the signature compounded the mystery: the pranksters signed themselves The Unknown. The letter was mailed in Odessa on the last day of February, 1832.

Balzac leaped at the bait, although the ladies in distant Russia had no way of knowing his reaction. The mystery, the apparent wealth of his correspondent intrigued him, and he was exasperated because she gave him no return address. Hoping to entice her, he printed a cryptic reply in the *Gazette de France*, and must have been disappointed when she failed to respond.

When spring came to the Ukraine, Mme. Hanska was able to enjoy the outdoors again and put her game out of her mind. In the summer of 1832 she and her husband paid an obligatory visit to St. Petersburg, which depressed them, and the approach of another Russian winter soon after their return home compounded their gloom. By November Eveline was ready to torment the distant M. de Balzac again, so The Unknown sent him another, even more provocative letter:

Your soul embraces centuries, monsieur; its philosophical concepts appear to be the fruit of long study matured by time; yet I am told you are still young. I would like to know you, but feel I have no need to do so. I know you through my own spiritual instinct; I picture you in my own way, and feel that if I were to actually set eyes upon you, I should instantly exclaim, "That is he!"

Your outward semblance probably does not reveal your brilliant imagination; you must be moved, the sacred fire of genius must be lighted if you are to show yourself as you really are, and you are, I know, what I feel you to be—a man superior in his knowledge of the human heart.

My own heart has leaped as I read your works. You elevate woman to her true dignity; love, in her, is a celestial virtue, a divine emanation; and I admire in you the sensitivity of soul which has enabled you to see this in me, and in all womankind.

Not satisfied with this effort, she continued to tease him. She had no intention of revealing her identity to him, and would remain The Unknown for the rest of her life. Nevertheless, even though she withheld her address, she felt that her fiery soul could commune with his angelic soul. Perhaps she could help him; in time she hoped to become his conscience, and it was possible that, through her, he would learn the eternal truths that governed the spirits of womankind.

The communication ended on an even more provocative note. She wanted to know whether he received the letter and gave her permission to continue writing to him. So, if he approved, she instructed him to place a small personal advertisement in the newspaper *La Quotidienne* addressing the message to one "A. l'E," and signing it H.B.

Balzac found the lure irresistible. The stationery, the crest and the lady's initials indicated she was a noblewoman. Her handwriting was firm, that of a young person, and her language indicated that she was highly educated. He promptly inserted a classified ad in the December 9 edition of the appropriate newspaper, writing, "*M. de B. has received the letter addressed to him; he has only today been able to acknowledge it in the columns of his journal, and regrets not knowing where to address his reply.*"

The classified ad caused rejoicings in Volhynia, and Mme. Hanska wrote another letter, going so far that her cousins joined in the protests of the governess. The joke appeared to be getting out of hand when she wrote:

In my eyes your genius appears exalted—but it should be divine!

From the moment I started to read your works I have identified myself with you and your genius. Your soul stands before me in shining clarity. I follow your progress step by step, and all that you write and do fascinates me.

Let me present to you my whole, essential being in a few words: I admire your talent; I honor your soul. I should like to be a sister to you.

Captivated but cautious, Balzac placed another message in the newspaper, but the ladies apparently realized they were going too far, and fell silent.

The ingenious author thought of another device that might intrigue The Unknown. A new, enlarged edition of the *Scènes de la vie privée*, which contained some additional stories, was already at the printer's, but had not yet been dedicated. So he took the stationery to the printer, who reproduced the tiny seal. Beneath it Balzac wrote the date, February 28, 1832, and the lower portion of the page contained the single line, "*As a silent token of my innermost feelings.*" The Unknown obviously read all of his books and, after seeing the flattering dedication, would write to him again.

As it happened, however, Mme. de Berny, living in retirement, was continuing to perform a function for her former lover that she had long enjoyed. When a book he had written reached its final stage of page proofs, Balzac could not force himself to read the copy, rightly fearing that he would continue to make changes in the wording. So Mme. de Berny did the work for him. Although now relegated to the role of dear friend and counselor, she was still a woman and still was tied to him by many emotional cords. So, without further ado, she eliminated the dedication page.

If Balzac was annoyed, as he must have been, he was in no position to argue with her and meekly accepted the deletion.

As it happened, however, Mme. Hanska needed no further prodding. She was startled by the messages in *La Quotidienne*, and realized the time had come to stop playing a game. She was tempted to enter into a genuine correspondence with Balzac, but her husband knew nothing of the prank she had been playing, and she was afraid that a man with his limited sense of humor would not appreciate the joke. Therefore, if she intended to continue, she would have to exercise extraordinary care in order to avoid unpleasant marital complications.

Some of Balzac's early biographers speculated at length on the change in Eveline Hanska's attitude, but there was nothing mysterious about her sudden shift. She was a sensitive woman, highly intelligent, with a genuine interest in literature, and she was flattered, just as lesser women had been and would continue to be, when one of the most talented of the younger authors of the day showed enough interest to respond to her communications. Nor should it be forgotten that she was bored.

She knew that discretion was paramount, however, if she planned to establish a real relationship of some sort with the French author, and the letter she sent to him in the early spring of 1833 was a far cry from the playful tone she had used previously:

I should like to receive an answer from you, but it is necessary for me to be careful, so careful, more careful than you can possibly know. It would be necessary for me to choose so many devious means of writing back and forth that I cannot yet venture to give you a binding promise. On the other hand, I do not enjoy the prospect of remaining in a state of uncertainty regarding possible exchanges of letters between us.

So I beg you to let me know at the earliest opportunity what possibilities you may be able to envisage for an unimpeded correspondence between us. I trust entirely to your word of honor that you will make no attempt to discover the identity of the recipient of your communications, for I should be lost if it were to become known that I am writing to you.

Deliberately or otherwise, she added to Balzac's sense of mounting excitement by informing him that she was planning to make a protracted journey in the near future that would bring her much closer to the borders of France. So there was a strong hint, if he cared to interpret the statement accordingly, that they might meet in person in the not too distant future.

Had Eveline received a letter from Paris, the entire Hanski household would have learned of the unusual event, and it no longer would have been possible to keep her husband in the dark. She had now reached the stage where she thought it might be dangerous if her cousins remained her confidantes, so she deliberately refrained from telling them what she was doing.

That left the governess, and Henriette Borel could be utilized as the ideal helper. She heard fairly frequently from her relatives in Switzerland, and on occasion she had received mail from Paris when a member of her family was visiting France. So no one at Volhynia thought it unusual when she received a letter from abroad. In addition, of course, Mlle. Borel was already compromised, having copied the letters that Eveline had written to Balzac. The poor woman was deeply disturbed when asked to continue the deception on a far different level, but her loyalty to Mme. Hanska made it impossible for her to refuse, and she agreed to act as the go-between.

Balzac was informed that the name he had been given was false, but his correspondent was taking no chances and asked him not to put his own name or return address on the outside of his envelope. Nevertheless he now had someone to whom he could write, and responded to the lady's invitation with an enthusiasm that should have warned her she was dealing with an impetuous, reckless romantic, a man whose approach far exceeded the mock-sentimental tone she had used when opening their correspondence.

He sent an immediate reply to Eveline's letter, and made no attempt to curb his own enthusiasm:

I am carried away by the feeling of confidence that your letter has inspired in me! Ever since I received it, you have been the subject of my most delightful dreams!

If you had been able to witness the effect your letter had on me you would have perceived at once the gratitude of a man in love, the heartfelt trust, the pure affection which binds a son to his mother, the sincere respect felt by a young man for a woman, and his delicious hopes for a long and ardent friendship.

His reply must have startled Eveline, who could have expected nothing so passionate. Before she had a chance to recover her balance Balzac wrote to her again, and she received his second letter only forty-eight hours after the first arrived. Cleverly aware that he was dealing with a woman, he increased the pressure on her:

In the midst of my incessant struggle, amid my labors and endless studies in the turbulent city of Paris where politics or literature absorbs sixteen or eighteen hours out of every twenty-four, unhappy though I am, and very different from the author of everyone's dreams, I have had charming hours which I owe to you. That is why, in gratitude, I dedicated the fourth volume of the Scènes de la vie privée *to you by putting your initials at the head of the final Scene, the one which I was writing when I received your first letter.*

But someone who is a mother to me, and whose wishes, even jealousies, I am bound to respect, has asked that this mute expression of my feelings be removed. I do not fear to tell you of this dedication and its deletion because I think you have sufficient greatness of soul not to desire an act of homage which would have pained a person as noble and great as the one who bore me, for she protected me amid the distresses and disasters which nearly caused me to die young.

Eveline Hanska was overwhelmed. What had started as a joke to while away a long Russian winter had unleashed a torrent of emotion directed at her by a man of great and growing literary stature. She, a nobody, was being offered a close friendship with one of the leading authors of the era. Mindful of her sister's relationship with Pushkin, she may have sought a measure of limelight in her own right, too. In any event, and whatever her motives, she maintained the correspondence, although she was careful not to reply too quickly to Balzac's letters. She was playing a devious game, and if Mlle. Borel received too many communications from Paris, others in the household might wonder, and some word of her activities might leak back to the ordinarily tolerant Baron Hanski. Certainly she knew that, in spite of his cultured veneer, her husband was still a powerful Russian nobleman capable of performing ruthless acts of great cruelty if his good name was even slightly dishonored.

Balzac, of course, was captivated, and kept up his end of the correspondence faithfully, even though he was actually increasing his already frantic work pace. In early 1833 he was completing the first volume of a large fiction project he was calling *L'Histoire des treize,* which deal with the secret societies which existed on every level of French society. He conceived the idea of a banding together a group of brilliant men who formed a society for the purpose of making themselves the masters of Paris, then of France, and ultimately of the world.

That was only the beginning. He was also at work on a series of novels, the *Études philosophiques,* and was beginning work on yet another series for a different publisher, the *Études de moeurs.* In addition the editors of the *Revue de Paris,* who were observing their part of the contract with him by paying him a monthly stipend, were demanding that he give them some short stories in return. Balzac obligingly turned out several, which were exceptionally well-received; the reading public recognized his mastery of the art of short story writing, and his reputation was enhanced.

Not even he could maintain the blistering pace he had set for himself, however, and he inevitably began to fall behind in his publishing deadlines. He was still spurred by his private demons, his ever-present need for money and the obsessive drive that gave him no opportunity to feel satisfied with his accomplishments, so he pushed himself still harder.

He gave up virtually all social life and once again became a hermit, leaving his house only when it was essential to meet a publisher somewhere for a brief meeting. He went to bed at eight o'clock every evening, and was awakened at midnight, when he started to work. With nothing but the usual gallons of coffee to sustain him, he labored without stopping until eight o'clock in the morning. Then he paused briefly for a light meal, and after a respite of no more than thirty minutes he went back to work again, continuing until four in the afternoon. From four to five he received business callers, who were urged to be brief in their dealings with him. At five he retired to a hot tub, and wrote for another hour or more while soaking. Then he allowed himself his only relaxation of the day, the hour that he took for his dinner, and immediately after he finished eating he retired for four hours before starting the whole, weary process again.

He continued to maintain a steady correspondence with Mme. de Berny, Mme. Carraud and other friends during this exhausting time, but his only real diversion consisted of the game he was playing with The Unknown in the distant Ukraine. Desperately seeking relief, he wrote to her in the summer of 1833:

I beseech you, tell me in that charming, catlike style, how your days are spent, hour by hour. Make me see it all. Describe the rooms in which you live, even to the color of the furniture . . .

Draw me a picture so that when I turn to you in thought I may meet you; so that I may see the tapestry-frame with the beginning of a flower, see you in all your hours. If you knew how often tired thought needs repose that is in some sort active, and how much good it does me to be able to indulge in a reverie that begins, "At this moment she is there, she is looking at this or that." I, who credit thought with the gift of being able to cover distances so completely as to abolish them! These are my only pleasures amid my ceaseless toil.

A new review, *L'Europe littéraire,* asked the busy author to contribute some literary and sociological essays, and he found time to oblige, turning out several brilliant pieces, among them one, "A Theory of Behavior," which won him respect in scientific circles. Then he turned to fiction for the review, which published the opening portions of what would become *Eugénie Grandet,* and his two regular publishers immediately claimed he was guilty of breach of contract, as he was not allowed to publish novels elsewhere.

Balzac fought hard, but was forced to agree when the court ordered the matter submitted to arbitration. The decision was made in favor of the publishers, and he had to stop printing portions of forthcoming novels in the new review. But he consoled himself with the thought that the book he considered the greatest of his novels, *Le Médecin de campagne,* would be published early in September, and would not only make him wealthy but would establish him as the greatest writer of the age. "I think I can die in peace," he told Victor Hugo. "I have done a great service for my country. To my mind this book is worth more than laws and victorious battles. It is the Gospels in action."

Without question *Le Médecin de campagne* was unlike anything he had ever written, and his central character, the enigmatic Dr. Benassis, was considered the spokesman for Balzac's personal opinions, a view that has prevailed from 1833 to the present day. His attitudes were a curious blending of the conservative and the progressive-liberal, and he looked simultaneously toward the past and the future.

Dr. Benassis was opposed to universal suffrage, believing it would lead to a class war between the bourgeoisie and the working class, which would be jealous of those directly above them in the economic order and would seek to take their comforts from them. Peasants and the city poor, Dr. Benassis said, were not any more vicious and grasping by nature than were other, more fortunate people, but the squalor and penury they were forced to endure made them hard and limited their vision. They had to be inculcated with a new spirit if civilization was to survive, and that task would require infinite skill and patience. The poor needed courage to face each new day, and could acquire it only if their lot improved, if they could find tangible evidence that they, too, were receiving benefits in return for their toil.

Le Médecin appeared as scheduled, and Balzac confidently wrote to Zulma Carraud, who had received an advance copy and loved the book, that he would be acclaimed as the new Voltaire, as the intellectual giant of the age. It was not too much to expect that the Académie Française, which annually awarded a prize, the Prix Montyon, for the best philosophical novel of the year, would give him the award.

The virtually universal reaction of the newspaper and literary journal critics momentarily stunned the proud author. Instead of writing a novel, as he should have done and had been expected to do, he had scribbled a confused maze on politics, morality and the social order. Instead of telling a story, as he had the proven ability to do, he had delivered a series of unconnected lectures on rural life, forestry and the economic order. The Académie delivered the final blow. *Le Médecin* not only failed to win the Prix Montyon, but was not even included on the list of eligibles that received serious consideration.

Balzac recovered from these blows very quickly, once again demonstrating that he possessed remarkable powers of recuperation. Other, far more glittering prospects occupied his mind, both of them holding out the promise of substantial returns. The first was purely personal, and involved The Unknown. He received a brief letter from Russia informing him that the lady was intending to pay a protracted visit to Neuchâtel, in Switzerland, and that, if he cared to go there, it might be possible for them to arrange a meeting.

He had no idea how much scheming Mme. Hanska had found necessary in order to bring off her plans. Neuchâtel was Mlle. Borel's home, and she had dangled a carrot before the eyes of the governess, who would enjoy a family visit provided she continued to co-operate with the great lady who made it her business to think of every angle. Once Henriette's promise had been obtained, Eveline went to her husband and suggested that the faithful governess be rewarded with a trip home. She added that the entire family needed a holiday, and suggested it was time that Anna, the Hanski daughter, enjoyed the benefits of travel.

The baron found the idea sensible, so the arrangements were made. The noble couple engaged a suite at the Hotel du Faucon, and a nearby villa was rented for Anna, the governess, Mme. Hanska's dependent relatives and the usual large retinue of servants with whom members of the Russian aristocracy traveled.

Unaware of these complicated arrangements, Balzac had a second, equally pressing reason to make the trip to Switzerland, and of all the business ventures he conceived, none demonstrated his genius more than the idea he originated and developed in the early autumn of 1833. It is no exaggeration to say that it was he who sired the basic plan that revolutionized the book-publishing industry in the United States and Europe a century later. Honoré de Balzac was the father of the modern book club.

His idea was similar in both principle and proposed execution to the book clubs of the present day. Readers would obligate themselves to purchase one volume per month from the organization Balzac intended to establish, and would pay the absurdly low price of one franc for each book purchased. The publisher—in this case Balzac himself, the former printer, who has an understanding of such matters—would earn himself a profit by printing books in mammoth editions, which would reduce costs. Sheer volume of sales would enable him to perform this publishing miracle.

He also needed thin, strong paper, similar to the rice paper made in the Orient, but experience had taught him that imported paper was prohibitively expensive. A short time before leaving the printing business, however, he had learned that a company in the town of Besançon, near the Swiss border, manufactured an inexpensive paper that was similar to the rice paper of the East. So, hoping to cut costs still more, he planned to travel to Besançon for the purpose of purchasing quantities of the stock.

Simple logic indicated that he could kill two important birds on one journey. He would go to Besançon, attend to his business there, and then go on across the Swiss border to nearby Neuchâtel. Not even those Paris newspapers that specialized in gossip about the prominent would even know he had left France, so he would be able to afford The Unknown the complete protection that her unexplained situation made necessary for her protection.

The sales of *Le Médecin* were disappointing and reflected the critics' adverse reaction to the book, but the peripatetic author, fledgling book-club publisher and hopeful lover-to-be was far too busy to brood. He made no changes in his work schedule and continued to write books and short stories at least eighteen hours out of every twenty-four. He organized a book subscription and publishing company, and his enthusiasm for the venture was so great that he sold numerous shares to relatives and friends who should have known it was unwise to give him money, among them his brother-in-law, the engineer De Surville, and Zulma Carraud, who had literally no funds to spare.

His letters to Mme. Hanska became still more intense. Now that it would be possible for them to meet, he wanted to take no risks that she might grow shy and back out at the last minute, so he wrote:

You, around whom I am fluttering as around a beloved illusion, you who are a pervading hope in all my dreams—you do not know what it means to a writer when he can enliven his solitude with such a sweet figure, whose form is rendered all the more charming by the elusive and indefinable quality of her being.

What do I really think of you? I love you, my Unknown! Why should this be? This singular circumstance is but the natural consequence of a life that has always been bleak and unhappy. If ever there was a man to whom this unique adventure had to befall, I am that man.

If you ask me to do so I will snap my pen in two tomorrow, and in the future no other woman will hear my voice. I shall request your indulgence only for my dilecta, *who is like a mother to me. She is already fifty-eight, and you who are so young cannot be jealous of her! Oh, accept all the feeling I have to offer you and guard my emotions like a treasure! Take charge of my dreams and make my longings come true!*

A more cosmopolitan woman would have called this gushing

stranger unstable, and would have gone to great pains to avoid him. But Eveline, in spite of her wealth and cultural background was lacking in the sophistication that came only from association with worldly people. The better part of her life had been spent in Polish and Russian rural retreats, and the rhapsodies of the great author filled her with wonder. As nearly as she could judge, he had truly fallen in love with her, even though they had not yet met, and she was still naïve enough to accept the seeming miracle at face value. It could not have occurred to her that the love-starved Honoré de Balzac was ready to throw himself at the feet of any woman who appeared to offer him the emotional refuge he sought.

The Hanski family went to Vienna in the summer of 1833, stopping there for several months while the baron renewed the friendships he had enjoyed in the Austro-Hungarian capital in his student days. There Eveline made her final, careful plans, and sent Balzac a letter instructing him to take quarters in the Hôtel du Faubourg when he reached Neuchâtel. She did not reveal to him that her own hotel would be located no more than a stone's throw away, and contented herself with a cryptic, final comment to the effect that he would be told how to proceed after he reached his destination.

He misunderstood the communication, and afraid that she was backing out, sent her an urgent letter:

Oh, my unknown beloved, do not distrust me, do not believe anything bad of me; I am a more wanton child than you probably imagine, but I am also pure as a child, and I love as only a child can love!

Balzac had to make his own arrangements with care. Not only did he want to avoid any mention of his final destination in the Paris newspapers, but there were people close to him who had to be kept in the dark. Mme. de Berny would react jealously, and might forbid him to make the trip. Zulma Carraud would be certain to disapprove of the adventure, and would write him long, scolding sermons. Unable to keep the secret of his coming good fortune completely to himself, however, he confided in his sister, and even speculated on the possibility that the lady's caution might be dictated by the proximity of a husband. Although Balzac was foolishly romantic, his middle-class common sense did not completely desert him.

He left Paris in early October 1833, and spent a few days at Besançon, where he arranged to buy the paper he needed for his book subscription venture, happily allowing himself to dig deeper into debt. Then he went on to Neuchâtel, and at the Hôtel du Faubourg a message awaited him. The Unknown had arrived, and he could communicate with her by writing to Mlle. Borel at the Villa André. The note made it plain, however, that his correspondent was not herself a guest.

Assailed by self-doubts now that the climactic meeting was at hand, Balzac couldn't help wondering whether she might laugh at him. She might share the view of fashionable Paris that his person was ugly, his appearance gross and his manners beneath contempt. If she mocked him he would find the pain unbearable, and if she turned away from him, he would be crushed.

He wanted to give her the chance to escape gracefully, so he wrote her a final letter, sending it to Mlle. Borel:

I shall go for a walk in the town from one o'clock until four. I shall spend all that time looking at the lake, which I do not know. I can arrange to stay here for as long as you are staying. Please send me a line to notify me whether I can write to her with safety, for I fear to cause you the least displeasure.

I beg you, tell me your true, exact name.

A thousand tendernesses. There has not been a moment, between Paris and Neuchâtel, which has not been filled with you, and I have gazed at the Val de Travers with you—and only you—in mind. It is enchanting, that valley.

X

According to a story that has been generally accepted for the better part of a century and a half, the long-awaited initial meeting of Balzac and Mme. Hanska was as romantic as either could have wished.

Balzac left his hotel promptly at one o'clock in the afternoon and crossed the street to the walk that ran parallel to the shore of Lake Neuchâtel. He was wearing a new suit of pearl gray with a matching hat, an embroidered vest and new boots, and he carried his turquoise-studded cane. Pretending to concentrate on the lake, he strolled a short distance, but slowed his pace when he saw a woman sitting on a stone bench overlooking the lake.

Studying her from a distance, he noted that she was young, and looked like a girl in her mid-twenties. Her blond hair shimmered in the sunlight, her aristocratic features were chiseled, and her brow was high; her lips were full, sensual, and that, too, was promising. She was wearing a velvet dress of violet, his favorite color, and over it had thrown a short cape of the same material and color.

She appeared to be deeply engrossed in a book, however, and did not look up as he approached. Sudden doubts assailed him, and he was afraid she wasn't The Unknown. Then he saw she was reading one of his books, and his heart beat more rapidly, but he was still a trifle uncertain, and started to move past her.

The lady's handkerchief fell from her hand and fluttered to the ground.

Balzac bent to retrieve it for her, and their eyes met; then, as he gave her the handkerchief, their fingers touched for an instant . . .

No biographer wants to spoil the perfect story, but the truth of the matter is that no details of the first meeting of Balzac and Eveline are known. In a letter he wrote to her ten years later, on the anniversary of their initial meeting, he made a passing reference to having seen her in the window of her hotel suite, and having been terrified by the thought that she might disapprove of him.

What matters is that the couple met, and that both were pleased. Eveline was too flattered by the great man's attentions to pay much notice to his unattractive appearance, and, in all fairness to her, she hadn't thought seriously of a romantic attachment. Certainly she had no intention of placing her marriage in even greater jeopardy and disgracing herself. As for Balzac, it did not matter to him that her figure was somewhat more plump than was the fashion, that her eyes were deep-set beneath heavy lids or that her neck was almost as thick as a man's. He had been prepared to fall in love with her, no matter what her appearance.

In the next few days any doubts that might have been lingering in the remote corners of his mind vanished. The lady was enormously wealthy, far richer than the most prominent of French duchesses! He met her husband, seemingly by accident, and discovered that the baron, who wore glasses and a coat with a fur collar, was middle-aged and in delicate health. Certainly he was pale and thin, almost fragile, so it was conceivable that he would depart the world within a reasonable time, leaving Mme. Hanska a widow.

Here was a situation infinitely more promising than the abortive romance with Mme. de Castries, and Balzac was filled with the desire to take full advantage of it. But he quickly discovered innumerable obstacles in his path. Neuchâtel was a small town, and there were few visitors there in October, so he constantly found himself in the company of one or more members of the Hanski party.

The baron, in particular, was always underfoot. A cultured man who loved literature, he was delighted to find the celebrated French author visiting the same resort, and rarely had he met such a captivating, witty speaker. He made it his business to seek out M. de Balzac at all hours of the day for chats and strolls, teas and lunches. He still followed his custom of retiring immediately after dinner, and his wife remained in their hotel suite with him. Little Anna was often on hand, as was her governess, and the two female cousins hovered nearby, hoping to pick up some pearl of wisdom dropped by the great author. Mme. Hanska was attended by two ladies' maids, and one or the other was usually within earshot. The handicaps were difficult for even the most impassioned and inventive of would-be lovers to overcome.

On October 12, 1833, five days after the monumental first meeting, Balzac expressed his feelings freely and fully in a letter to his sister Laure:

I have found here everything that can gratify the thousand vanities of the animal called man, of which the poet is assuredly the vainest variety; but why do I say vanity, when it is nothing of the sort? I am happy, very happy in thought, honorably happy, if still no more.

Alas, there is an infernal husband who has not left us alone together for an instant in five days! He whirls constantly, dancing between his wife's skirts and my waistcoat. Neuchâtel is a small town where a woman, a distinguished foreigner, cannot move a step without being seen.

I feel as though I were in a furnace. Restraint does not suit or become me.

The essentials are that she is young and lovely, that she has the most beautiful hair in the world, a smooth, deliciously soft skin, an adorable little hand and a naïve heart—and imprudent almost to the point of flinging her arms around my neck in the sight of the whole world.

I say nothing about the colossal wealth. What is that by comparison with a masterpiece of beauty which I can only liken to the Princesse de Bellejoyeuse, but infinitely more so? A glancing eye, which, when one meets it, acquires a voluptuous splendor. I am intoxicated with love.

If Eveline had thought in terms of a platonic relationship with her French admirer, she soon changed her mind. Even when they were in the company of others he found ways to communicate privately with her, sometimes looking at her, sometimes whispering to her, sometimes squeezing her hand. She discovered it was pleasant to flirt with him, and responded in kind to his covert advances.

On two occasions the couple managed to shed other members of the Hanski ménage for an hour, and enjoyed a walk together along the shore of the lake. But they never lost sight of the fact that they could be seen by the citizens of Neuchâtel, among them Henriette Borel's relatives, as well as by Baron Hanski himself, if he happened to glance out of his hotel window. So they behaved circumspectly, and if their hands occasionally touched, it appeared to be accidental.

At last there came a day when they made an opportunity for a slightly more promising gesture. Balzac accompanied the Hanski family and their retainers on a picnic, and the author managed to send most members of the party ahead, while he walked far to the rear with the baron and baroness. Eventually they came to the crest of a wooded hill, beyond which stood a little valley that nestled on the shores of the lake. Would it be too cool there to spread the picnic linen? Balzac wasn't sure, and neither was Madame. The baron, who had no idea he was being manipulated, volunteered to go ahead and test the site, saying he would beckon if it was satisfactory.

He started downhill, and as soon as he vanished into the trees, Balzac and Eveline stepped behind the trunk of a large, protecting tree, and there they embraced and kissed. That night the lady sent a reckless note to Balzac at his hotel:

Villain! Did you not see in my eyes all that I longed for? But have no fear, I felt all the desire that a woman in love seeks to provoke, and if I did not tell you how ardently I have hoped for you to come to me one morning, it is because I have been so awkwardly lodged. That place is too risky; elsewhere it might be possible. When we meet again in Geneva, my adored angel, I shall have more talent for our love than ten persons would need in order to be called talented.

Eveline's letter and her response to Balzac indicated that she reciprocated what he was already calling the grand passion of his life, and it was true that she was making plans for a later meeting in Geneva. But there is evidence to indicate she may have been amusing herself partly out of boredom, partly because of his own impetuous wooing, but that her seeming passion was as false as the color of her hair. For a number of years she had been bleaching it, but grew tired of doing so around this same time and was pleased to discover that Balzac, at least, preferred her as a brunette.

Before setting out on her journey she had corresponded with her brother, who lived in Warsaw, and had confided that she expected to meet the great author. The young Count Henri Rzewuski had visited Paris as recently as the preceding year, and a number of stories about Honoré de Balzac having come to his ears, he passed them along to his sister. Mme. Hanska reminded him of them in a letter she sent him before she left Neuchâtel.

He had informed her that Balzac was a gross person who ate with his knife and blew his nose in his napkin. Well, she wanted to tell that the first report was true, but the second was false—although she had expected that, at any time during any meal the Hanskis had eaten with him, he might make the story come true. She could also confirm the fact that he was a glutton; in fact, she had never seen any human being eat so much at a single sitting, and he had consumed enormous meals whenever he had sat down at the same table with her. Nevertheless, she said, she was inclined to forgive him because this very quality of enthusiasm for whatever he was doing set him apart from lesser men and undoubtedly was responsible for his achievements as an author. She seemed to be of two minds.

Balzac was living in the clouds, however, and referred to her as "my beloved, the only woman that the world holds for me." Not even his return to Paris in a jolting coach on a journey that lasted four long days in mid-October 1833, brought him back to earth. In fact, an unexpected windfall increased his euphoria.

Few of the world's truly great literary figures have ever been less well received by their contemporaries than Balzac. He not only succeeded in alienating the critics, the majority of whom refused to regard him seriously, but most publishers were leery of him. This attitude was not completely unjustified, of course, word having passed through the industry that he made too many commitments and therefore had to be hounded repeatedly before he could be half-cajoled, half-compelled to complete a project. But now, on his return to Paris from Neuchâtel, he learned that one publisher, at least, keenly appreciated the potential business investment that his work represented.

That publisher, not surprisingly, was a woman. Mme. Charles Béchet, a wealthy widow and the daughter of a prominent publisher, was an attractive, intelligent and shrewd businesswoman, who believed that the market for Balzac's works was as yet virtually untapped. She had learned of his ambitious plans to bring out a multivolume series under the general title of *Études de moeurs,* and she requested a conference with him immediately after his return.

Balzac held a number of meetings with Mme. Béchet, and the result was an agreement to publish twelve forthcoming books. These would include new editions of *Scènes de la vie privée,* as well as several volumes of the as yet uncompleted *Scènes de la vie de province* and *Scènes de la vie parisienne.* The first volume of novellae and stories about provincial life was already finished, and one more story was needed for the second volume. Balzac went home and, working for twenty-four hours without pause, turned out an eighty-page novella about a commercial traveler, which he called *L'Illustre Gaudissart.*

He completely failed to recognize the worth of his own work, and thought of the tale as just another piece of competent storytelling. What he did not realize was that he had captured the rough-hewn, Rabelaisian spirit of a new breed of middle-class Frenchman, and that the story would become a classic.

The one thing that was very much on his mind was the compensation he received from Mme. Béchet. She paid him an advance royalty of thirty thousand francs, which was an enormous sum, larger by far than any other author of the period, Victor Hugo included, had been paid up to that time. As always, he used the money unwisely, and after paying a portion of his most pressing debts—except the vast amounts he owed to his mother—he went on new spending sprees and managed to compound his indebtednesses.

Balzac's personal life was even more complicated than his financial existence, and no period better illustrates the tangled involvements he created for himself. He came home from Neuchâtel convinced he had fallen madly in love with Mme. Hanska, and not only told his sister and such friends as George Sand that he had found the great love of his life, but also took Zulma Carraud into his confidence.

At the same time he maintained his steady correspondence with Mme. de Berny, who remained loyal to him, and, suffering from ill health, began to make peevish demands on his time and affections. What becomes difficult to accept is that he elected, at precisely this time, to dedicate *L'Illustre Gaudissart* to Mme. de Castries, of all people! He could not tolerate the thought of losing whatever place in her life he had created for himself, and the dedication was an attempt to restore their friendship. What is even more remarkable is that he succeeded, at least to an extent, and thereafter he and Mme. de Castries corresponded sporadically, always quarreling, and on rare occasions spent a few, mutually venomous hours together.

Even more astounding is a situation that remained a secret for many years. George Sand noted that Balzac told her about a girl who had entered his life, "a sweet person, a most innocent person who had fallen like a flower from the sky, who visits me in private, asks for no letters, no attentions, but simply says, 'Love me for a year, and I will love you for the rest of my life!' "

Neither George Sand nor those to whom she repeated the words accepted Balzac's claim at face value. They had grown accustomed to his exaggerated accounts of various incidents in his life, and assumed that, once again, he was allowing his imagination to get the better of him for the sake of telling a story. But, incredible as it may seem, his claim was true.

The girl was both young and beautiful, and was only twenty-four in 1833, when she had her brief affair with Balzac. She was Marie Louise Daminois du Fresnay, the wife of a prominent attorney who was a member of an old and honored family. He was regarded as a leading member of his profession in Paris, and had been married for about two years. His impressionable bride had written Balzac a letter after reading one of his books, he had invited her to call, and they had promptly initiated their secret affair.

Marie Louise was one of the few women in Balzac's life who wanted and expected nothing from him, but she received a gift from him that was unique. A romantic girl who loved his books and was thrilled by his interest in her, she came to his house in the Rue Cassini once or twice each week, and Balzac interrupted his work long enough to have relations with her. She went to great lengths to prevent her husband from learning of the affair, and Balzac revealed her name to no one.

What makes the relationship incredible is that Balzac continued to take Marie Louise to bed after his return from Neuchâtel, when he was proclaiming his love for Mme. Hanska. Then, in November, Marie Louise told him she was bearing his child; for several months she had slept with no one else, her husband included, and was positive the baby was Balzac's.

He accepted the news with equanimity, and together they decided it would be wise to pass off the child as Du Fresnay's. The ruse succeeded, and virtually none of Balzac's contemporaries ever learned that he had sired an illegitimate child by a married woman. Almost nothing is known about his subsequent relations with Marie Louise, whether he continued to see her or ever met his only child. On occasion he sent a gift to Marie Louise through the years, identifying her only as "a friend."

But, late in 1833, he did dedicate *Eugénie Grandet* to her, saying:

TO MARIA. *May your name, you whose portrait is the highest adornment of this book, stand here like a sprig of consecrated box, culled from no matter what tree, but certainly sanctified by religion and replaced, ever green, by pious hands to protect the house.*

It is useless to speculate on the possibility that Eugénie Grandet really was a portrait of Marie Louise. Nothing is known about the girl, there are no portraits of her in existence, and it would appear that she never corresponded with anyone. She drifted briefly into his life, gave birth to his child, which bore the name of Du Fresnay, and vanished again into anonymity. Balzac never acknowledged the child's paternity, so it must be assumed that Marie Louise's deception was successful and that her husband believed himself the father.

The ultimate significance of this sordid little episode in the life of Honoré de Balzac is that it casts doubt on the sincerity of his relations with any woman. On the other hand, it would be a mistake to view with too jaundiced an eye his relations with Mme. de Berny, Mme. Hanska or any of the other ladies who played major roles in his life. His capacity for self-delusion was as infinite as his convictions were passionate, and while dealing with any woman he had the ability to believe whatever he wished. He did not think of himself as inconstant while informing each of several ladies, more or less simultaneously, that she was the only woman in his life. All he had to do was think of Eveline Hanska, or Laure de Berny, and instantly she became absorbingly important to him. It was as though he applied to his women the same intense powers of concentration that made it possible for him to work on so many books simultaneously, devoting his mind and emotions exclusively to each while he was actually at work on it.

All in all, Balzac was happier in the autumn of 1833 than he had ever been. The Béchet contract would enable him to work in earnest on the *Comédie humaine*, and he said of the project, "It will have its echo in our world of grudging envy and stupidity. It will rouse the choler of all those who so presumptuously believed that they could walk in my shadow."

He corresponded regularly with Mme. Hanska, using the convenient Mlle. Borel as his letter-drop, and made definite plans to spend two weeks in Geneva with her. He made it clear he was relying on her to get rid of her husband and other members of the Hanski party from time to time so they could enjoy the intimacies that had been implicitly promised during their brief Neuchâtel encounter. He also spoke frankly about his work and his financial situation. One day he received a payment of five thousand francs from Mme. Béchet, a portion of his advance royalty, but his creditors were so alert that by the following morning there wasn't a sou left in his purse.

Mme. Hanska, who knew nothing of his financial habits and spendthrift tendencies, made an embarrassed gesture and offered him one thousand francs, the allowance she had just received from her husband. She explained she had no money of her own, and was dependent on the baron for all she received.

Balzac thanked her effusively, but would not accept either a gift or a loan from her. Her offer, he told her, meant everything to him—and nothing. "*What,*" he asked her rhetorically, "*is a thousand francs to a man who needs ten thousand every month?*"

He also made it his business to maintain cordial relations with Baron Hanski, and knowing that the Russian nobleman was a collector of autographs, sent him an original manuscript of Rossini's. At the same time he requested the husband's permission to present Mme. Hanska with the original manuscript of *Eugénie Grandet.*

The permission was gratefully given, of course. What the baron did not know was that Balzac lightly penciled the date when he expected to arrive in Geneva on the back of the title page.

Busy on so many books that he had to postpone his journey, Balzac also started to work on a book he intended to dedicate to Eveline. In one of their Neuchâtel conversations she had mentioned that she thought he sometimes wasted his substance on frivolous works, and she returned to the theme in a number of her letters. He was dismayed when she informed him she had just purchased a copy of the recently published *Contes drolatiques,* and he made excuses for the book, assuring her of the seriousness of his basic purpose. Apparently he was afraid she would believe that a frivolous author would be a frivolous lover.

As a consequence he plunged into the writing of the book that would prove his love, and his vigor and dedication were frightening. He planned to call the novel *Séraphita,* and it was the most abstruse, mystical and convoluted effort he had ever attempted. His scene was Norway, which he had never visited, and which he knew only by reading several indifferent French books on the country. He was influenced by the works of Swedenborg, whom he had never read, and with whom he was acquainted only through the reviews of the works of the Scandinavian philosopher which had appeared in various literary journals. He planned to explore what he considered to be the essence of mysticism, and would demonstrate that the spiritual and material aspects of man's nature were but two manifestations of what he believed to be the united or whole man. Of man's two aspects the spiritual was by far the more important, and the material, which man discarded as his spirituality became more intense, was the ultimate in human offal.

The story was relatively slight. Balzac's principal characters were two angels, a male and female, whom he envisioned as himself and Eveline. They mated, and produced Séraphitus-Séraphita, a double or twofold being, who was both man and woman. This hermaphrodite embodied the best of both sexes, the drive of the male and the balance of the female, the intelligence of the male and the beauty of the female, the strength of the male and the tenderness of the female. This twofold being is truly angelic, and therefore rises to heaven, there to dwell permanently. There are clues without number in the finite world of material man that will lead him to the infinity of the spiritual world, and the very process of seeking them will enable to find them. But he cannot achieve the infinite without making this effort, which is ultimately responsible for his transformation.

Grappling with the immediate problems of finishing overdue book manuscripts, placating creditors, maintaining a heavy correspondence and struggling with the mystical complexities of *Séraphita* occupied more of Balzac's time than he had envisioned, and he had to postpone his departure for Geneva again, then again. He was not able to tear himself away until December 21, three weeks later than he had planned, and on Christmas Day he finally settled into the room at the Hotel d'Arc that Eveline had reserved for him.

There he found a note from her, asking whether he really loved her; with the letter was a gift that he wore for the rest of his life as a good luck charm. It was a handsome gold ring which had a secret compartment inside its dome, and in it she had secreted a tiny lock of her hair. When he slipped the ring onto his finger he was able to assure himself that his love for the lady soon would be consummated.

Balzac had planned to remain in Geneva for two weeks, but the problems that arose in his relationship with Mme. Hanska made it necessary for him to stay longer, and he lingered for a total of six weeks, postponing his departure until early February 1834. What made it possible for him to delay his return to Paris was his remarkable, self-disciplined devotion to his work. No matter how much Mme. Hanska distracted, infuriated, encouraged and depressed him, he spent a minimum of twelve hours each day at his desk. Not even the great romance of his life could take him from his work for more than a few hours at a time.

It could not have been easy for him to concentrate. Mme. Hanska was causing him totally unexpected problems. In his imagination she had fallen into his arms, and they had initiated the affair that her attitude and correspondence had seemingly promised. To an extent, at least, she kept her word: she had been cunning in making her arrangements, and frequently spent time alone with him. But she astonished him by resisting his physical advances.

For the better part of one hundred and fifty years various biographers of Balzac have debated whether Eveline Hanska's love for him at this time was genuine or spurious, whether she was afraid to become his mistress or whether she fought with herself. The question appears to be something of an oversimplification, and the facts indicate that the struggle, if that is what it was, grew out of a many-faceted character.

The bored wife of a provincial Russian nobleman was eager to participate in an affair with one of the most brilliant men of the age. Eveline was a passionate woman, many years younger than the semi-invalid husband with whom she rarely had relations, so she was eager to taste the erotic delights Balzac so persistently offered her.

On the other hand, she was no fool, and was learning her would-be lover's faults. Not the least of them was his lack of discretion. She had already discovered, in her correspondence with him, that he too often referred to women in his past, and she suspected that, if she pursued his hints about them, it would be possible for her to identify these ladies. She followed a rule as sound as it was simple, and knew that what he had done to others he might do to her. If he boasted, even obliquely, that he had conquered her, she would be ruined. Baron Hanski was a proud, old-fashioned man who would unhesitatingly banish an unfaithful wife to a remote house in some far corner of his distant realm, and there she would rot for the rest of her days. No affair was worth taking the risk that she might spend the rest of her days as a hermit and social pariah.

Other factors also made her hesitate. She admitted—at length in a letter to her brother, Count Rzewuski—that Balzac possessed great charm, that he was a fascinating companion and that he made her feel desirable, a sensation that was new to her. On the other hand, she could see he was pressing far too hard in his attempts to persuade her to share his bed. His protestations of love were too ornate, too flowery, too overwhelming, and her common sense caused her to doubt his sincerity. Too often she caught him telling little lies, none of which was important in itself, but all of which, when combined, made her wonder if he ever meant what he said.

She realized he was something of an opportunist, and she could not help but become annoyed when he refused to accept a negative answer. Her own gentle, aristocratic background caused her to resent his bourgeois aggressiveness, his never-ending boasts that he was the greatest author on earth, the leading intellect of the century and, above all, the best lover of the day.

Eveline was something of a snob, which she admitted, and Balzac's manners offended her, just as they had offended many others of her class. She freely admitted he wrote books that would live for centuries, but his genius did not excuse his boorishness, his braying laugh, his sloppy appearance or his monumental appetite.

Although she was vain and sometimes light-headed, her feet were nevertheless planted firmly in the world of reality. She needed and demanded the time to sort out her conflicting emotions and to reach her own decision. But Balzac was unable to realize in real situations the deep understanding of women he demonstrated in his books. Impatient in all of his amorous dealings, he was the victim of his own passionate nature. Wanting

Eveline immediately, he pressed her when she hesitated, and thereby injured his own cause. His praise of her virtues became louder, the declarations of his undying love became more vehement, and his demand for a consummation of their love became increasingly shrill.

Even before they had met he had made up his mind that they would share a love as classical as that of Eloise and Abelard, and he was hurt when she insisted that she needed the opportunity to evaluate their relationship for herself. His ardor still flattered her, and sometimes, spurred by her own desire for adventure, she came perilously close to succumbing to his advances, but each time she managed to hold firm. Balzac's frenzy increased as his frustration mounted, and his irrational conduct gave Eveline further pause.

Her cousin, a Countess Potocka, came to visit the Hanskis in Geneva for a few days, and Eveline presented Balzac to the lady, who was exceptionally handsome and personable. He paid far more attention to the countess than the circumstances warranted, and Eveline expressed her jealousy, which caused him to become even more attentive to the visitor. On the eve of the countess' departure he and Eveline quarreled, and his despair was so great he threatened to return to Paris.

Balzac's threat seemed to weaken her resolve, and his hopes rose again. He worked each day from noon until midnight, slept for four hours and then worked again until breakfast, which he took with the Hanski family at their hotel. He spent his mornings with Mme. Hanska, enduring the presence of her husband when necessary, and for several days he had been in such low spirits that the baron had assumed he was ill.

Now, however, he sensed the change in Eveline's attitude, and excusing himself earlier than usual, returned to his hotel room and wrote her a letter in which he heaped endearment on endearment. There was no reply through the long hours of the day, but at midnight, when he was ending his work and preparing to go to bed, a tap sounded at his door.

It was January 26, 1834, a date Balzac remembered for the rest of his life. Eveline Hanska, clad in a dress of gray velvet with a fur-collared, matching cloak, was capitulating at last.

She spent the rest of the night with him, sneaking back to her own hotel shortly before dawn, and both of the lovers were pleasantly surprised. Balzac, as other women had discovered, was an expert in the erotic arts, and Eveline proved to be an eager pupil whose skill and fervor matched his. Some of Balzac's biographers have expressed the belief that he extracted a promise of marriage from Mme. Hanska before her pre-dawn departure, as his subsequent correspondence indicated. But his testimony in such matters is demonstrably unreliable, so whether an exchange of vows took place is a matter of conjecture. In any event, she appeared to accept his ecstatic planning with placid, passive calm, and by not contradicting him seemed to agree with him.

Balzac could not sleep after Eveline made his dreams come true, and wrote her the most impassioned of all the love letters he ever penned. She was his "beloved love," "the most adorable of all Heaven's angels," the light of his spirit, his "eternal inspiration." With a single caress she had brought him to life, and never before had he known the secret meanings of either life or love. Their love-making had been a combination of "honey and fire."

It appeared to be true that Eveline fulfilled all of the secret requirements that had been his dream since he had started to write, if not earlier. In book after book he had spelled out his ideal wife-mistress, a great lady of warmth and sensitivity, intellect and common-sense intelligence, someone who would be, in turn, a mother, a sister, a daughter—and who behaved like a reckless wanton in bed. No man, above all Honoré de Balzac, could ask for more.

So much of his fantasy had already materialized that he could not resist writing the rest of the book in subsequent letters, which filled page after page of his large-sized manuscript paper. He knew, he said, that she would follow him to Paris, that for his sake she would give up her husband, her position in the world, the fortune she would inherit and even her child. She would obtain a divorce, even though the remains of her reputation would be shredded, in order to live honorably as Mme. de Balzac. Even if the pressures of society forced them to live elsewhere than in Paris, she would not care, and would willingly share his exile with him.

But he would not permit her to make these sacrifices for him, he wrote. His own love forbade it, and he begged her to regard the future "through sensible eyes." They were still young, and would not become aged in mind, body or spirit for another thirty years. So they could afford to wait for the permanent joys of a life together. Baron Hanski, however, was suffering from ill health, and "pure logic" made it seem likely that he would die within the next five years. At the outside, even if he lingered far longer than expected, he could not live for more than a decade, and that would give the lovers the next twenty years together.

The fortune she would inherit from her husband meant nothing to him, Balzac wrote, abandoning the dream of a lifetime in a bald lie. His books would earn him vast sums of money, more than enough to support his wife in the great luxury to which she had been accustomed by birth and marriage. And he could not tolerate the thought of a scandal that would result in her separation from her daughter. The love of a mother was sacred, and he intended to respect it, protect it and cherish it.

While waiting for the convenience of the baron's death, to be sure, they would see each other as frequently as possible, and he urged her to join him in making the necessary arrangements that would tide them over the next year or two. Eveline had mentioned a forthcoming visit to Italy, so he would join her and the baron there. Then they would look forward to the next step.

His new mistress, who had no desire to break up her home, be deprived of her daughter or lose her marital inheritance, was relieved by her impetuous lover's conclusions. Although it thrilled her to think of herself as Balzac's mistress, she was still sensible enough to want to keep her position as the Baroness Hanska. So she seconded his plan to join her in Italy, and dangled a fat carrot before his eyes: within the next year the Hanskis would return to Russia, and she would make the necessary arrangements for him to pay a prolonged visit to Volhynia, where he could work in solitude—and make love to her when the rest of the household was asleep.

Balzac never told anyone his reasons for avoiding an immediate marriage, but they were obvious. Certainly he had no intention of losing the vast fortune that the baron's widow would bring with her when she became his wife. He had already estimated, in a letter to his sister, that the Hanskis were worth "millions of francs," and it was sweet to dream of a luxurious, debt-free existence. His own bourgeois background was also responsible for his reluctance to become a principal in what obviously would be a sensational scandal. It was permissible to enjoy an affair with a married woman, but it was another matter entirely for a middle-class Frenchman to be the cause of an aristocratic divorce, and to become the lady's husband. He and Eveline would be objects of curiosity and contempt no matter where they went, and he didn't want to subject either of them to the world's permanent scorn. He had concluded it was far better to wait.

For the present, however, Baron Hanski was very much alive, and the danger of creating a scandal still remained if his suspicions were aroused. So Balzac made it his business to exert all of his considerable charm in his relations with the cuckolded husband during the last ten days of his stay in Geneva. He invited the baron to walk with him, and flattered him by showing him some stories for a new edition of the *Contes drolatiques* he had written since coming to Switzerland. This was a high honor. Balzac never allowed anyone to see his work until he had revised it repeatedly and was satisfied that it was in a final form, but he broke his own rule for the baron.

Hanski was pleased, recognizing the honor, and replied at great length when Balzac sought his advice. The Russian nobleman who had never written or edited a line in his life gave his wife's secret lover the benefit of his most profound thinking on the art of creating lasting literature. And Balzac, gritting his teeth, listened by the hour, pretended to accept the words of wisdom and thanked the baron for them.

Becoming increasingly adept in throwing sand into Hanski's myopic eyes, Balzac wrote a letter to the baron and baroness on February 8, the day of his departure from Geneva. He was grateful for their friendship, and never had he known such carefree happiness as he had enjoyed in their mutual company. Never before had he been able to escape from the concerns of an exacting profession that weighed down his soul. He had known them for only a short time, in the course of brief visits to Neuchâtel and Geneva, but he had ample reason for believing them to be his dearest friends.

The farewells of Balzac and the Hanskis were touching. The baron gave his delightful French friend several expensive gifts, among them an inkwell of solid gold. Forewarned by Eveline, Balzac was prepared, and returned the gesture. Hanski received a handsome walking stick with a gold head, little Anna was given some toys that were mechanical marvels, and the blushing, guilt-ridden Henriette Borel was the recipient of a warm winter coat with a fur collar, the finest item of apparel she had ever owned. But Balzac's gift to Mme. Hanska was modest, as it would not have been seemly to give a personal gift of value to a married lady. Only Eveline and the shocked governess recognized the audacity of Balzac's brazen touch: he gave the lady a set of writing paper and envelopes.

Gently prodded by a reminding wife, Baron Hanski extended a cordial invitation to his friend to join the family in Italy during the coming months. Nothing would give him greater pleasure than the renewal of their relations.

Mme. Hanska mildly echoed her husband's words.

Bowing politely in her general direction, Balzac shook the baron's hand, and then, in a casual display of friendship, lightly kissed the baroness on the cheek.

Departing on the noon coach to Paris, Balzac carried with him a store of very bright memories and the most glittering promises for the future that he had ever entertained. He was taking no chances that the word about his affair might leak out, and had even stopped writing to his sister about Eveline. He carried his new mistress' letters in a little oak casket she had given him, and thereafter always kept the key on a chain around his neck, never leaving it anywhere and hiding the casket in the safe that held his most precious manuscripts. Years passed before Zulma Carraud finally divined the true nature of his relationship with Eveline, and he went through countless gyrations to prevent Mme. de Berny from learning the facts. As he well understood, secrecy was vital.

He also took with him a portfolio filled with manuscripts, and could congratulate himself on how smoothly his writing had gone. *La Duchesse de Langeais*, his damning novel about Mme. de Castries, was in final form. He had turned out some of his best stories for the new *Contes drolatiques*, and he had completed the better part of a draft for a major contribution to the *Comédie humaine*, which he was calling *Le Cabinet des antiques*. He had also written a long section of the difficult *Séraphita*.

In all, Balzac had enjoyed an exceptionally profitable holiday.

XI

When he returned to Paris in mid-February 1834, Balzac discovered that a number of people close to him had undergone important changes in their lives. The most serious situation was that of Mme. de Berny, who had been gravely ill, and he hurried to Nemours to see her. Although her letters had warned him that he might not recognize her, he had not accepted her statements literally, and her appearance shocked him. She had "aged a quarter of a century in a single month," and had become wrinkled and gaunt, an old woman who walked with the aid of a cane and spoke in a quavering voice. He spent a few days with her, probably motivated by his guilts, and then wrote to his sister:

Even if she should recover her health—as I hope she will—it would always be painful for me to watch the melancholy decline into old age. It is as if Nature had avenged itself suddenly, and at one stroke, for this woman's prolonged resistance to the laws of life and of time.

Other problems struck equally close to home. Mme. de Balzac had made a foolish investment and had lost the last of her savings. She was now destitute, and was forced to live with her daughter and son-in-law, with whom she had been staying for periods of varying length as a visitor. Laure de Surville and her husband thought it only right that the successful author whose style of living cost him more than one hundred thousand francs per year should contribute to his mother's support, and they also reminded him, as did Mme. de Balzac herself, that she would be solvent if he repaid the sum of more than one hundred thousand francs that he owed her.

Balzac's reaction was one of innocent, outraged hurt. His creditors gave him no peace and dared to interrupt his work. He was plagued by bill collectors whenever he set foot outside his own house. He was scraping together small amounts of money whenever he could, in order to obtain brief respites from his financial worries. Certainly it had not occurred to him that his own mother would turn on him at a time when he was depending on her kindness, generosity and understanding, but if she insisted on creating a scandal and sending him to a pauper's prison cell, he could not stop her.

The wrangle continued for several weeks, and eventually was solved in a manner that was satisfactory only to Balzac. He agreed to pay the De Survilles one thousand francs per month as his share of his mother's support, but insisted they were fleecing him. He also allowed himself to be persuaded to continue paying his mother the five hundred francs per month he received from the *Revue de Paris*. It was a calamitous day, he said, when a man's own flesh and blood conspired against him, and taking advantage of his tender nature, robbed him of the pittance he needed to keep a roof over his head and put simple food on his table.

Yet another difficulty caused him still more concern. His sister and brother-in-law were going through a crisis in their marriage, and Balzac was the ostensible cause of the dispute. De Surville thought the peripatetic author was a bad influence on Laure, and ordered her to stop seeing him. Laure had no intention of breaking relations with her beloved brother, but was afraid to defy her husband openly, so she contrived to meet Balzac without De Surville's knowledge.

The indignant engineer obviously did not believe that he himself was prey to Balzac's malevolence, and continued to see him openly, meeting him for a meal or a business chat once every week or two. On these occasions Balzac was forced to listen to unending complaints about his sister's driving ambition, her refusal to let her husband work out his vocational destiny in his own way. Then, in his secret meetings with Laure, he heard in detail that De Surville was lazy, that money meant nothing to him and that he was content to drift.

Years before, Balzac would automatically have taken his sister's part and defended her to the end, but he was becoming more objective as well as more mature in his judgments. Laure might still be the adoring little sister, although he suspected she was enjoying his success vicariously. But he realized she was becoming more like their mother every day. He felt sorry for De Surville, aware that the man was leading a barren life because he was married to a woman incapable of giving him love.

In spite of the unhappiness of those who were dear to him, Balzac was able to shrug off their problems and concentrate on himself. He was in love with the woman of his dreams, who loved him in return, and no man could ask for more. He wrote to Eveline each day, no matter how busy his working schedule, and in the course of a single year sent her more than one hundred and fifty thousand words, most of them assuring her of his undying love for her.

Yet he exercised uncharacteristic restraint, and mentioned her name to no one. Zulma Carraud, whose father had just died and who was having a difficult time bearing her newest child, invited him for a visit and told him at length about the privacy he would enjoy when working in Major Carraud's new house. Balzac declined, as he knew she would see his incoming and outgoing mail, and wanted to keep the secret of his affair with Eveline Hanska from her.

He was equally careful in his dealings with his friends. Most French authors of the period boasted to their intimates of their sexual and romantic prowess, and one's amatory success was equated with one's literary standing. Dumas bragged so incessantly that others discounted his exploits, George Sand emulated the men and revealed her indiscretions, and even Victor Hugo, who may have bedded more members of the opposite sex than most of his colleagues combined, immodestly permitted himself the luxury of admitting that he occupied himself with two or three—or even more—women each day of his life.

Balzac went to the other extreme. He spent long hours convincing George Sand that he led a totally celibate life, and not until years later did she discover that ladies of questionable virtue visited his house regularly and attended to his physical needs. She had no idea of Eveline Hanska's existence, either, and when she urged him, as she did in 1834, to find a woman of charm, beauty, social position and wealth with whom he could fall in love, he insisted that such a woman existed only in his imagination.

He was equally reticent in his dealings with Théophile Gautier, the distinguished critic, poet and essayist, with whom he was becoming very friendly. Gautier, himself a writer of considerable stature, had a genius for recognizing the literary worth of his contemporaries, and was one of a very few who realized that Balzac was emerging as one of the giants of the age. Balzac was grateful for the extension of a hand to him by a peer, and until the end of his life he considered Gautier one of his true friends.

Maintaining the same posture he had taken with George Sand, however, Balzac told Gautier that his life was monastic. He went out of his way to cover up his relationship with Eveline by expressing the wish that he might find some beautiful amenable woman who would understand him. Gautier revealed to him the details of his own love life, but Balzac did not reciprocate confidences. He was motivated, in part, by the desire to protect Mme.

Hanska, knowing her own life would be ruined if her husband learned of the affair. Yet something deeper prevented him from revealing his affair with Eveline, either in correspondence or conversation, with those who were closest to him.

He had been free enough in his revelations to Zulma Carraud about Mme. de Castries, for example, but his only references to Mme. de Berny in his letters to his friend had been oblique. It appears that when a woman really meant something to Balzac, he refused to share any part of the relationship with anyone.

Mme. Hanska wasn't the only cause of his rejoicing in the winter of 1834, and another event helped him put the troubles of Mme. de Berny, his mother and his sister out of his mind. *Eugénie Grandet* was proving to be the most successful book he had ever written, the booksellers of Paris and the provincial cities couldn't keep it in stock, and copies were being purchased at a rate that would make it the most successful novel of the year. To some extent the critics shared the attitude of the public, and a majority grudgingly admitted that Balzac had written a first-rate story. They carped, to be sure, finding elements of which they disapproved, but they accorded him the most favorable reception they had yet given him.

Balzac's friends were ecstatic, and Delphine de Girardin summarized their views in a letter, saying, "*What talent, what talent! Oh, great Balzac!*"

Encouraged by his redoubled fame and the increased royalties being paid him, he plunged into work with renewed fury that eclipsed his previous efforts. He plunged into two major novels, *César Birotteau* and *La Vieille Fille,* turned out *La Recherche de l'absolu* in three months, made considerable progress on *Séraphita,* wrote *Père Goriot* in forty days, did one novella, followed it with two others, and put the plot outline of *Le Lys dans la vallée* on paper. He also wrote the whole of his *Lettres aux écrivains français du 19ième siècle,* and worked on a long play in collaboration with Jules Sandeau, with Balzac doing most of the writing.

Not even Honoré de Balzac could keep up that blistering a

pace without paying for it, and late in April he collapsed. Dr. Nacquart was afraid he was suffering from what was called brain fever, a disease about which virtually nothing was known, and insisted that his patient take a complete rest. A reluctant Balzac left Paris to take a holiday with the Carrauds at Frapesle, where the major had been made commander of the army garrison. He proved unable to conquer his work habits, however, and "rested" by walking in the garden with Zulma for an hour each day, then relaxing for more than two hours at dinner with both of the Carrauds. Otherwise he made no changes in his usual schedule, and remained in his room, writing at his usual frenzied pace.

Meanwhile Mme. Hanska was enjoying the protracted visit to the West that helped her forget the dreary winter snows of the Ukraine. She and the baron, accompanied by their large retinue, visited Venice, Florence and Naples, where she went sightseeing, spent hours each day in the shops, tried a different restaurant every night and had her portrait painted. She dutifully answered Balzac's letters, although it was impossible for her to maintain his tempo. She managed to write one in reply to every three she received.

The tone of her correspondence was even more significant than its frequency. She described her activities, told him about various purchases she had made and lovingly spelled out the menus of meals she had eaten, but she rarely made more than a few perfunctory personal remarks. She showed scant interest in his work, and her comments in reply to detailed accounts of books in progress were vague.

But she never failed to demand more and still more letters from him. She herself might allow several weeks to pass without writing to him, but she upbraided him sharply when his schedule occasionally overwhelmed him and made it impossible for him to post a letter for several days. As a number of Balzac's biographers have noted, Mme. Hanska appears to have been less interested in Balzac, the man, than she was in receiving communication from Balzac, the author.

Balzac's increased flow of letters created a problem for him, making it difficult for him to communicate with her through the faithful Henriette Borel. The situation was further complicated by the censors in the various Italian states, men who took their work seriously and assiduously opened every letter addressed to anyone in their countries.

Balzac found an ingenious solution by writing openly to both of the Hanskis in what were, on the surface, joint letters. These were friendly communications, filled with chat about his various activities, but he managed to slip in remarks whose meaning his mistress alone would divine. A favorite was recounting a dream of the previous night, and again and again he found himself in the Hotel d'Arc in Geneva, where he stared out of the window at the view, perhaps, or toasted his good friends from Russia in steaming coffee, or even tossed fitfully on his lonely bed.

The theme of loneliness played a major role in his letters. He led a celibate life, totally devoid of even social friendships with women. He spent all of his days and nights alone, and sometimes he wished he might find a wife who would relieve the loneliness of his bachelor dwelling. He had a dream about a lady with black hair and swore eternal fidelity to her, but she vanished from sight when he awakened; nevertheless, he would remain faithful to her, as he had in the dream.

It was fortunate that Baron Hanski was neither romantic nor suspicious, and it may be that the Russian nobleman did not bother to wade through the thick letters, of which Balzac filled page after page in a small hand. His own sightseeing occupied him, he moved at a leisurely pace in order to conserve his strength and he probably wasn't interested in the sentiments expressed at such length by the family's friend in Paris. Writers were verbose, which he supposed was one of their failings.

Mme. Hanska took her lover's protestations with the proverbial grain of salt. In spite of her lack of experience she was shrewd, and knew that anyone who talked so much about his fidelity had something to hide. She had discovered during their brief affair that Balzac was an expert in the art of love-making, and realized he had acquired his experience somewhere. It is possible, too, that she enjoyed the power she exerted over him. All she had to do was hint in a letter that he had been unfaithful to her, and his self-righteous, self-exonerating replies filled semi-concealed pages of his next letters. It was fortunate for her, too, that her husband was paying scant attention to the correspondence.

In May 1834, Eveline finally caught Balzac. He was in such high spirits and robust health after his visit to the Carrauds, where he had worked no more than sixteen hours per day, that he kicked up his heels. He conceived the ideas for what would materialize as two of his major books, *Les Mémoires d'une jeune femme* and *Une Vue du monde*. He also relaxed his schedule sufficiently to spend one or two evenings each week on the town, dining at a fashionable restaurant, attending the opera or the theatre and then going on to a chic gathering place for supper.

On these occasions he always escorted a beautiful young woman, usually one or another of Paris' leading courtesans of the day, and these activities were duly noted by the gossip writers of at least a dozen of the city's newspapers. Honoré de Balzac had become newsworthy, and any public appearance he made with a lovely companion found its way into print.

So he made himself look ridiculous when he wrote to the Hanskis that he was living in gloomy solitude, going nowhere and seeing no one. Eveline, who continued to read the Paris newspapers that had given her solace in the remote vastness of her Ukranian estate, had proof he was gallivanting, and taxed him for telling lies.

But Balzac was capable of handling any situation when he was dealing with a woman, and his reply to her accusation was a tribute to his genius:

The proprietors of theatres and restaurants will do anything to encourage patronage. My recent success emboldens them to believe that my presence encourages others to follow my alleged example, so it is with much amusement that I read I have been seen here or there, always accompanied by some lady whose very existence is as mythical as her supposed beauty. I am forced to laugh when, after working without pause for a day and a night, I read in the newspapers that I have been enjoying a night's pleasure at a theatre I have never visited or a restaurant I have never frequented. I must attempt to acclimate to the thought that this is the price one must pay for fame in our supposedly honorable, civilized society.

Eveline Hanska was unable to prove he was lying, and subsided until the next flurry appeared in print. Yet when she complained again, Balzac replied in the same vein. She became very annoyed, however, when there was a veiled reference to a young lady of high social station who, it was rumored, paid private visits to the author of *Eugénie Grandet* at his home. But Balzac took that charge in his stride, too, and told her:

There are women who plume themselves on being of some consequence in my life and boast that they pay me secret visits. I would find these calumnies amusing were it not for the indiscretion of these women, who try to increase their stature at my expense by informing gullible members of the press that they are my mistresses. Were their frivolities not beneath me, I could almost wish that I might spend an evening with one of these ladies, but the truth of my situation is that never was solitude more complete than mine.

Here I sit, far removed from any other member of the human race, as completely alone as any woman in all the yearning of her love could wish me to be.

Mme. Hanska wisely rejected these fantasies, but did not belabor the point. It is possible she didn't care what he did, or with whom, and was merely whiling away an occasional idle hour at his expense.

Balzac had no idle hours, and his life was further complicated, in the late spring of 1834, by the unexpected reappearance of his half brother, Henry. Two years earlier the family had rejoiced when Henry had written from Mauritius that he had married a beautiful heiress and would have no worries for the rest of his life. But Henry, like Balzac, was a congenital liar.

Without warning Henry *de* Balzac (he, too, had adopted the new name) emerged from the blue waters of the Indian Ocean, accompanied by a homely, pregnant wife, ten years his senior, and her child by a previous marriage. She had inherited a small fortune, but Henry had allowed the money to sift through his fingers in a manner worthy of his elder half brother and had also emulated Balzac by accumulating debts in excess of one hundred and fifty thousand francs.

Balzac shuddered when he saw his sister-in-law and said to De Surville, "Did he really have to travel more than five thousand miles to find a wife like that?"

Laure de Surville, ever mindful of her blood ties, obtained an apartment for the newcomers in the same building in which she and her family were living. Her husband demonstrated his family loyalty, too, by finding work for Henry on his own current project, a new bridge in Normandy. And Mme. de Balzac sold her last remaining parcel of real estate so her youngest could meet some of his obligations.

"Mama," Balzac said unfeelingly, "is receiving her just punishment for her love child."

But his bark was far more vicious than his bite. He increased his mother's allowance to one thousand francs per month, knowing that the additional funds would find their way into Henry's pocket. And when the baby was born he presented the infant with an expensive bassinet, a cup and plate of solid gold—and a leather-bound set of his books. He was proud of his ability to act as the principal support of the entire family, including the half brother he had always loathed. Laure accused him, in several letters, of being secretly pleased by the various failures Henry had suffered, but Balzac refused to dignify her charge by replying to it.

There were sound business reasons for believing he could support a great many people. An ambitious young publisher, Edmond Werdet, had just brought out a new edition of *Le Médecin de campagne*, and it sold so well in the wake of *Eugénie Grandet* that Werdet, emulating Balzac, borrowed to the hilt so he could publish a minimum of twenty-five forthcoming Balzac works. The latter was so enthusiastic over the prospects that he abandoned his book subscription scheme and paid out money of his own to buy back the rights, from other publishers, to various of his works which had not yet been published. He would become Werdet's partner, and would not only receive his author's royalties, but would also share in the publisher's profits.

He seemed to thrive in an atmosphere that would have made it impossible for most of his colleagues to work, and made particularly good progress on the newest of his Philosophical Studies, *La Recherche de l'absolu,* in which he returned to a now familiar theme. His protagonist was an enormously wealthy man of Flemish descent, Balthazar Claës, who becomes fascinated by chemistry. Claës becomes obsessed by the desire to isolate and break down the element of which all matter is composed, the atom. Possessed by demons of his own making, Claës spends his fortune, and is reduced to selling the family's collection of priceless paintings. He ruins the lives of his children, destroys the wife he loves more than anyone else, and ultimately causes his own death as he fails in his effort to isolate the absolute.

The book was filled with vast quantities of accurate material on chemical developments, and was a testimonial to the thoroughness of Balzac's research. He read many books on the subject, including a number of the latest technical volumes published in Paris, and he conferred at length with two Academicians who were distinguished chemists. His readers, he believed, had a right to expect the truth.

La Recherche de l'absolu, long considered one of Balzac's finest books, is also significant because of a statement that echoes the author's own sentiments regarding the domestication of a genius. Claës is speaking to his wife, but it is really Honoré de Balzac telling the world how he himself feels when he says:

A great man should not have a wife or children. You must tread your unhappy path alone. Your virtues are not those of ordinary people. You belong to the world; you can never belong to a wife or family. You drain the soil around you like a great tree!

Huge trees put out many branches, and one on which Balzac expected to earn the fortune that continued to elude him was in the theatre. Victor Hugo's plays had earned large sums of money and made him financially independent; what Hugo could do, Balzac also could do. He was conscious of his own lack of theatrical knowledge, but had found someone who would supply it. Jules Sandeau, the part-time actor who had been living with George Sand, had just been dismissed by the lady, and Balzac had not only given him a home in the house on the Rue Cassini, but, as we have seen, was collaborating with him in the writing of a play. The joint effort progressed poorly. Sandeau was lazy, far more interested in acquiring a new wardrobe so he could approach theatrical managers for work than he was in writing, and the exhausting regimen of his partner overstrained his intellectual and emotional capacities. He felt like a man who was drowning, he told friends, and he and Balzac spent more of their time quarreling than they did in reducing their idea for a play onto paper.

La Recherche de l'absolu was published very quickly. Mme. Béchet had invested so much money in Balzac that she required a prompt return on her money. But the public again demonstrated a lack of interest in the Philosophical Studies, and the novel was a financial failure. Balzac, who had become convinced that, after *Eugénie Grandet*, he could do no wrong, was bitterly disappointed. The fault, he decided, was entirely that of the publisher: the book was badly printed, sellers didn't receive copies until long after the advertised date of publication, and insufficient efforts had been made to woo the critics. He told his friends what he thought of Mme. Béchet, but that wasn't enough. He had to tell her off personally in a direct communication, and wrote her such an unpleasant letter that their relationship immediately cooled.

It was another letter, however, that almost did him far greater harm. In July 1834, the Hanskis and their entourage left the Italian states for Austria, intending to spend the autumn and winter in Vienna before returning to the far-distant Ukraine. When they had last visited Vienna, Balzac had written to Eveline via Mlle. Borel, and as the Austrian censors were not interested in love letters, he immediately stopped writing letters to both of the Hanskis, and instead sent one intended only for the eyes of his mistress:

Oh, my angel, my love, my life, my happiness, my dearest, my treasure—how dreadful this enforced reserve has been! What joy it is to be able to write to you now from heart to heart!

Our separation has been a nightmare I can no longer endure, I shall fly to your side. I shall hasten to you like the wind, although I cannot possibly give you an exact date this far in advance, since the journey will demand titanic exertions on my part. But I love you with superhuman force!

Do you realize we have been separated for six months? I have suffered six months of longing, six months of pent-up love, and now I must kiss the divine brow, touch the beloved hair of which I have worn a lock so carefully, next to my heart.

Is it too much to ask for three days at your side? Three days of your sweet, beloved company will give me life and strength for a thousand years!

These sentiments were only a sample of the emotional fervor that filled many pages. Precisely what Balzac said is unknown, as only the fragmentary notes which he copied are still extant. The original letter itself found its way into a fireplace of the house in Vienna that the Hanskis were renting. The details of what happened when the letter reached its destination are not known, either, but in some way the communication fell into the hands of the baron.

There were some nasty scenes, and then the justifiably angry Baron Hanski wrote to Paris, demanding an explanation. Balzac, who believed in telling the readers of his books the truth, was caught short, but his imagination helped him solve one of the most difficult problems he had ever encountered, and the trapped genius accomplished the impossible. As nearly as he could judge from the outraged baron's letter, Mme. Hanska had admitted nothing to her husband, so he proceeded on this explanation.

Mme. Hanska, he wrote, was "the purest of beings, an utter child, and although clever, is very naïve." One day in Geneva—he could not recall the circumstances—she had remarked that she would like to see what a real love letter looked like. He had promised to send her the material discarded from a recent novel, but in the press of work after his return to Paris had forgotten the matter.

Then, just recently, he had happened to glance through the pages of his novel, *Les Chouans*, which would be reprinted soon in a new edition, and a letter from the hero to the heroine had reminded him of Mme. Hanska's request. Therefore he had picked up his pen and had dashed off a mock love letter.

Only an idiot would have accepted this feeble a fabrication, but Balzac promptly compounded his invention. The day before the baron's letter had reached Paris, he wrote, he had received an extremely indignant letter from Mme. Hanska, who obviously had forgotten her playful request in Geneva. She had reminded him of her virtue—and her loyalty to her husband was so great that no man required any such reminder. Now she would refuse to speak to him.

Reaching still deeper into his bag of tricks, Balzac struck his final, most brilliant blow. He still thought of the baron as his friend, and was devastated. Writing as one gentleman to another, he begged his friend's help. Would the baron do him the great favor of intervening on his behalf with the good Mme. Hanska, and try to convince her that he had been joking? Carrying the request to its ultimate conclusion, he declared:

Mme. Hanska's indulgence would provide a noble demonstration of the foolishness of my conduct. It would show what a saint she is, and that would be my consolation.

He was sending along a copy of *La Recherche de l'absolu,* together with the original manuscript of the book, as a token of his friendship, and could only hope he had not forfeited that friendship. He begged the baron to pass along these tokens to his wife. If the Hanskis rejected that friendship, however, he trusted that they would burn both the book and the manuscript, and would forget him. The letter ended on a dejected, pathetic note:

Even if it should be possible for Mme. Hanska to grant me the complete pardon I do not deserve, I will never be able to pardon myself for having hurt or offended, for as much as a single moment, such a noble soul. It will no doubt be my fate never to see you again, but I should like to assure you how deeply I would regret that; I do not possess so many really affectionate friends that I could afford to lose one of them without shedding a bitter tear.

Whether Baron Hanski was a fool who was taken in by this inspired gibberish or a very wise man who pretended to be a fool is unknown and cannot be determined. It well may be that Mme. Hanska was successful in convincing her husband that, regardless of the state of Balzac's affections, she had no romantic interest in the homely, overweight, egocentric little French author. Perhaps the baron realized he would serve his own best interest by glossing over the matter. After all, he and his wife would be returning home in a few months, and after their long sojourn in the West probably would not leave Russia again during his lifetime. Certainly he had no desire to end his marriage on the basis of such relatively flimsy evidence, and could not have wanted to make himself a laughingstock by naming the unprepossessing Balzac as his wife's lover.

So he made the best of the embarrassing situation. After delaying a month, during which time Balzac slept on a figurative bed of needles, the baron wrote him a brief, jovial letter. Adopting a hearty, man-to-man tone, Hanski made light of the "misconstrued" letter, indicated that he had intervened with his wife and urged his friend to hope for the best.

Balzac wanted to reply by return mail, but his common sense told him to wait. A character in one of his books who was as innocent as he pretended to be would not hasten to leap into the breach, but would await the lady's pleasure.

The lady allowed him to sweat for a few more weeks. There is no way of determining whether Mme. Hanska's delay was deliberate, whether she was too busy with her social life in Vienna to spend an hour at her writing desk, or whether discretion prompted her to play her role casually. But the fact of the matter is that another month passed before she, too, sent Balzac a letter, its tone indicating that she had shown it to her husband.

Of course she forgave the dear friend of her husband and herself. She hoped he wouldn't believe her too silly or naïve, but he could imagine how shocked she had been when she had opened the envelope written in his familiar hand and had read his passionate declaration of his love for her. She was pleased the misunderstanding had been cleared away, and she wanted to assure the good friend of the Hanski family that their affections toward him were unchanged in any way. In fact—and she added this as a casual, almost careless afterthought—they would be delighted to entertain him as their guest if he found it possible to make the journey to Vienna before they left for their home in the Ukraine early the following spring.

Balzac's reply indicated that he had recovered his own dignity. He was delighted he had been forgiven, and he would resume his letter-writing so he could tell his friends about the inconsequential events that filled his insignificant life. He was deeply touched by Mme. Hanska's kind invitation, and hoped he would be in a position to accept it in the not too distant future. For the present, however, he was chained to Paris by the demands of his publishers, who seemed to think he was a machine capable of delivering endless streams of manuscripts at their request. He would let them know as soon as he saw his way clear to make the long journey.

Mme. Hanska at first believed his reluctance to come to Vienna was a sham invented for her husband's benefit, but Balzac soon indicated to her, in the private letters he began sending her again via Mlle. Borel, that he had told the literal truth. He could not leave Paris at present.

Mme. Hanska accused him of having found another woman, someone he preferred.

He denied the charge, and swore eternal love and fidelity.

If he loved her, she wrote, he would come to Vienna.

After a number of evasive exchanges Balzac finally broke down and admitted the truth of his situation. Even though he was earning large sums of money it was pouring out faster than it came in, and he could not afford to make the journey.

The quicksands into which he had stumbled were no less dangerous because they were familiar. He was not only supporting his mother and contributing substantially to the living of his half brother, but had resumed his wildly extravagant spending habits. He had supposedly rented the apartment on the ground floor of the house on the Rue Cassini for Jules Sandeau, but was decorating it to suit his own extravagant tastes. Francs poured out by the tens of thousands for furniture and drapes, lamps and Oriental rugs, dishes and glassware, and above all, for the shockingly expensive, useless bric-a-brac that had become his passion. It was time for a man in his position to change his wardrobe, and he bought a dozen new suits, a pair of greatcoats, new hats and shoes and shirts and cravats—and, of course, innumerable pairs of the yellow leather gloves that already filled a chest of drawers.

Mme. de Balzac thought her son had taken leave of his senses, Laure begged him to spend less, and Zulma Carraud wrote letter after letter urging him to curb his extravagances. Dr. Nacquart spent an entire day with him, and still was not quite convinced that he should be allowed to wander where he pleased; it might be better for him, the doctor said, if he were confined in an institution.

The physician's observation was not as far-fetched as it might seem. There were periods in Honoré de Balzac's life when a spirit close to madness seemed to possess him, and it was reflected in his spending of money as much as in the pressures he exerted on himself to turn out vast quantities of work. In the autumn of 1834, when his debts were mounting astronomically, he was spending at a reckless pace, knowing he was digging himself deeper into debt.

He was also working harder than ever before in his life, partly because he wanted money, partly because he wanted a breathing space in his self-inflicted schedule long enough for him to visit Eveline Hanska in Vienna, on the anniversary of their Geneva affair. It was in precisely this period that he wrote with a blinding speed greater than any he had previously achieved, and in precisely one month and ten days turned out the complete manuscript of what was to become one of his greatest and most enduring masterpieces, *Père Goriot*. The accomplishment is so dazzling it is useless to wonder, as so many critics have done, what kind of a book *Père Goriot* would have been had he spent more time on it. Balzac could only work at his own pace, and the speed of his writing was irrelevant to the quality of the material he wrote.

The theme was familiar, and is best summarized in Balzac's own words: "Passion does not compromise; it accepts every sacrifice."

There was no single plot, and Balzac emphasized his theme by telling a series of interlocking stories, each of which would have been a complete short novel in itself. Goriot, whose name was used in the title, was a middle-class man with a limited income who wanted his daughters to enjoy every luxury. For their sakes he scrimped, saved and gave them all his possessions; eventually he was ruined, and his daughters, like King Lear's, deserted him.

The principal setting was that of a boardinghouse owned by Mother Vacquer, where many of the principal characters lived, and it was destined to become one of the most famous pensions in history. Among the tenants was a former convict, Vautrin, who lived there under an assumed name, and who wanted to conquer the world. Here is another of Balzac's familiar themes. Vautrin's ambitions mirrored his own, although the character was cold and unemotional, hence a product of the author's imagination.

The essence of Balzac's heightened realism was expressed by Vautrin: "I defy you to walk two steps in Paris without encountering the most despicable intrigues . . . That is life as it really is. It is no more beautiful than a kitchen, it stinks as badly, and you are forced to dirty your hands if you want to cook anything. There are no principles here, but only events—accidents and coincidences and acts committed by the desperate; there are no laws, but only circumstances. The superior man allies himself to events and circumstances so he may use of them for his own purposes."

Balzac felt a kinship with Vautrin, to a degree, but his own sense of morality would not allow amoral and criminal acts to go unpunished. Vautrin's own vaulting ambition caused his ultimate downfall.

A character even closer to the author was a young Gascon, Rastignac, who was a symbol of innocent purity when he first came to Paris, and he was shocked by the corruption, depravity and poverty he saw everywhere. His attitude was similar to that of the author himself in his youth, and the circumstances of his apprenticeship and early vocational struggles resembled Balzac's, too. Rastignac vowed to conquer Paris on his own terms, but soon discovered that compromise was necessary and almost lost himself in a world where morality was unknown. But he clung to his own principles, which was difficult; yet at the end of the book the reader does not know whether he might stumble in his pursuit of the heights.

The last of the stories was that of Rastignac's cousin, Claire de Beauséant, a beautiful and great lady whose entire life was wrapped up in that of the lover whom she worshiped. The lover deserted her and she was lost, a woman who deteriorated into an empty shell and lived for the sake of form rather than trying to enjoy the substance of life.

Balzac wove a large number of minor characters into *Père Goriot*, and many of them reappeared in later books as principals. Similarly, some of the major characters were seen again in minor roles. Rastignac, in fact, had been introduced briefly in the pages of *Peau de chagrin*. It was this utilization of character that enabled Balzac to create the over-all tapestry of the *Comédie humaine*, and many of his books can be regarded as sequels, in that the plot of one frequently grew out of a story that preceded it. The technique has become familiar in the past century and a half, but no one has ever used it more effectively than its originator.

Balzac not only surpassed his previous efforts when he wrote *Père Goriot,* but knew precisely what he was doing and believed implicitly in his ability to create the effects he wanted to achieve. Laboring twenty hours per day on the book, snatching only a few hours of sleep, gulping down endless cups of strong coffee and eating while continuing to write, he realized he had climbed to a new summit. "*This book will be regarded for centuries to come as a masterwork,*" he wrote to Eveline Hanska.

His self-confidence was so great that he found a way to meet some of his contractual obligations. He convinced the editors of the *Revue de Paris* that *Père Goriot* was his best effort, and they agreed to publish the novel in serial form. But they, too, had a problem, that of filling the empty pages of immediately forthcoming issues, so the first chapters appeared before Balzac actually completed the book.

Late in December he collapsed and spent several days in bed, sleeping for long hours at a time and awakening only to eat. His family situation was easing somewhat, which gave him greater peace of mind. He was especially relieved when his mother went to Chantilly to make her home with a friend. Henry was in Normandy, working, and had taken his wife and children there, so Balzac found it unnecessary to spend any time with the half brother he despised.

He continued to worry about Mme. de Berny, and early in January 1835, as soon as he recovered his own health, he paid her a visit of a few days. His worst fears were confirmed when he discovered she was suffering from a fatal illness, and he sent a heartbroken letter to an old mutual friend:

My life is threatened at its source. If that light from Heaven is taken from me, every day will be less bright. She is, as you know, my conscience and my strength; she prevails over all like the sky, like the spirit of faith, of hope.

I do not know what to do. She does not know what her illness is, but she realizes only too well that she is dying.

Balzac indeed felt lost, and it is difficult to doubt the sincerity or depth of his feelings. Predictably, he turned with even greater violence in the direction of Eveline Hanska, for here was a man who could not survive without the love—or imagined love—of someone who would be both mother and mistress:

You will be, if she should be taken from me, the one and only person who has ever opened her heart to me.

XII

Père Goriot lived up to Balzac's fondest expectations and was an overnight sensation. The *Revue de Paris* sold out overnight, and an additional fifty thousand copies were printed, but they quickly vanished, too. Plans were rushed to bring out the hard-cover copy of the complete book, and customers hurried to the booksellers by the thousands to place advance orders. There could be no question about the success of the book, and Balzac enjoyed his greatest triumph.

The critics failed to join in the applause, however. With the notable exception of Théophile Gautier, they damned the novel. Many of the reviewers were shocked by the author's harsh cynicism, claimed that he did an injustice to all Parisians, and remarked that he violently exaggerated the life and manners of the city. But the reading public obviously ignored the bad notices, and Balzac was confident that *Père Goriot* would earn what any other author of the period, Victor Hugo included, would have considered a comfortable fortune.

Immediately prior to the publication of the hardcover version of the book, Balzac completed another, shorter novel, which he called *La Fille aux yeux d'or*. It was also a story of contemporary Paris, in which he dealt boldly and frankly with a theme that no one else dared to touch: lesbianism.

It has been said that he was writing about George Sand and the actress Marie Dorval, and there may be an element of truth in the assertion. Jules Sandeau, who was still close to Balzac, had lived with George Sand for a long time. After they parted, he had enjoyed a brief affair with her friend, Marie Dorval. These relationships parallel those of the principal characters in *La Fille*, but there are strong echoes of the metaphysical in the novel, too, as well as hints of the fusion of male and female that appear in *Séraphita*.

La Fille shocked the women in Balzac's life. Eveline Hanska thought it disgusting, and Zulma Carraud wrote the author an indignant letter in which she said she refused to read the book. Laure de Surville reacted in the same way. The gossips of Paris soon became busy, and it was inevitable that questions should be raised, in whispers, regarding Balzac's own sex life. Jules Sandeau was still living with him while they worked on their play, *La Grande Mademoiselle*, and many people knew his recent history with two women who were commonly regarded as lesbian lovers. Balzac and Sandeau dressed extravagantly, lived in a house so ornately furnished that it was a travesty, and occasionally gave dinner parties more lavish than the banquets of the wealthiest aristocrats.

On the basis of the rumors created by this flimsy evidence, various attempts have been made through the years to "prove" that Balzac was a homosexual, and the complicated relationship of Vautrin and Rastignac in *Père Goriot* is cited as justification of the contention. But a claim of this sort is spurious. Balzac was writing about every type of human relationship, and because he did not shrink from dealing with the homosexual, in either men or women, is certainly no proof that he himself sometimes preferred men to women as bedmates.

His correspondence with Sandeau in no way bears out the rumors about them. Their friendship was casual, and even a minute examination of details in their letters fails to reveal any data of significance. As every serious student of Honoré de Balzac well knows, women were his obsession, along with his work and his need to spend money.

In fact, he and Sandeau spent only a few months under the same roof, although the world assumed that both of them were dwelling in the house on the Rue Cassini throughout all of 1835, as well as during the final months of the previous year. This was not the case. Sandeau lived in the house, as did Balzac's cook and valet, but the author took himself elsewhere, deliberately allowing the world to think he was still making his home there, and maintaining the fiction by acting as the host at various dinner parties there.

In actuality he had moved to a secret hideout in the Rue des Batailles, which at that time was not in Paris itself, but in the suburb of Chaillot. The reason for the elaborate deception can be found in his ever-mounting debts.

As a result of his incurable spending habits, his financial situation once again had become hopeless. *Père Goriot* and *Eugénie Grandet* earned him enormous sums of money, the former bringing in almost one hundred thousand francs over a period of several years. But he had told Eveline Hanska the literal truth when he had written to her that he required ten thousand francs a month. Unable to live within his budget, he made his situation worse. Not only had he failed to repay his mother one sou of the one hundred thousand francs he owed her, but he continued to pour out money for luxuries, then carelessly made no attempt to pay for them. By early 1835 he owed various creditors at least fifty thousand additional francs, although some sources indicate the total was closer to seventy-five thousand. His finances were in such a muddled state that no one, least of all Balzac himself, knew precisely how much he owed his creditors.

When he entertained at a dinner party, serving vessels, flatware, goblets and the plates from which guests ate the rare delicacies imported from the far reaches of the world were made of solid silver. Every inch of available space was crowded with furniture and bric-a-brac, all of which Balzac fondly insisted was worth many times what he had paid.

His turquoise-studded walking stick became so famous that he decided to add to his collection. Late in 1834 he had a cane made of silver, and he used it frequently, even though it was so heavy he wielded it with difficulty. Undaunted by the experience, he had another cane fashioned in 1835, this one of gold, and he obviously enjoyed creating a sensation on the streets when he went out for a stroll. Eventually, several years later, he bought yet another walking stick that was the height of folly; the handle was a rhinoceros horn, which was set with a dazzling array of precious gems. He feebly excused the extravagance by explaining that the jewels made it possible for him to grip the handle firmly.

His secret move to the Rue des Batailles was motivated, in part, by Balzac's desire to escape from the creditors who were again appearing each day at his door, and who lingered there for hours in the hope that they might catch him as he left or returned home. Literally no one except a very few highly trusted friends, relatives and business associates knew where he was really living.

There was a second reason for his move, and this was so absurd that no one would have believed it had he written about it in one of his novels. The Garde Nationale, the military service in which every able-bodied, eligible citizen was expected to serve, had recently been reorganized, and serious attempts were being made to force men of every station to do their duty. Honoré de Balzac was a bachelor who had neither a wife nor legitimate children to support. The assistance he was giving his half brother Henry meant nothing to the authorities, and as his mother was now living in Chantilly, he could not claim her as a dependent either.

Therefore the authorities considered him eligible for active service and late in 1834 sent him a notice ordering him to report for duty as a sentry at the Paris arsenal. Balzac was stunned, then indignant; apparently the Garde Nationale did not realize it was dealing with one of the world's greatest living authors. He wrote an angry letter, then forgot the matter. But the Garde Nationale did not. He received a second letter, then a third. His evasions were regarded so seriously that this last communication was signed by a general, who warned him that he would be sent to prison unless he accepted active service.

Balzac had no intention of climbing into an ill-fitting uniform and spending a month trudging up and down outside the arsenal while carrying a heavy musket and bayonet. Not only would he look ridiculous, but he couldn't afford to lose a month's working time. The secret dwelling was the answer to this problem, too, and the Garde Nationale could ransack Paris searching for him but would not find him.

Balzac's precautions were worthy of an obsessed character in the Philosophical Studies. The apartment was leased in the name of a fictitious Mme. Durand, and it was her name that appeared beside the bell rope. One manservant accompanied Balzac into hiding, and it was he who answered the ringing of the bell. Only those who gave the appropriate sign and password were allowed to enter.

One who touched the lobe of his left ear with his right hand and said, "An omelet requires six eggs and seasoning," would be admitted. Three days later only those who touched the tips of their noses with the heel of their left hands and said, "The grapes in Cognac are off to an exceptionally slow start this season," would be permitted to pass the guardian of the gate. All others, regardless of their missions or their seeming legitimacy, were turned away without an explanation.

Balzac left virtually nothing to chance. The first two floors of the building were unoccupied, and although none of the windows was broken, a casual passerby could stare in through the dirty glass and swear that no one lived in the place. But those who were admitted soon were astonished. After climbing two flights of dirty, rubble-strewn stairs, they paused while a door of heavy oak was unbolted and opened. Then they walked down a narrow corridor which was so dark they could see nothing, and finally a set of heavy drapes was thrown aside.

The visitors then found themselves in an apartment that was unique in all the world. The walls were quilted, those of the sitting room in rose-colored satin, those of the huge bedchamber in white, those of the kitchen and tiny dining room in pearl gray, and those of the master's workroom in a somber brown linen. The quilting, as Balzac happily explained to his visitors, made it impossible for anyone in the street below to hear a sound emanating from the apartment.

The furnishings were lavish beyond compare, and Jules Sandeau, who visited the place soon after the work of decorating was completed, later wrote that he thought he had wandered into the private palace apartment of the Sultan of the Ottoman Empire. The most prominent item of furniture in the sitting room was a huge divan, covered in rose-colored watered silk, and the canopied bed in the adjoining chamber was so large that four people could have slept in it. The master of the house, it appeared, did not intend to spend all of his waking hours working on his manuscripts.

Only a handful of people lived in the immediate neighborhood, but Balzac nevertheless reduced the risks of discovery to a minimum. Two or three days each week his manservant, inconspicuously dressed, went out by way of the front door to purchase food and attend to other necessary errands. But Balzac himself never used the front entrance, and went out only after dark, when heavy blinds had been pulled over the windows to conceal the light created by the lamps burning inside. He used a rickety rear staircase that opened onto a blind alley, and although he could not be seen from any adjoining building as he descended or ascended, he invariably concealed himself beneath a cloak of dark gray wool and a hat with a broad brim he could pull over his eyes. Neighbors might see an occasional visitor, but—aside from the manservant—they never caught a glimpse of the building's tenant, and they had no idea the place was furnished to resemble an imaginative author's concept of terrestrial paradise.

Balzac had relatively little opportunity to enjoy his luxurious surroundings, however, because he worked at his usual frenetic pace. He was bearing down in earnest on the writing of *Séraphita,* and spent a minimum of twelve hours each day at the battered writing desk he had brought with him from the Rue Cassini. Never content to occupy himself with only one project, he also initiated a half-dozen others.

One was *La Fleur des pois,* ten short stories that would make up the newest set of the *Contes drolatiques.* Another was *Le Lys dans la vallée,* in which he probed deeper into the psyche of woman, and yet another was a variation on the same theme, *Les Mémoires d'une jeune mariée.*

Le Lys was of particular interest to him. It concerned a great lady, noble and virtuous, who was based to some degree on Mme. Hanska. She was married to an exceptionally unpleasant man, and he assured Eveline in his secret correspondence that he was not using Baron Hanski as his model for the character.

His need for money kept his nose buried in his manuscripts, and he was unable to keep his appointment in Vienna at the end of January. But he promised repeatedly that he would break free as soon as possible and would join her.

Strains were becoming evident in the relationship. Mme. Hanska wrote him infrequently now, and her short letters gave him only the vaguest outlines of her activities. Her tone, in the main, was irritable, and she had good reason to be annoyed. The baron was growing weary of his protracted sojourn abroad, and wanted to return to his own manor house in the Ukraine. His wife was reduced to finding one excuse after another to delay their departure, and did not know how much longer it would be possible to remain in Vienna. If Balzac had no intention of meeting her, she declared, she wished he would be generous enough to admit the truth to her at once, and she would not resent his candor. If he planned to come, however, she urged him to waste no time. She reminded him that she was playing a devious game, and emphasized that each delay increased her own jeopardy.

Balzac replied by swearing his eternal love and vowing to fly to her side as soon as his vocational and financial circumstances permitted. What he carefully neglected to mention was that he was in the first throes of one of those minor romances that were so necessary to his well-being, this one with a fascinating and beautiful young English girl married to an Italian nobleman. The lady was living in Versailles, and he spent at least two evenings each week visiting her, surreptitiously leaving his secret apartment by the back stairs, then walking several blocks to the spot where his carriage and driver awaited him.

By the time that spring arrived, Balzac realized he would never be able to leave Paris unless he obtained a substantial loan, so he went to his new publisher, Werdet, for it. Unfortunately for both of them Werdet was temporarily out of funds but applied to Baron James de Rothschild for a loan. Always one to leap when the opportunity was right, the baron agreed, and Werdet pledged half of the stock in his company as security. According to legend, Rothschild warned him, "Be careful when you loan money to Honoré de Balzac. He's irresponsible, and runs through gold the way a fish swims through water."

Armed at last with hard cash, Balzac set out for Vienna in early May, traveling in a style that befitted a great author. He rode in his own luxurious carriage, which was pulled by a team of four horses and driven by his own liveried manservant. He stopped at Heidelberg for a brief visit with the Austrian ambassador to France, with whom he had become acquainted, and paused for other short visits with members of the German nobility in Stuttgart and Munich.

In mid-May, after spending ten days on the road, Balzac finally arrived in Vienna, and the members of the ancient Austro-Hungarian nobility could scarcely contain their smiles. He was attired in a blue coat with gold buttons, a waistcoat embroidered in gold, and wore gold buckles on his shoes beneath his voluminous trousers of heavy silk. The Hanskis had engaged a room for him at the fashionable Hotel zur goldenen Birne, a short distance from the mansion they were renting. Hungarian princes and Bohemian dukes were satisfied with small rooms in the hotel, but the French author who wanted to impress a foreign capital with his wealth and stature complained to the management that he was being lodged in a clothes closet. So the most sumptuous suite in the hotel was turned over to him, and there he luxuriated for the three weeks of his stay. In all, the entire journey cost him the staggering sum of more than fifteen thousand francs.

In some respects the trip was worth the expenditure of every penny, but in other ways it was a major disappointment. Certainly his reunion with Mme. Hanska was anticlimactic. The pace of life in Vienna was far more hectic than it had been in Geneva, and aside from the many invitations that inundated and delighted Balzac, Eveline wanted to show him off to her own friends.

When Balzac wasn't being taken somewhere on his own, Mme. Hanska had him in tow, and exhibited him at dinners, receptions, lunches and tea parties. He begged for an opportunity to spend time alone with her, and whenever they returned to the Hanskis' rented house the baron was on hand, affable and courteous, ready for a chat. Not once was it possible for the couple to sneak away in order to renew their illicit romance, and the most Balzac could manage was an occasional stolen kiss in a carriage. No matter how badly he wanted her, or how much she allegedly wanted him, circumstances made it impossible for them to go to bed together.

How much of this was the baron's doing and to what extent Eveline herself was responsible is difficult to determine. The baron would have been stupid had he allowed them any privacy, and he appears to have kept a smiling, alert watch. As for Mme. Hanska, a determined and clever woman might have found a way to snatch an hour with her lover on occasion, so the suspicion arises that she did not make a genuine effort. Only twice in three weeks did she enter his hotel suite, and both times she was escorted by her husband. Members of her entourage usually were in attendance, even on a short carriage ride, and one afternoon, when Balzac went to great lengths to arrange a drive in the Prater, Vienna's great park, Eveline brought her daughter along for the airing.

One conclusion is inescapable. Mme. Hanska had enjoyed her daring fling in Geneva, but, having bound the impressionable

French author to her—to the extent he could be bound to anyone—she had no desire to renew their intimate relationship. Her husband was on guard, regardless of his casual acceptance of Balzac's labored explanation of his impassioned love letter, and she had no intention of placing her marriage, her reputation and her enormous inheritance from her husband in jeopardy.

There were glittering compensations, however, that caused him to forget his frustrations. Vienna, which considered itself the most cosmopolitan of all the world's great capitals, paid a thunderous salute to the genius of Honoré de Balzac, the man who was recognized on the boulevards and in the smart cafés of Paris only when he carried one of his outlandish walking sticks. Members of the highest aristocracy vied with each other in giving dinners, receptions and balls in the visitor's honor, and the Polish, Bohemian and Hungarian nobility joined in the chase.

Prince Metternich, the most influential of Europe's rulers not only invited the French author to his palace, but sent his own carriage to fetch the guest. In awe, Balzac spent the better part of an afternoon with the great Chancellor in his study, discussing world affairs and literature, and Metternich told him a story which Balzac later used as the central plot of his play *Pamela Giraud*.

Only the authors of Vienna, their attitude similar to that of the French literary critics, failed to pay homage to the visitor. Balzac met only a few minor writers. He was a pioneer far in advance of his times, and the novelists and playwrights of Austria were not yet ready to accept his brand of super-realism.

No matter how great his popularity with the aristocrats, to be sure, he managed to grind out his daily quota of work. He changed his writing schedule to suit the circumstances, and arose each morning before dawn, then put in six hours at his desk before his first social engagement of the day. He forced himself to return to *Séraphita* late every night, after his return to the hotel, and labored on his manuscript for several additional hours, until total exhaustion forced him to fall into bed.

He lost no opportunity to broaden his own knowledge. He carefully inspected the interiors of a number of Vienna's famous ancient palaces and studied the priceless art works he saw there. He also visited a number of battlefields in the vicinity of the city and made extensive notes, which he used when writing his novel *La Bataille.*

At the end of three weeks he sent an unhappy note to Mme. Hanska, saying:

There is not an hour, not a single minute that we can call our own, and I am in despair. I have grown weary, even ill, at the sight of other people. These hindrances put me in such a fever of despondency that the best thing I can do is to hasten my departure and go home.

This communication does not sound like the Balzac who obsessively pursued a goal and who relished the attentions of the world's mighty. It was not his inability to spend time alone with Mme. Hanska that spurred his departure from Vienna but his lack of funds. He had been spending money at such a rapid rate that he had barely enough in his purse to see him and his manservant back to Paris. According to one of the innumerable Balzac legends, he was penniless on the day he left, and had to borrow some coins from Mme. Hanska in order to tip the hotel employees who stood in a line at the entrance to bid him farewell. It is impossible to verify or refute the story.

What is far more important is that Balzac spent more than a week on the road returning home, and during this time he began to realize the folly of his journey. His feeling of pleasure dissipated, and the entertainments that had been given for him became jumbled in his memory. He had spent fifteen thousand francs in return for a few of Mme. Hanska's kisses, and he had the uneasy feeling he was beginning to lose her. He did not yet know it, of course, but another seven years would pass before they would meet again. Worst of all, he had made a shambles of his writing schedule, and he knew he could not obtain money for future books until he began to produce solid chapters of those for which he had already drawn considerable sums. He had to deliver

Le Lys dans la vallée to Werdet in the immediate future, and *Mémoires d'une jeune mariée*, on which he had barely started, was long overdue; in fact, Mme. Béchet was becoming annoyed with him, and was threatening a lawsuit.

Family complications awaited him in Paris. His well-meaning sister had pawned his valuable silver in order to pay some of his most pressing debts, and unless he redeemed the treasure he would suffer an even more staggering loss. But he could not upbraid Laure, who was seriously ill, and De Surville, afraid she would become too excited, refused to allow Balzac to see her. Meantime Henry had resigned from his job in Normandy. The work had been too hard and the compensation too small. Now he was back in Paris, with a wife and two children to feed, and he threatened to destroy himself unless his half brother helped him. Balzac who had enough problems of his own, suggested that Henry find another position. Paris was growing rapidly, business enterprises were expanding, and positions of many kinds were opening. Henry heard the advice, cursed Balzac and stalked out, swearing that his body would be found floating in the Seine the next morning.

Balzac was far too busy to look. He plunged into *Le Lys*, the story of a young couple who loved each other but refused to go to bed together because of their respect for conventions. The young man drifted into an affair with a fascinating young English girl, and the heroine, regretting her own sense of morality, died a bitter death. The plot was basically simple, but Balzac recreated the spirit of youth, and his portrait of the girl in love was one of his finest character studies.

He finished the novel in July, seeing no visitors whatever in his Rue des Batailles hideout, and knew he had to take a short respite. First he paid a visit to the frail Mme. de Berny, to whom he showed a copy of the manuscript of *Le Lys*, and was elated when she called it sublime, his finest work. "*I can die in peace now,*" she wrote him after he had gone on to spend a few days with the Carrauds, "*having become sure that you wear the crown I have always wanted to see on your head.*"

Returning to Paris after taking a holiday of less than a week, Balzac turned to *La Fleur des pois,* the title of which he changed to *Le Contrat de mariage.* It was a story of lawyers good and bad, old-fashioned and progressive, a subject he knew from his own experience. He also promised Mme. Béchet two additional books, *Illusions perdues* and *Le Cabinet des antiques,* and showed her just enough of the manuscripts to squeeze another payment out of her.

In October he paid Mme. de Berny another visit, and his worst fears were confirmed. She was failing rapidly, and he needed all of his self-control to maintain his composure in her presence. "I am drunk with grief," he told his mother after his return to Paris, where she was nursing Laure de Surville. But Mme. de Berny's physician told him the patient well might live for another year, and he was somewhat comforted, not realizing he would never see her again.

His tangled finances required his full attention. Balzac borrowed what he could scrape up from Dr. Nacquart, Dablin, Mme. Delannoy and several other old friends who still had faith in him and believed he would repay them. He also arranged to have all the books he had done in his youth under a pseudonym reprinted, and received an advance of ten thousand francs for them. Now the word was sure to make the Paris rounds that he had written drivel under the name of Horace de Saint-Aubin, but Balzac didn't care. His present work spoke for itself, regardless of what he had done when he had been starting his career, and he needed the ten thousand francs.

Late in the autumn of 1835 he became involved in a raging dispute with Buloz, the publisher of the *Revue de Paris,* and one of the most prominent men in the industry. The opening chapters of *Séraphita* had just appeared in the *Revue,* and readers were complaining that it was so oblique they couldn't understand it. Buloz asked the author to substitute another story for it.

Wildly indignant, Balzac not only refused, but also took *Séraphita* away from Buloz and gave it to the accommodating Werdet to publish. But he continued to do business with Buloz, who was publishing *Le Lys* in another of his literary journals, the *Revue des Deux Mondes*. Eager to take the story away from a man who had "insulted" him, Balzac soon found a convenient excuse. He discovered that Buloz had sold *Le Lys's* serialization rights to a literary journal in St. Petersburg, a common practice at the time, although perhaps contrary to a strict interpretation of his contract. He might have received payment for the sale in due time, and in any event was heavily in debt to the publisher, but his nerves were frayed because of Mme. de Berny's decline, and he made an issue of the matter, withdrawing *Le Lys* and filing suit against Buloz.

Balzac's literary friends thought he had taken leave of his senses. There were no laws against slander, and Buloz could crucify him in print. Furthermore, no court would dare to hand down a verdict against one of the country's most prominent publishers, who could make life miserable for a magistrate, too. And Buloz, they predicted, would win the support of other authors who depended on him for contracts.

The prophecies soon came to pass. Buloz filed a countersuit, claiming that Balzac had failed to fulfill his contractual obligations, and simultaneously launched a campaign of ridicule in both of his journals. Every story harmful to Balzac's reputation and dignity that had ever been whispered in the cafés of Paris found their way into print, along with new tales, many of which were invented out of whole cloth by gossip writers on Buloz's staff. The newspapers made the most of the case, and gleefully reprinted every scurrilous item that appeared in Buloz's journals.

But Balzac would not retreat, and showing greater courage and tenacity than anyone had anticipated, insisted on pressing his case, even though the dispute was eating into time he should have spent at his writing desk. Then the case came to trial, and as anticipated, a dozen prominent authors, among them Eugène Sue and Alexandre Dumas, took the stand and testified against Balzac. It was common practice, they declared, for a publisher to sell foreign rights, and whether an author received a payment for the sale depended exclusively on the publisher's generosity.

Théophile Gautier, who wrote regularly for the *Revue de Paris*, demonstrated his independence of spirit as well as his friendship for Balzac by refusing to take the stand. It was rumored that Buloz threatened to retaliate, and no one was surprised when, a few days later, the *Revue* dismissed Gautier as a critic.

Only two of Balzac's colleagues had the courage to take the stand in his behalf. Victor Hugo, whose success was so great and whose stature was equally overwhelming, delivered a long, reasoned plea. It was possible, he said, that some publishers made the payment of foreign rights sales to an author dependent on their own largesse, but this was wrong. He had no objection if the publisher, a businessman who was taking the original risk, shared in these rights, but he thought it morally and legally wrong if the author failed to participate in the profits earned by his own brainchild.

Hugo also argued that a publisher could not compel an author to produce the book which he had promised to write. Creative efforts were not shoes or glassware or swords. They grew out of the writer's intuitive, subjective approach to his subject, and sometimes even a work that had been planned with care and executed with professional skill failed to jell. If the writing of a book could be reduced to a formula, every author would achieve success every time he wrote a book.

The other author who testified in Balzac's behalf was the fiery George Sand, who observed the amenities by wearing a dress into the courtroom instead of her usual trousers. In a long, emotional outburst she told the truth that everyone else was reluctant to speak. Buloz was a bully who forced authors to do his bidding because they were afraid they would lose lucrative markets if they crossed him. Balzac had been subjected to cruel abuse and vilification in a press campaign that had been carried out in an attempt to intimidate, harass and embarrass him until he dropped his suit. Authors were mere serfs who were forced to bend their knees before their masters, the publishers, but serfdom had been abolished in France, and those who wrote for their living were entitled to the same rights and the same protection under the law granted to other citizens.

To the astonishment of the general public as well as the literary world, the court ruled in Balzac's favor. Buloz was forced to pass along the small payment he had received from the publisher of the St. Petersburg review. Of even greater significance was the landmark decision that, thereafter, influenced all author-publisher relations. When an author agreed to write a book for a publisher on a certain subject, he was obligated to do his professional best to live up to the terms of his contract. If he found he could not treat the subject to his own satisfaction, however, it was his inherent right to withdraw the work, in which case he was required to repay to the publisher any royalties that had been advanced to him up to that time.

The elated Balzac went out for a celebratory dinner with Hugo, Gautier and George Sand. Thanks to his own stubborn courage and that of his friends, the very principles on which French book publishing was based were changed.

A number of concrete results soon manifested themselves. Werdet brought out his edition of *Séraphita,* and although readers still found the book abstruse, murky and in some sections almost impossible to comprehend, the vast publicity it had received resulted in a brisk sale. In all, Werdet brought out three printings before public interest declined, even though the initial reaction of readers had indicated that the book would suffer the fate of the other Philosophical Studies.

Of even greater significance was a new, mad scheme that took shape in Balzac's mind as a result of the trial, and it might be wise to pause in order to examine the strange mental processes that led him into so many bizarre ventures. Virtually everyone who has studied the life of Honoré de Balzac in detail has agreed with the contemporaries who knew him best, among them the three friends who helped him win his case against Buloz, that the line separating reality and fantasy in his thinking was finely drawn.

He enjoyed fooling others, even in the most trivial matters, but ended only by fooling himself. Gautier wrote of an occasion when Balzac was giving one of his elaborate dinner parties, and at the end of the meal served as a liqueur a dry white rum that had come from Martinique. "This rum," the host proudly told his guests, "came from a cask that the Empress Josephine herself brought to France from Martinique when she came here to live."

The others pressed him for details, but he refused to elaborate, and everyone present knew he was playing another of his little jokes, weaving a fantasy for his own amusement as well as that of his guests.

Gautier was the last to leave at the end of the evening, and Balzac urged him to take another drink before he departed. Gautier agreed, and asked for another glass of the superb rum from Martinique.

An expression of alarm tinged with regret crossed Balzac's face. "Don't think me too selfish," he said, "but I must hoard that rum. I only brought it out so everyone could enjoy a small taste, but I want to make it last as long as possible. After all, it was a personal possession of Josephine's when she was a young woman, so it is a precious possession."

Having told a story, he immediately believed it himself, and his fantasy became reality.

He applied this process to every aspect of life. In his relationship with Mme. Hanska, for example, he convinced himself, long before they met, that they were madly in love and were soulmates destined for each other. Nowhere was this transformation of fantasy into reality more pronounced than in the realm of his business relations.

No sooner had he won his case against Buloz than he convinced himself the publisher was discredited. Since both of his journals had lost standing with the public, the time had come for the appearance of a new review that would capture the imagination and win the loyalty of a vast body of readers. It would be fitting if the publisher of that journal were Honoré de Balzac, the David who had "destroyed" the mighty Philistine of the publishing world.

Balzac happened to know of a publication that suited his needs. It was a sad little review called *La Chronique de Paris*, and was published and edited by a man of no financial or literary standing,

William Duckett. The journal had virtually no readers and was on its last legs, but this did not deter the daydreaming Balzac. In the waning days of 1835 he purchased *La Chronique* for the trifling sum of one hundred and twenty-five francs.

The review was printed by Max de Béthune, the founder of what would later become one of the great publishing houses of France, and Balzac, forming a new company, enthusiastically offered Béthune a one-eighth interest in the corporation, in return for which he would have to put up no funds. Balzac obligated himself to supply all of the money needed for the venture, fifty thousand francs, but he refused to permit this trifling detail to halt or hamper him.

Balzac, the new editor-publisher, intended to write a short story or novella for the journal each month, and the mere presence of his name in the publication, he declared, would guarantee a long list of subscribers. He persuaded a somewhat reluctant Victor Hugo to contribute an occasional piece, he talked Gautier into becoming an editor as well as a contributor, and he painted the future of the review in such glowing terms that Gustave Planche, one of the most distinguished book critics of the period, agreed to join the merry band. Planche had just been embroiled in a salary dispute with Buloz, and his presence on the staff doubly insured the opposition of the powerful publisher to the new enterprise. Alphonse Karr, a brilliant essayist and literary critic, was inveigled into casting his lot with the *Chronique*, and Henri Monnier, already noted artist, was persuaded to become chief cartoonist. Public curiosity was aroused when it was learned that so many men of standing were going to take part, and, precisely as Balzac had already predicted, subscriptions flowed into the office.

Fascinated by his new toy, Balzac hired as his assistants two young men of excellent family backgrounds and no proven ability, Count Ferdinand de Gramont and the Marquis de Belloy, both of whom promised to bring in funds from relatives. Gramont managed to raise ten thousand francs, Belloy produced another five, and subscribers sent in ten. Balzac obtained an additional twenty from the long-suffering, almost unbelievably patient Mme. Delannoy. He assumed all of these debts himself, thereby adding to his personal burden.

But he shrugged off the financial obligation as of no consequence. He was going to pay himself a salary of twenty-five thousand francs per year, and his share of the profits would net him at least seventy-five thousand more. So the repayment of the debts would be no more than a technical transfer of minor sums.

He threw himself into the project with his customary vigor, supervising every phase of the publication, editing every word that appeared in print and writing a number of stories that were among his best. *Facino Cane* first appeared in the *Chronique*, as did *L'Interdiction* and *La Masse de l'athée*, a superb story about a surgeon that captured the essence of what impels a man to enter the medical profession.

For the first half of 1836 Balzac devoted most of his time to the journal, and much that appeared in it, the work of others as well as his own, has survived the test of time. There can be no question that the *Chronique* was first-rate as a critical review, in its fiction and in its reviews of books, theatre and opera. Once the original public curiosity abated somewhat, however, the journal was forced to settle down to a period of long, slow growth. Buloz could have told his euphoric competitor that successful literary journals were not built overnight, but required years of slow, careful nurturing. And Balzac lacked the capital to sustain losses for several years before the *Chronique* would begin to earn substantial sums.

The daydream began to evaporate, but Balzac was determined to make a success of the venture and gave a series of dinner parties at the house on the Rue Cassini. His newest idea was to sell a number of his shares in the journal—a minority interest, to be sure—to various wealthy persons. He was laboring under one self-imposed handicap: he imagined that all Paris believed him to be extremely wealthy, so he could not admit his need for funds and had to seek fresh capital in oblique ways. The efforts failed.

His financial situation grew more desperate than ever. He could not recover his silver from the pawnbrokers, he was remiss in his payments to his mother, and he made no attempt to help his half brother. The royalties that came in from his books had to be given to the most pressing of his creditors, and he was virtually penniless.

Then a new catastrophe struck. One day in the summer of 1836 a squad of the Garde Nationale that had been lying in wait for him managed to apprehend him, and he was hauled off to a prison for minor offenders, known as the Hôtel des Haricots. Balzac was as disgusted as he was miserable. The Garde Nationale, he declared, was made up of greengrocers, and he was forced to share a large cell with a number of laborers incarcerated for the same offense, these men preferring to spend two weeks behind bars rather than lose a month's wages while serving in the Garde.

Honoré de Balzac let it be known, repeatedly and in his loudest voice, that he was the close friend of Prince Metternich and other prominent European rulers. He was the intimate friend of the Duke de Fitz-James and other French aristocrats. He was one of the intellectual leaders of the entire Western world, and by all odds was the most distinguished of living French novelists.

The harried warden isolated him in a private cell, and all at once Balzac began to enjoy himself. Karr, Planche, Gautier and Jules Sandeau all came to dine with him, bringing various delicacies. The rest of his meals were supplied by the Vefour, acting on the instructions of Werdet. His plight was highly publicized, and many people who considered him a martyr sent him gold coins and even jewels, all of which he forwarded to his cane maker with instructions to make him a new walking stick studded with them as a memento of his incarceration. And when he wasn't otherwise occupied, he spent long hours of glorious solitude working on various book projects and stories for the *Chronique*, the weary warden having supplied him with the necessary paper and ink for his purposes.

After two weeks of delightful incarceration Balzac returned to the outside world, hailed as a hero by the liberal press. He immediately began to think in terms of going into politics and running

21. Madame Delphine de Girardin, wife of the most powerful French publisher in Balzac's era, and herself a famous hostess. (Maison de Balzac; Lauros-Giraudon)

22. Countess Eveline Hanska, Balzac's mistress-of-a-moment, pen pal for many years and, ultimately, his only wife. (Musée Balzac; Photographie Bulloz)

23. Baron Hanski, the cuckolded husband. (Musée Balzac; Photographie Bulloz)

24. (Below) The Hanski estate in the Ukraine. (Maison de Balzac; Lauros-Giraudon)

25. Eugène Sue, Balzac's friend and rival. (Culver Pictures)

26. (Above right) Balzac (left) and Théophile Gautier (right) visiting the actor Frédérick Lemaître. An 1840 watercolor. (Historical Pictures Service, Chicago)

27. (Right) An 1840 letter from Balzac in which he refers for the first time to his work as "La Comédie humaine." (Roger Viollet)

as a candidate for the Chamber of Deputies, a notion that soon evaporated under the pressures of far more immediate concerns. It should be noted that in his fourteen days of imprisonment he managed to spend a grand total of nine hundred and eighty-seven francs for his meals and a variety of other luxuries that made his sentence palatable.

Balzac's troubles were far from ended. Mme. Béchet, who despaired of ever getting the manuscripts he owed her, went to court and obtained an order directing the author to deliver two novels to her within the next three weeks or return the enormous advance royalties he had been paid. He had no way of raising thirty thousand francs, either in that short a period or in a year, so he had to go into isolation again.

"I have been ordered to write both *Les Héritiers Boisrouge* and *Illusions perdues* in the span of twenty days," he announced. "So shall it be!"

To the astonishment of the literati, many of whom flatly refused to believe he had done so much in so short a time, he actually wrote Part One of *Illusions perdues* in the required three weeks. His canvas was so crowded in the novel that what he had planned as a single novel eventually became two related but separate works. The real miracle of *Illusions perdues*, however, is that it ranks as one of his greatest efforts, and, according to many students of Balzac, is the single finest novel he ever wrote.

Briefly, the story is that of a young provincial who is the victim of his own illusions. He is convinced he is one of the greatest poets of the age, and when he comes to Paris a wealthy and aristocratic woman uses him for her own purposes while encouraging his illusions, and then discards and ruins him.

The basic setting of Part One is Angoulême, a town Balzac observed with infinite care when he visited the Carrauds. He understood the subtleties of social ramifications, he knew the people and their ambitions, and he was able to describe in great detail every street, every house. Lucien Chardon, the exceptionally handsome son of poor parents, adopted his mother's aristocratic maiden name, De Rubempré, much as Balzac himself added a *de* to his own name. Lucien resembled him in many ways, but he was careful to avoid a physical similarity. In fact, Lucien's brother-in-law, David Sechard, who, with his wife, Eve, was devoted to the young man, was a printer who bore an almost startling physical resemblance to the author. It is fascinating to note that David bankrupted himself for Lucien's sake.

The brilliant Lucien, whose great weakness was his ever-present need for a woman's love, had an affair with the rich, self-assured Mme. de Bargeton, who was more than fifteen years his senior. Balzac could not have helped but think of Mme. de Berny while writing about the intricate relationship of this ill-matched couple, and although Lucien's personality and needs are similar to the author's in many ways, he made certain that no one would associate Mme. de Bargeton with his own first mistress.

Lucien became Mme. de Bargeton's spiritual captive, and for the sake of her own vanity she made him masochistically dependent on him. Eventually, growing tired of her sport, she abandoned him to his own devices, penniless and far from home.

Balzac realized he could not end his story of Lucien at that point, and felt compelled to write Part Two. Lucien went to Paris, where he became a member of Louis Lambert's circle of artists, authors and philosophers, all of them idealists. The most high-minded member of the group was Daniel d'Arthez, a man of strength, courage and patience, in whose nature the author saw his own best qualities. These young men believed in the pursuit of art for its own pure sake, but in an attempt to impress the fashionable members of the artistocracy Lucien became a writer of trash. He became famous and wealthy in his own right, and was even a major force in the making and molding of public opinion, but he sold his own soul in the bargain, only partly realizing that he had made himself into a literary prostitute.

Nothing Balzac ever wrote was more devastatingly candid than his portrayal of the Parisian literary world and its false standards, its mores and its warped goals. He revealed, as no one before him had ever done, the reality behind the books, the literary journals and the newspapers that made Parisians think they were the best-informed, most widely read people on earth. Had nothing else won him the enmity of his colleagues, *Illusions perdues* would have been sufficient to damn him in their eyes forever.

He emerged from the hard struggle of writing the novel to find his own private world in chaos. Members of the *Chronique* staff were suing for their back wages, the suppliers of paper and ink were screaming for their money, and even his Rue Cassini landlord threatened to evict him within twenty-four hours unless he paid his back rent of five hundred francs at once.

He found the five hundred francs and kept a roof over his head, but that was the best he could manage. "*My enemies surround me on every side,*" he wrote Mme. Hanska, "*and for the moment it appears they have triumphed. But they shall not win this war against me! I will not permit it!*"

Never had his affairs been in a more pathetic or precarious state. Juggling finances like a magician gone berserk, he rearranged his debts, paying off his employees and closing the doors of the *Chronique*.

But when the dust settled he still owed Mme. Delannoy twenty-five thousand francs, and left other creditors with their palms outstretched, demanding an additional thirty thousand francs he didn't possess.

It would have taken a financial wizard to escape from the morass of debts, and Balzac's genius obviously did not lie in that direction. It was his books that were making him immortal, and, as he continued to assure Mme. Hanska in long letters, his love for her, pure and steadfast, was elevating him to new heights. What he failed to mention was that he was finding surcease from his woes in another complicated affair.

XIII

Frances Sarah Lovell, known to her family and friends as Fanny, was young and slender, blond and beautiful. The daughter of a substantially situated Wiltshire squire, she was the granddaughter, on her mother's side, of an Anglican bishop, and her family was as respectable as it was prominent. Fanny married above her own level when she became the wife of the Count Emilio Guidoboni-Visconti, the scion of an illustrious Milanese family who could trace their proud Tuscan ancestry through more than one thousand years of turbulent history.

Fanny, as sensuous as she was aristocratic, first met Honoré de Balzac at a reception given at the Austrian embassy, and he was attracted to her as soon as he learned that her uncle by marriage was the premier Duke of Milan. Fanny was accustomed to engaging in affairs, in part because of her own inner need for excitement, in part because of her husband's indifference to her private relationships. Emilio's great passion was music, his own violin in particular, and he made it his practice to play with the symphonies and other orchestras of Paris, Milan, Vienna and Berlin. Even when attending the Paris Opera he quickly slipped out of his box and took his place with the musicians in the pit.

Fanny was just emerging from an affair with a Polish prince when she met Balzac, and the gossips of Paris said she was debating whether to take a French count or an English earl as her next. She was a trifle surprised when Balzac threw himself at her in his customary headlong fashion, and she hesitated. He was not the type of man to whom she had ever granted her favors.

But he prepared for a siege in his usual manner, and wrote to Zulma Carraud:

For some days I have been under the spell of a very encroaching personality, and I do not know how to escape from it, for I am helpless to resist anything that pleases me. The lady has been avoiding me, not knowing she is wasting her own time and mine. I have made up my mind in this matter, and no matter how much she may resist me, I assure you I intend to become far better acquainted with her.

He penned the lines in the early spring of 1835, before going off to Vienna, but had to postpone any action until long after his return. He paid frequent visits to Fanny—and to her husband—at their Versailles home, but his writing schedule, the difficulties of editing and publishing a literary journal and his imprisonment by the Garde Nationale interfered with frequent trips. He felt relieved when Emilio decided that living in Versailles kept him too far removed from his music, and moved into the elegant Guidoboni-Visconti townhouse in Paris.

Balzac, who had just finished the exhausting task of writing the *Illusions perdues*, turned to Fanny with a vengeance in the autumn of 1836. He sent her long letters assuring her of his eternal love and fidelity, communications that might have been carbon copies of letters he was addressing to Mme. Hanska at the same time. Identical ideas, phrases and whole sentences appeared in both sets of correspondence.

Fanny Guidoboni-Visconti was no impregnable fortress. She had read a number of Balzac's books, had enjoyed them and was genuinely impressed by his extraordinary talent. Experienced in the ways of illicit love, she saw through his protestations, and was amused by his persistence. Soon thereafter, just as Balzac himself had so confidently predicted, the fortress fell.

He did not change his tune when writing to Eveline Hanska, to be sure, and continued to speak of the lonely life he led. But his Russo-Polish paramour of a few Geneva days had learned to read between the lines, and doubly insured her own interests by maintaining her subscriptions to a number of Paris newspapers. When she learned that he was no longer attending the Opera with Olympe Pélissier, but was sitting instead in the Guidoboni-Visconti box, she made a few discreet inquiries, and found out all she needed to know when she was told there was a Countess Guidoboni-Visconti who was young, lively and beautiful.

She promptly charged Balzac with double-dealing. His replies were models of hurt innocence, and he swore to her that every word she read was a lie. He was acquainted with the countess, to be sure, but only because her husband was his friend. "If I had time to know the lady better, which I do not," he said, "she would be like a sister to me. Her attitudes are like those of a child, and do not appeal to a weary man of thirty-seven."

Having disposed of Eveline's doubts to his own satisfaction, Balzac felt free to concentrate on Fanny. In some ways she was the perfect mistress: her passion was as intense as his, and her skill in the erotic arts was as great; she was fond of him, although not in love with him, and displaying no traces of jealousy, made no demands on him. She received him warmly, both in public and private, but if he was busy and could not meet her, either at her house or in his secret apartment on the Rue des Batailles, she was content and made no complaints.

For more than a century Fanny was more or less ignored by Balzac's biographers because she played such an unobtrusive role in his life. She was his mistress for five years, and it was she who offered him both friendship and money in his hours of greatest need, but she wrote him very few letters, so little was known of her own feelings toward him. There was nothing mysterious in the relationship. Fanny had an independent mind of her own, and Balzac stimulated her intellect. She was highly sexed and found him the most satisfactory bed partner she had ever known. She saw through his façade of boastings, garish clothes, overdecorated apartments and outlandish walking sticks, and there are indications that her strongest feeling for him was a sense of sympathetic pity.

Fanny's independence was more than intellectual. She made no attempt to hide her affair with Balzac from her husband, on whom she made no demands; if he wanted to stray she would not interfere. She was also indifferent to the opinions of Paris and London society of her private life. If she elected to engage in an affair, it was her own business, and she shrugged off gossip. This attitude enabled her to be candid in her relations with Balzac, and as a result he became equally honest with her. He had become adept at subterfuge in all of his dealings with women, but Fanny taught him a new approach to life, and he found it difficult—as well as absurd—to lie to a bed partner who not only laughed when he told her about his problems with other women, but actually tried to help him by advising him how to handle them.

Fanny's open manner and refusal to engage in petty deceptions made it obvious to anyone who saw Balzac sitting beside her at the Opera that they were very good friends. She placed her hand on his arm and held it there. She leaned toward him, whispered something in his ear and simultaneously stroked his face. The newspaper gossips noted the familiarities and duly recorded them.

Mme. Hanska read the accounts, and her letters to Balzac became increasingly indignant.

His replies were bland. "*I have not been to the Opera in months,*" he told her. "*I so abominate the women of Paris that I will have nothing to do with them, and remain bent over my work for eighteen or twenty hours each day.*"

In the spring of 1837, after Balzac and Fanny had been immersed in their affair for several months, he escorted her to a reception at the Austrian embassy. There he met several Viennese nobles, friends of Eveline's with whom he had become acquainted on his trip to Austria. A number of high-ranking Polish aristocrats were also present, and he realized it was inevitable that they, too, should know the Hanskis. Fanny was pleasantly and casually possessive toward him, and he had no doubt that a number of letters soon would be on their way to the Ukraine. Determined to ward off nasty complications, he sat down that same night and sent a "frank" letter to Eveline:

Mme. de Visconti, of whom you speak, is the most charming of women, and one of infinite and exquisite kindness, of a refined and elegant beauty, who does much to help me endure life. She is gentle but very firm, unshakable and implacable in her ideas and her dislikes. She is a person to be trusted. She is not wealthy, or, rather, her fortune and that of the count are not appropriate to the splendid name they bear, for the count is the representative of the first branch of the legitimized sons of the last duke, the renowned Barnabo, who left only bastards, some legitimized and others not.

My friendship with Mme. de Visconti is one which consoles me for many reverses of fortune, but, alas, I see her only rarely. You cannot conceive of the privations to which my work condemns me. Nothing is possible in a life as hectic and hard-pressed as mine, and when one goes to bed at eight in the evening, to arise again at midnight, there is no opportunity for visits with even the dearest of friends.

I can perform no social duties. I see Mme. de Visconti once in a fortnight, and this is a real grief to me, as she and my sister are my only true, kindred spirits. My sister is in Paris, Mme. de Visconti is at Versailles with her husband, and I scarcely ever see either. Can that be called living? You are in the wilderness at the farthest end of Europe, and I know no other women in the world.

To be always dreaming, always waiting, always hoping, yet find-

ing no relief from my loneliness; to see the brave days pass and youth being plucked from one, hair by hair; to hold nothing but empty air in one's arms—and then be accused of being a Don Juan! It is too much. What a fat and empty Don Juan!

Fanny was indeed very firm and had an opportunity to prove her devotion to Balzac, which she accomplished in a sensible, businesslike manner. His creditors were harassing him day and night, and it was imperative that he leave France for a time, but he had no money, and Fanny found a way to kill several birds with one stone. Emilio was encountering difficulties in obtaining various sums of money owed to him by several beneficiaries of his late mother's estate, so she suggested that he send Balzac to Italy as his emissary, and reward him with a generous percentage of all he collected.

Balzac left at once for Turin but did not travel alone. Even while accepting Fanny's lifesaving help and lying to Eveline about it, he could not resist becoming involved with yet another woman in what proved to be the most bizarre and extraordinary adventure of his life.

The lady was Caroline Marbouty, the wife of a provincial official and the daughter of a prominent attorney. She was in her early thirties, and her slender, almost boyish figure made her look still younger. Balzac had first become acquainted with her when she had come to him with an autobiographical story, written under a pseudonym, and he had published it in the *Chronique*.

Caroline had spent nine years with her husband and had given birth to two daughters, but her life had been a constant frustration. An incurable romantic, she had written poems and novels, but her husband had refused to read any of her handiwork. Boredom led her into an affair with a man of prominence, and after they broke up she went to Paris with her daughters, whom she placed in school there, and lived on the proceeds of an estate her mother had given her. For all legal purposes she was still married, but lived as she pleased, and at the time she met Balzac she was looking for fresh romantic adventures.

When the journey to Italy materialized for Balzac, Caroline was so eager to accompany him that she offered to contribute five hundred francs to help defray expenses. He was reluctant to accept the offer, in part because he didn't want the generous Fanny to learn he was traveling with another woman, and also because he was afraid word would leak back to Eveline.

But Mme. Marbouty was as resourceful as she was determined, and made a daring suggestion. He had told her on a number of occasions that her figure was as supple as that of a young man, so she offered to disguise herself as a man and accompany him as his valet.

The idea so appealed to Balzac's love of intrigue that he found it overwhelming, and accepted. Entering wholeheartedly into the conspiracy and apparently never stopping to think of the scandal that would ensue if the ruse should be discovered, he sent Caroline to his tailor, who quickly made her a complete wardrobe of man's attire.

Jules Sandeau accidentally saw the beginning of the journey. Knowing that Balzac was leaving for Italy, he went to the apartment on the Rue des Batailles to bid his friend farewell. Just as he reached the building a hired carriage pulled up at the door, and a beautiful young woman, whose hair was cut short like a man's, hurried inside. Sandeau hesitated, not wanting to interrupt a last-minute pre-departure rendezvous, but he lingered nearby, and in a short time the young woman emerged from the building again, dressed from head to foot in man's clothing.

She was followed by Balzac, who was using the front entrance in daylight for the first time. The coachman and Balzac's manservant hoisted the boxes containing the traveler's clothing onto the coach, and he drove off with his "valet." What Sandeau did not know was that Caroline was carrying some of her own clothing in the carriage, too, for use in case of emergency need.

No character who ever emerged from Balzac's imagination enjoyed more adventures than did the author himself on his strange journey to Turin. He and "Marcel," as they decided to call

Caroline, applied for a night's lodging at the monastery of the Grande Chartreuse, but the monks took a searching look at the "young man," and denied the couple admittance. Caroline's disguise, it seemed, was not quite as effective as she and Balzac believed.

She took revenge on the monks by going to a nearby stream, and, in full view of the monastery windows, stripped off her clothes and bathed in the river. According to the accounts she herself wrote, in letters to her mother and in a book that was published after Balzac's death, Balzac followed her to the bank of the river, but she saw him approaching and demurely dressed again before he reached her side.

Caroline also emphasized in her letters to her mother that her relationship with the kind and jolly M. de Balzac, her generous patron and friend, remained platonic on the entire journey. His only interest was in perpetrating a huge joke, and knowing she was a married woman, he took care to respect her at all times. Those acquainted with the proclivities of M. de Balzac may accept this story for whatever it may be worth.

The couple reached Turin without further incident, and were given the best suite in the city's finest hostelry, the Hotel de l'Europe. There Caroline occupied the large, main bedroom, while Balzac took a somewhat smaller chamber. There was a connecting door.

The arrival of the celebrated author, which was duly announced in the local press, caused a stir in Turin reminiscent of Vienna's excitement. The prominent aristocrats of the city sent their servants to the hotel with invitations to dinners and luncheons, tea parties and receptions and balls. The most distinguished author in the Piedmont, Count Frederico Sclopis, paid a call on his colleague, and was so charmed he made arrangements for Balzac to meet the other authors and artists of the region.

Unable to resist the temptation, Balzac insisted that Caroline accompany him on all of his social rounds, and in almost no time her identity as a woman was revealed. But she kept up her masquerade and continued to dress in a man's attire.

The Turin aristocracy liked to believe they knew the world, and they had heard of a renowned French author named George Sand who cut her hair short, wore trousers and smoked cigars. So a number of people jumped to an obvious conclusion when, a few days after the couple's arrival in the city, Caroline jokingly accepted a cigar offered to her after a lunch in Balzac's honor. She was amused, but Balzac became uneasy. The joke was beginning to have too many repercussions, and might get out of hand, so he vigorously denied that Caroline was George Sand. The Piedmontese were equally stubborn, and clung to the conviction that she was the unorthodox French author, their belief strengthened by the knowledge that George Sand and her current lover, Alfred de Musset, the young dramatist, poet and novelist, recently had made a tour of Italy. At various social functions the literati of Turin sought Caroline's opinions on books and poetry, particularly the work being produced in the Italian states, and Balzac was forced to rescue his companion from embarrassment.

The charade did not prevent Balzac from fulfilling his mission in Turin. He met one of the most prominent attorneys in the city, and action was taken at once to press Count Emilio Guidoboni-Visconti's claims on his mother's estate. Fanny had been shrewd in her choice of an emissary. Balzac worked as hard and as faithfully as he would have labored in his own behalf. The wheels of justice, in the Piedmont as elsewhere, turned at a snail's pace, but Balzac made greater progress than even he in his optimism had anticipated, and he accomplished far more than Fanny and her husband expected.

Meanwhile his hosts and hostesses continued to pay court to Caroline almost as intensely as they lavished attention on Balzac, and his nervousness increased. Word was sure to seep back to Paris, and he shuddered when he thought of the stories the newspapers would print. There would be untold complications if the press declared he had been traveling with George Sand, and even greater problems if they wrote that his companion was a beautiful young woman masquerading as the author.

His solution was typically dramatic. Sclopis was giving a large party for the visitors on their last night in Turin, and Caroline appeared for the evening dressed, for the first time, as a woman. She wore her finest gown, a hat that was not only the current Paris rage but concealed her short hair, and was expertly made up. She looked ravishing and created a sensation. Yet the Piedmontese present did not know that the real George Sand was far less attractive, and clung to their illusion.

Balzac, demonstrating one of those quirks of temperament he sometimes exhibited, arranged the itinerary for the homeward journey so they would pass through Geneva, the city of Mme. Hanska and Mme. de Castries. He and Caroline not only took a suite at the Hotel d'Arc, but remained there for two days.

During that time he sent a reply to a message from Count Sclopis, who had written to ask that his regards be conveyed to the lovely lady. The letter was the first tentative thrust in the direction of the line Balzac intended to take in the event that Paris had heard of the escapade. He wrote:

As for my traveling companion, she is a charming, witty and virtuous lady who, being able to escape for twenty days from domestic tedium, has flown to me for shelter in inviolable secrecy. She knows that I love another, and in this she had found the surest of safeguards. As you no doubt observed, we travel as friends, not as lovers, and the lady's secret is as safe with me as is her virtue.

The virtuous pair seemed reluctant to end their idyll, and continued their homeward journey at a leisurely pace. Balzac had spent only four days on the road when traveling from Geneva to Paris after leaving Mme. Hanska, but he and Caroline made so many overnight stops they needed ten days.

For the rest of their lives Balzac and Mme. Marbouty insisted, separately but with equal emphasis, that they had never become lovers during the twenty-six days they spent together. They were bound together by the innocent pleasure the masquerade afforded them, and by the poetic love of beauty they shared as they viewed their surroundings. Their claim elevated as many eyebrows in their own day as it raises the better part of a century and a half later.

If they did become involved in an affair, it was short-lived, and they saw each other infrequently thereafter. Six years later Balzac dedicated *La Grenadière* to Caroline Marbouty, saying, "*To Caroline. To the poetry of the journey, from the grateful journeyer.*"

That dedication made it necessary for him to "explain" the situation in a letter to Mme. Hanska, who was certain to see the book, and he wrote to her in an emphatic tone:

The poetry of the journey was poetry and nothing else. I will tell you candidly how it was, and when you come to Paris I will prove it to you for your punishment. You will see that I have never had any taste for such women—who inspire the lines of the old comedy—Upon my word, Chevalier, may I be branded a rogue/If that devilish nose is not turquoise blue! It is the line I always use, and I set a whole salon laughing with it when someone asks me my opinion of an unattractive woman.

This lady was a mere acquaintance of mine, and I came to know her through Mme. Carraud, her intimate friend. I have not seen her since our journey, nor have I had any desire or wish to spend additional time in her company. I will admit to you freely, however, that as for her wit, it was charming, and as for her intelligence, it was considerable. Do not, I beg you, misinterpret a jest that was as pure in its execution as it was innocent in its conception.

Balzac long made it a practice to avoid telling Mme. Hanska anything but a censored version of what he considered the "truth," and several discrepancies in the letter are obvious. Caroline was an exceptionally lovely woman, and was anything but homely. As for her alleged friendship with Mme. Carraud, there is no evidence to indicate that she and Zulma ever met.

In any event, tragic news awaited Balzac in Paris after his escapade, which was not unusual. Drastic changes seemed to take place in his personal life when he was absent from the city. He returned home to find a letter from Alexandre de Berny awaiting him, and the son of his first beloved wrote that Mme. de Berny had died in her sleep. Beside her had been a special copy of *Le Lys dans la vallée*, which he had ordered bound for her and had sent her shortly before his departure. She had read it, enjoyed it, and had been reading it again when she had drifted off into her last sleep.

Balzac blamed himself for not having seen her in many months, even though she had forbidden him to visit her when she had looked so ravaged by illness. His guilt became even greater when he learned that Alexandre had hurried to Paris in search of him when the end had drawn near, only to discover that he was making a protracted journey and would remain abroad for a month or more.

He was equally distressed to learn that, the night before her death, Mme. de Berny had ordered her son to burn all of the many hundreds of letters she had received from Balzac over a period of years. She had watched them burn in the hearth, and had sighed quietly when they had been reduced to ashes. The letters had been her property, so she had been entitled to do as she pleased, but Balzac felt deep pangs of regret. He was the greatest of living authors, so his letters to the woman who had been his first and principal love for such a long time would have been priceless, a boon to the many who would write about him after his own death. Fortunately he had kept copies of a great many of his letters, and he took pains to put them in a secure place. No matter what one may think of his vanity, his evaluation happened to be right.

He paid a visit to Mme. de Berny's grave, and spent a half day standing beside it, unable to halt the sobs and tears that welled up within him. Then he returned to Paris, and immediately wrote to Mme. Hanska:

I make you her heiress, you who have all her noble qualities . . . her invariable wisdom . . . But, my dearest, do not aggravate my distress with humiliating doubts; believe that calumny is easily visited on a man so heavily beset, and that now and hereafter I must permit anything to be said about me without allowing it to trouble me. In your latest letters, you know, you have believed accusations which cannot be reconciled with what you know of me.

Even in Balzac's grief it is obvious he realized that Mme. Hanska was anything but the heiress to the place that Mme. de Berny had held in his life. His first love, recognizing his genius as well as his weaknesses, had forgiven his many slips, and at the very least led him to believe she accepted his pitiful lies, evasions and half-truths. She had been supremely conscious of the need to sustain his ego, knowing it would have been impossible for him to write if his fragile belief in his own talents had been damaged or destroyed. In large measure he had been right when he had written that Mme. de Berny was responsible for all he had accomplished.

Mme. Hanska was a poor substitute. Her own desires in her relationship with him were self-seeking, and nothing in her attitude indicated an understanding of his vocation, his problems or his inner needs. Apparently it did not occur to her to make the attempt to achieve such an understanding, either, and although it may be harsh to say that she wanted the scalp of a great author as an ornament, but was indifferent to him as a man, her correspondence over a period of many years and her subsequent actions in no way indicate otherwise.

She demanded fidelity from him, granting him only the right to spend brief periods with prostitutes and courtesans for the relief of his physical needs, but insisting that his emotions remain uninvolved. Had she known Balzac better she would have realized that it was impossible for a man of his temperament to comply with her rule. But she thought only in terms of her own desires, and harassed him unmercifully through the years with her suspicions, her charges of infidelity and her accusations. He was guilty, to be sure, but was far less to blame than she made him out to be, and she was always ready to believe any tidbit of gossip harmful to him.

Unable to obtain the balm he needed from Mme. Hanska, Balzac found his consolation in his work, and in five nights and days wrote three of his finest short works, the *Secret des Ruggieri, La Perle brisée* and *La Vieille Fille.* It was astonishing that he could concentrate, but his compulsive drive was so great he literally willed everything but his manuscript of a given day out of his mind.

Certainly the death of Mme. de Berny was a major milestone in Balzac's life and career. He quickly realized he was bereft, that no one could really take her place, and that he stood alone in the world. After his first sense of shock passed and his panic subsided, he took stock of himself and his situation, and was not encouraged by what he found.

He had written thirty books, some of which had been translated into as many as a dozen languages, and he continued to cling to the belief that he towered above all other authors of the age, graciously conceding that only Victor Hugo was in his same class. Yet he had accomplished only a fraction of what he wanted to do, what he had to do if the *Comédie humaine* was to take its rightful place in the body of world literature.

He was forced, too, to the rueful conclusion that his personal situation had deteriorated in every way. He had earned vast sums of money, to be sure, but he had spent every penny, and his debts were far larger than they had been when he had entered his life's career in earnest. He also realized he was ruining his health: he was becoming grossly overweight, his hair was turning gray, belying his scant thirty-eight years, and his endless cups of coffee were causing chronic stomach pains.

His physical condition twice caused him to become alarmed in the early months of 1837. One day, while working at his desk, he became violently dizzy and then dropped unconscious. Less than a month later he collapsed in the street only a short distance from the house on the Rue des Batailles, and two neighbors, who hadn't even known he lived there, had to help him home.

He realized the time had come to change his way of living, but he was the prisoner of his own habits, desires and perverse insistence on doing precisely as he pleased. At the beginning of 1837 his debts, aside from what he owed his mother, amounted to a staggering sixty thousand francs. Instead of living more sanely, however, he decorated the attic of the house in the Rue des Batailles, spending a small fortune on furniture, drapes and quilted satin walls. He not only kept the house in the Rue Cassini he didn't need, but when several bailiffs and creditors learned of the existence of the hideout on the Rue des Batailles, he also rented a room in a small residential hotel under an assumed name and spent the better part of his time there in solitude, telling no one the secret.

He was growing too old to waste his energies chasing romantic fantasies, but instead of cutting down he added to his already complicated love life. He continued to send long letters to Mme. Hanska with astonishing regularity, and he saw Fanny Guidoboni-Visconti at least twice each week. He told her he had decorated the attic bedroom exclusively for her, and she enjoyed the place so much that she visited it regularly.

He also became involved simultaneously in several other affairs. One was with an aristocratic young lady from Britanny, Hélène de Valette. Another was with someone known to posterity only as "Louise," and the mere fact of her existence is confirmed exclusively by the copies he kept of his voluminous correspondence with her. When he went to bed with someone other than a trollop he felt compelled to write her long letters assuring her of his love for her and telling her how hard he was working.

Courtesans were also playing an important role in his life. On a number of occasions he gave elegant dinner parties at the house on the Rue Cassini, and all of the women present were ladies of elastic virtue. Balzac reserved the after-dinner company of two of these lovely, compliant ladies for himself, and after retiring with them, gave vent to all the excesses of his erotic imagination. Never one to waste material he deemed worthy of inclusion in his books, he subsequently used them as models for two of his most debauched characters, both of them courtesans.

Dr. Nacquart warned him that he was driving toward a complete physical collapse that might prove fatal, but he paid no attention. So much remained to be done on the *Comédie humaine* that he had to keep working as long as he could write. Bill collectors were driving him to distraction, and their efforts impelled him to race in the opposite direction. He continued to pour money into the decorating of the house on the Rue des Batailles, and meanwhile began to think seriously of giving up all of his Paris residences. In their place he might buy an estate worthy of his stature somewhere in the country, an hour or two removed from the city and beyond the reach of bailiffs. He had no spare time, but began to inspect homes for sale and plots on which he might want to build.

He continued to court the ladies, too, snatching brief periods here and there for his liaisons, entertaining Fanny in private and acting as her public escort, writing long letters to Eveline and to the mysterious Louise.

In addition to his other problems, he had become the sole support of his family. His mother needed his help, and he sent her every franc he could spare. He continued to give money to Henry, and made a gift of two thousand francs to the son of his late sister, Laurence, who needed the money to obtain a higher education. Laure de Surville and her husband also needed a loan, and he gave it to them without hesitation.

Fanny, the most generous and perhaps the most perspicacious of his many mistresses, watched with growing concern as he ran steadily downhill. Even though he went to bed for no more than a few hours each night, he could not sleep. His hands trembled, and he could not write until he drank several cups of coffee strong enough to gag an ordinary palate. His usually fluent speech became halting, and when he became excited he could not stop blinking.

The time had come, Fanny decided, for another journey abroad. Her husband's case had been transferred to Milan, so she made the arrangements for Balzac to go there as Emilio's agent, armed with the appropriate powers of attorney. Again, all of his expenses would be paid, and he would receive a percentage of the entire sum collected.

Balzac grasped hard at the straw of hope the semi-holiday offered him. In his disconsolate frenzy he had given thought to the idea of going off to the manor house of the Hanskis in the Ukraine and burying himself in work there until the storms buffeting him subsided. But Milan was nearer, and he would not be removing himself for a year or two from Paris, the center of his universe.

XIV

The aristocratic ladies of Milan and a few of their husbands welcomed Balzac with open arms when he arrived in the city in mid-February 1837. Apparently Caroline had wanted to accompany him, but he had escaped scandal and didn't want to take any more chances; Théophile Gautier had planned to go with him, but had to change his plans at the last moment, and Balzac traveled alone.

His reception in Milan was as enthusiastic as that which Turin had tendered him. He attended performances of La Scala with princes, the Austrian governor-general gave a dinner party in his honor, he rode a horse provided by the Austrian commander-in-chief, and a handsome young princess took him for long carriage rides to discuss literature and her own romantic problems. The leading sculptor of the city, Putinatti, presented him with a bust of himself, which he promptly sent on to Fanny.

No matter how active his social life, Balzac did not ignore his mission, and proved he was an able man of business as long as he was dealing with other people's money. He brought the case to a satisfactory conclusion, and won more than one hundred thousand francs for Emilio, his own commission amounting to approximately eleven thousand welcome francs. The signatures of several persons living in Venice were required before the final agreement became binding, and he was so anxious to conclude the matter that he went there himself.

Balzac and Venice did not take to each other. The jaded seaport had been entertaining celebrities for centuries, and the press, resenting the delirium of the newspapers in Milan and Turin, treated the author with a discourtesy reminiscent of Parisian gossip writers. A heavy rain fell steadily for the first forty-eight hours of his three-day visit, and he was happy to conclude his business and depart.

An unplanned halt in Genoa on his homeward journey caused long-range repercussions. All travelers were placed in quarantine, and the indignant Balzac was held as a virtual prisoner in a hotel which, he said, was unfit for common thieves. But during this enforced stay he met an Italian businessman named Pezzi who had an idea that sparked his always feverish imagination. A huge fortune, Pezzi told him, awaited enterprising men in the interior of the semi-cultivated island of Sardinia. There, in ancient times, the Romans had operated silver mines, taking only the pure ore and leaving huge slag piles behind. Those piles contained ore worth many millions of francs, and the only reason the Romans had left them had been because of their inferior refining processes. So Balzac overnight had a new business goal, the recovery of silver from the old Roman mines in Sardinia, a project as sound as any of the others into which he had ventured.

His health was improving, and having spent more than a month on his travels, he decided to prolong what he called a holiday, even though he was spending eight to ten hours each day working on a number of manuscripts. He was putting the finishing touches on *César Birotteau*, working alternately on the manuscripts of

La Femme supérieure and *Gambara*, and on days when he felt lazy he polished *Illusions perdues* and laid out the plots of *La Haute Banque* and *Les Artistes*. These activities which would have kept another author busy for years, were scheduled for completion within a few months.

He turned south again and went to Florence, but remembering his chilly reception in Venice, elected to visit the city incognito. While sightseeing there he also worked on the basic ideas for two plays. The theatre was of no real interest to him, but he turned back to it again and again because he knew a successful play would earn him far more money than any book.

Finally he turned homeward again, traveling by way of Switzerland, and braced himself for new problems when he reached Paris, where his worst expectations were realized. The De Survilles had gone bankrupt, and Balzac's brother-in-law was making a fresh start as an engineer. Henry claimed to be destitute, although he had taken a leaf from the notebook of his half brother and had bought his family new furniture. And Mme. de Balzac had written her son a pathetic letter from Chantilly:

Your journey to Italy is a very long one, my dear Honoré, and it is a long time since I have seen you or have had news of you. I cannot grow accustomed to such treatment.

In spite of your many promises it is more than two years since you last wrote to me, and I must learn of your whereabouts and your activities from the newspapers which the dear ladies of Chantilly bring to me when your name appears in them. If I do not complain you say I do not care, and if I complain you call me a nuisance. Oh, it is sad to have become useless, my son, and not to be sufficiently loved.

My son, since you have been able to find money for such friends as Sandeau, for mistresses, jeweled canes, rings, silver and furniture, your mother may, without presumption, remind you of your promise to repay your debt to her, and, at the least, to contribute small sums to her welfare. She has waited until the last possible moment before doing so—but that moment is now at hand.

Mama succeeded in shaming Balzac, a feat no one else had ever been able to accomplish, and as soon as he collected the eleven thousand francs due him from the Guidoboni-Viscontis for the estate settlement, he sent his mother three thousand, the largest single amount he had ever presented to her.

As for the rest, it was for spending. He knew he could not have paid off more than a tiny fraction of his debts with it, which would have been tantamount to frittering it away, so he preferred to use it to buy the luxuries that gave him his only pleasure in life.

Necessity forced him to try to set his house in order. Werdet had gone bankrupt, and Balzac signed a contract with a new publisher, Bohain, who demanded substantial portions of two books, *La Femme supérieure* and *La Maison Nucingen* before making more than a token payment of the fifty thousand franc advance he agreed to pay. Alphonse Karr had become editor of the new *Figaro*, and was willing to pay twenty thousand francs for a serialization of *César Birotteau*—provided that Balzac finished it. The book that excited the author most was *Gambara*, another of the Philosophical Studies on a now-familiar theme, that of a composer who is a genius, a man whose music becomes so intricate and abstruse that no one else can understand or appreciate it.

The most immediate problem was that of finding a place to work. The bill collectors had discovered the hideout on the Rue des Batailles, and had unearthed the secret of the room in the little residential hotel, too. Excluding what he owed his mother, Balzac's debts now exceeded seventy-five thousand francs and were still mounting. He would have fled the country again but had no money to take him anywhere. He thought of going into hiding with the Carrauds, but knew the secret of his presence in a small provincial town would leak out in a very short time, and that the bailiffs would follow him. His luck appeared to have evaporated.

Previously, someone had always come along at the last moment to rescue him, and this time it was the Guidoboni-Viscontis. Fanny sympathized with his predicament, and offered him asylum in a small apartment on the top floor of the new townhouse that had just been built for the count and countess on the newly fashionable Champs-Élysées. Emilio proved to be remarkably understanding, and the amateur musician felt a kinship with the man he considered a fellow artist.

Fanny displayed considerable courage when she gave Balzac a refuge. Many people knew of their affair, but certain rules of propriety were observed in these matters, and her own reputation would be ruined if anyone learned he was living under her roof. In addition, her own credit standing would suffer if the bailiffs found the latest hiding place of their prey.

Balzac refused to let such trifles worry him, however, and moving into the Guidoboni-Visconti house late one night, after the rest of Paris had gone to bed, he happily set up his battered writing table in the tiny sitting room of his suite and went to work. Hiding from everyone except Fanny and one or two trusted servants, he did his best work under pressure, as always. In a month he wrote all of *La Femme supérieure*, and the following week he turned out a novella and several short stories based on his observations of the Italian aristocracy.

La Femme supérieure was based on his own sister and brother-in-law. Célestine Rabourdin was married to a civil servant, an amiable man who had a genius for administration and loathed the complex workings of bureaucracy. Ambitious for her husband and family, Célestine drove Rabourdin in an attempt to force him to improve their lot. In the process she attracted the attention of her husband's superior, who would have given Rabourdin a coveted promotion if she would have an affair with him. Célestine struggled to retain her virtue while at the same time trying to obtain her husband's promotion, and all the while Rabourdin himself sealed his own doom by making suggestions for the overhauling of the government's antiquated procedural systems that were lucid, cogent and eminently sensible.

The novel was a social comedy, and Balzac enjoyed himself as he scored the whole bureaucratic order. He thoroughly understood the old-fashioned workings of government ministries, and he struck a responsive chord in thousands of readers who had been frustrated and infuriated by red tape. *La Femme* was an immediate, overwhelming success.

It proved impossible to keep Balzac's hiding place a complete secret, of course. A housemaid who was engaged to a bill collector told her betrothed where to find the culprit, and the following day he was trapped. He had to pay a bill of thirteen hundred francs, which he didn't possess, or be taken off to jail. Fanny saved him, as she did on a number of other somewhat less dramatic occasions.

Life became unbearable in July 1837, when the Garde Nationale, which failed to appreciate literature and still wanted him to stand sentry duty, discovered his new hiding place. This was the last straw, and he scampered off to Touraine, where his familiar room in the house of the Margonnes awaited him.

There he completed *César Birotteau*, a novel of the middle class that is still regarded as one of his greatest masterpieces. It was the story of an honorable man who found himself in debt through no fault of his own other than his honesty, and whose subsequent attempts to recoup his good name and fortune through a series of speculations led him to disaster. In relieving himself of his own frustrations, Balzac simultaneously turned out a gem.

By September he also completed *La Maison Nucingen*, and funds began to appear. He received his fifty thousand franc advance for the two books, and also received an additional twenty thousand for the serial rights to *César Birotteau*, the largest sum ever paid to an author for these rights up to that time.

With money in his pocket, Balzac felt he could face the world again. He had enough to finance his own investigation of the Sardinian silver mines, for instance, and soon would be wealthy enough to thumb his nose at his creditors. He had no intention, naturally, of using any of his royalties to pay off even a portion of his debts.

He could solve all of his immediate problems, he decided, by buying a house in the country, a place close enough to Paris to enable him to visit the city when he pleased, yet far enough to keep him beyond the grasp of bill collectors and the Garde Nationale. What's more, he would have a home to offer Eveline after the Baron Hanski died and left her a wealthy widow.

He found precisely what he wanted in a little village, Ville-d'Avray, a short distance from Versailles on the Paris road, where the trees were thick and tall they reminded him of a forest. Best of all, he would be situated only a short distance from the Guidoboni-Viscontis, which was an important consideration, particularly as Fanny and Emilio, for unfathomable reasons, offered to finance the purchase.

Balzac plunged into the project with boundless enthusiasm. He bought a small cottage from a weaver, intending to use it as a guesthouse, and then purchased five acres of surrounding land. He moved into the guesthouse temporarily, and hired a builder to put up a new, suitable dwelling for him. He had been pained to learn that creditors had seized the furnishing of the house on the Rue Cassini and his hideout on the Rue des Batailles, but he had salvaged his books, his papers, his wardrobe and his collection of walking sticks, so the rest did not matter. What he had done once he could do again, and he considered himself an expert in the buying of furniture, which may have been an accurate estimate.

According to Balzac's own figures, which are still extant on several sheets of manuscript paper, the entire project, including the building and furnishing of the new house, would cost a modest forty thousand francs. He had spent, so far, somewhat less than twelve thousand for the cottage and adjoining properties, and had paid the builder a scant fifteen hundred in advance.

He wanted and needed no sumptuous palace, he wrote Eveline Hanska. He was an unassuming man who lived simply, a man whose needs were approximately those of an untutored peasant. All he required were a stove on which he could cook and warm the house, a plain bed on which he could rest for a few hours each night, and a chair in which he could read or daydream about his beloved. These few items, along with his worktable and chair, were sufficient. Later, when his bills for the new house and furniture were mounting at a dizzy rate, he thought it unfair of Mme.

Hanska to belabor him with pointed quotations from his own letters.

Balzac's preoccupation with money matters in 1837 is understandable; although his earnings were greater than ever before, he was thrashing ever deeper in quicksands of his own making. It is not surprising that at the end of the book he had just completed he restored the principled César Birotteau's good name and cleared him of debt. Nor is it to be wondered that in *La Maison Nucingen* he approached the same basic problem from a completely different aspect.

Here was the story of a financier who was hard, cunning and calculating, a man who believed that laws were made for lesser people. Nucingen was a banker who manipulated the stock market for his own benefit, who allowed the trusting and innocent to be ruined, and who achieved such great success that he was made a baron. This reward must be contrasted with the sad fate of César Birotteau, who worked so hard on the treadmill that, although he repaid his debts and won back his honor, he killed himself by working too hard.

It has been said that in these two books Balzac was writing a condemnation of the capitalism of his era, but that is going too far. He took a cynical approach in both books, and was saying in effect, "Chicanery pays dividends, but honesty does not." What he was condemning, however, was the selfish nature of man, not a particular economic system. Above all, perhaps, he was revealing his own inner feelings, and may have realized, as he advanced into middle age, that he might end his days in the manner of César Birotteau rather than that of the wealthy Nucingen.

Early in 1838 Balzac acquired a new vice. A coolness had developed in his friendship with George Sand when he had become the champion of Jules Sandeau, but he now shared her low opinion of her former lover, whose indolence had forced him to call off their collaborative playwriting effort. Balzac wrote his old friend a cordial letter, she replied in the same tone, and a short time later he went off to pay her a visit of several days at Nohant, where she had acquired a house.

The two writers who led the most unorthodox of personal lives talked of their craft, compared ideas, sought each other's professional advice and gossiped. George Sand had behaved foolishly in her relations with Franz Liszt, the great composer and pianist, and his intimate friend, Marie d'Agoult, and after telling Balzac the story she regretted her inability to make use of it as the basis for a novel. He requested the privilege, which she gave him, and the story later became his *Les Galériens de l'amour*.

Balzac's new vice was smoking a water pipe. George Sand offered him cigars, which were too strong for him, so she urged him to try a hookah, which she frequently used. He became an enthusiastic convert. Tobacco, he later wrote, sharpened his perspectives and clarified his imagination, enabling him to put his thoughts on paper with greater precision. He also believed that smoking a hookah would make it possible for him to lessen his consumption of coffee, this new moderation would cure him of his stomach ailment and get rid of the pains that now plagued him regularly. By the time he learned that smoking had no effect on the quantity of coffee he drank, it was too late, and he found he had added a new bad habit to the old.

Some of Balzac's early biographers hinted that he and George Sand became lovers during his visit to Nohant, but their only evidence was the promiscuity of both parties, coupled with the belief that they would not have been able to resist the temptation while spending several unchaperoned days together under the same roof. The claim does not hold up under close examination. Scores of letters were exchanged by the pair in the years that followed, and there is no hint of intimacy in any of them. They remained good friends who exchanged views and offered each other advice. Both possessed such flamboyant temperaments that, had they been lovers, they would have found it impossible to refrain from dramatizing the relationship in their correspondence.

Late in March, Balzac returned to his weaver's cottage and tried to block out the hammering and sawing as the builders continued their work on what he repeatedly referred to in his correspondence with Eveline Hanska as his "humble little house."

But their proximity made it so difficult for him to concentrate that he left them to their labors and went off on what may have been the most insane of all his ventures, his attempt to gain control of the Sardinian silver mines and work them.

The basic idea for the venture was sound, as were all of his other attempts to earn a fortune. Two or three years after his abject and absurd failure a consortium of wealthy businessmen was formed, some of Europe's best mining engineers and metallurgists were hired, and within a decade the company refined enough of the abandoned silver to earn profits the equivalent of nine million dollars.

But Balzac had no idea how to put his basic idea into practice, and he lacked the funds to organize a company that would operate on a large scale. Worst of all, he was handicapped by his lack of technical knowledge. He knew nothing about mining, smelting, testing and refining ore, the transportation of the refined product or the state of the silver market. He launched his one-man venture with the optimism of an adolescent who would find the abandoned mines, purchase the otherwise worthless land at a low price from owners who had no other use for the property and would be glad to get rid of it for a pittance. Then, when the mines were his, he would form his company, obtain financial support and, perhaps, hire an expert or two to assist him. But his correspondence made it clear that he intended to direct the entire operation himself.

Balzac went to Marseilles in late March 1838 and after a delay of several days sailed from Toulon for Sardinia, via Corsica, where he was detained for five days by quarantine officials. He visited the birthplace of his idol, Napoleon, wandered around the primitive town of Ajaccio, which he enjoyed, and read several books which he obtained in the local library.

Obtaining passage on a fishing boat, he completed the last leg of his journey, and found still more obstacles ahead. Sardinia was a rough, undeveloped country, most of it consisting of thick, almost impenetrable forests. There were no roads, only a few prickly paths led to the interior, where the mines were located, and there were no hotels, inns or other facilities for visitors.

A new experience was in store for the adventurer. He purchased quantities of smoked fish and a local hard bread, the only food available, and used cash from his dwindling stores to purchase a blanket, an ax and other supplies. Although he hadn't ridden in years, he rented a horse, and went off alone into the interior. He was scratched by briars, ate his meals at the side of the trail and slept in the open, hating every moment of the journey.

After two difficult days and nights, he reached the abandoned mines, which were located near a small town called Nurra. It had been his intention to take "samples" of ore back to Paris with him, but the sight of high mountains of slag unnerved him, and he went off for local help, hoping to find someone who would be able to tell the difference between ordinary rocks and low-grade ore.

The disappointment was in Nurra. He discovered that the mines were no longer abandoned. Pezzi, the businessman who had first told him about the mines, had become so enthusiastic after listening to Balzac's flowing description of the fortune they would make that he had obtained a government permit to work the mines. A company of financiers had already been formed for the purpose.

Cursing man's ingratitude to man, he started off on the long homeward journey. By the time he reached Genoa he was almost penniless, so he went to Milan, where he had been accorded such generous hospitality, in the hope that he could borrow enough money to enable him to reach Paris.

Milanese society had lost interest in him, but two members of the nobility treated him with great kindness. Prince Porcia insisted on giving him a room in the Porcia palace, which made it unnecessary for him to rent a hotel room, and Countess Bolognini, knowing he was virtually destitute, invited him to dine daily with her and her family.

The isolation Balzac unexpectedly enjoyed gave him the opportunity to return to work, and he immediately began to write the first segment of what would become one of his best books, *Splendeurs et misères des courtisanes.* This story, *La Torpille,* was that of a brothel inmate, who fell in love with Lucien de Rubempré, who had been the protagonist of *Illusions perdues.* She left the brothel and spent three happy months with him, but tried to commit suicide when she was recognized. The attempt failed, and a sympathetic priest sent her off to a convent school, where she would be taught to lead a new life.

Girardin had agreed to serialize the story in *La Presse,* but the redemption of a prostitute at a convent was too much for even his progressive tendencies. Fortunately Werdet had reorganized his business affairs and recovered from his bankruptcy, so he published *La Torpille* later in the year.

Balzac never forgot the kindness of Countess Bolognini and Prince Porcia, and dedicated both *Splendeurs et misères* and another of his great books, *Une Fille d'Ève,* to them. "*Although the French are charged with frivolity and forgetfulness,*" he wrote, "*I am Italian in my constancy.*"

Reaching Paris in time for his thirty-ninth birthday, he found that, once again, a tragedy had occurred during his absence. The Duchess d'Abrantes had died in penury, and had been buried in Père-Lachaise, the pauper's cemetery.

She had meant nothing to him for a long time, and certainly he had never loved or admired her as he had Laure de Berny, but her passing made him more conscious than ever of his own advancing age. His letters to Eveline Hanska, although still filled with self-pity that might arouse her sympathies, took on a genuine pathetic quality. He was growing old, he told her, and found few real satisfactions in life. He had done only a small fraction of the work he needed to accomplish, and although he wanted the joys of marriage, domesticity continued to elude him. Soon his advanced age would make it impossible for him to find anyone willing to marry him, even though no man had ever been more suited to connubial life.

He took consolation in his "little" house, which he called Les Jardies, and to make sure none of his invited guests missed the place, a block of black marble inscribed with gold lettering told them they had reached their right destination. The building itself, which Victor Hugo described as a bird cage, consisted of a living room, dining room and kitchen on the ground floor, a second story with two bedrooms, a third floor similar to the second, and, at the top, a solarium with windows on all sides that would be used as the author's workroom. Always mindful of the wisdom of leaving himself a means of escape from the Garde Nationale and his creditors, Balzac had two staircases built into the place, one a conventional set of indoor stairs, the other a sturdy but odd-looking outdoor set.

No man could have chosen a less suitable site for a house. The property plunged down to a gully directly behind the building, so a set of extensive and very expensive retaining walls had to be constructed in order to prevent the earth from giving way at the rear of the house. Whenever a heavy rain fell there was a land-slide, the retaining walls frequently suffered damage and had to undergo extensive repairs, and there was always a very present danger that the walls would collapse.

The area on both sides of Balzac's property was crowded with tall trees, but not as much as a shrub stood on his land, which had been used for grazing. He had been proud of his sagacity when he had selected his building site, and had boasted that he had been spared the expense of cutting down and uprooting trees in order to put up the house. Now he discovered that, by some freak of nature, the soil on his land was unlike that of the territory around him, and no trees would grow there.

Balzac solved that problem by bringing in several tons of rich topsoil, which gardeners laid for him at a high cost; then the rains would come, the topsoil would wash down to the bottom of the gully, and he would be forced to repeat the dreary process. He insisted his soil was the best in France, however, because there were no trees to shade the property, which caught the benefit of the sun all day.

It was inevitable that he should dream up a new scheme that would make him rich, and when he described his plan to Théophile Gautier he became so enthusiastic that, in his own mind, his idea was already a reality. His notion was astonishing, to say the least: he intended to install a pineapple plantation on his property. Pineapples were a luxury food, imported from the Caribbean, and were prohibitively expensive. In fact, the average price in the Paris markets fluctuated between twenty and twenty-five francs for a single pineapple. But the pineapples of Les Jardies would be so plentiful they would flood the market, and the happy proprietor would open his own retail store for the exclusive purpose of selling his product at an unprecedented price of five francs per pineapple.

Balzac would accomplish this miracle, he said, by erecting a version of a hothouse to protect the pineapple plants in cold weather. All he would need would be a glass roof and glass walls; the sun would keep the interior warm.

The dream had already taken on substance in his own mind, and he insisted that Gautier accompany him to Montmartre for the purpose of finding a suitable shop he could rent as an outlet for his pineapples. He located precisely what he wanted, and described the interior after he rebuilt and redecorated it. Gautier had a difficult time restraining him when he wanted to take a lease on the place immediately.

Gardeners did their best to disillusion the would-be pineapple planter by telling him the soil beneath his greenhouse would be so cold that his trees would die. But Balzac refused to listen to such defeatist talk, and for years he persisted in dreaming about his plantation. Gautier wrote about a visit he paid to Les Jardies on a chilly winter day when the snow in the bare yard was piled high and a fire was burning in every hearth. The undaunted Balzac ignored the weather and excitedly paced up and down before the fire, describing the mechanics of his scheme.

He estimated that he had enough space for twenty thousand pineapple trees, so in the period of five years he would grow one hundred thousand pineapples, even if each tree yielded but one. The entire cost, including the purchase of the trees, would be one franc per tree—a figure he apparently plucked out of thin air. By selling the pineapples for five francs each, he would show a profit of four hundred thousand francs, in return for virtually no effort on his part. Then he would be wealthy enough to pay off all his debts and have enough left so he would be able to write only the books that interested him; never again would he be forced to worry about earning money.

In the meantime, however, he was so busy signing contracts for new books that he needed someone to help him. He decided to hire an assistant, someone who would learn his style and would turn out the first draft of various works, which would be carefully outlined for him in advance. He found the man he wanted in Charles Lassailly, a young writer recommended to him by Lamartine, but they failed to hit it off together from the start. Lassailly could not accustom himself to his employer's hours but was expected to be at work himself whenever Balzac sat at his own desk. Within a few months the weary Lassailly was forced to admit total defeat and return to Paris.

During this time Balzac turned out a play, *L'École des ménages*, and among those who liked it was a crippled young artist and writer named Jean Laurent, who used the professional name of Laurent-Jan. He immediately became Lassailly's successor. Laurent took up residence at Les Jardies and stayed for two years, during which time he did not collaborate in the writing of a single line. He made himself useful to the harried Balzac, however, and acted as a combination chief of household and personal manager. When he could get his hands on royalties that were flowing in, he unobtrusively paid off some of his employer's more pressing debts, and when there were no funds available, he diplomatically stalled the bill collectors, who were surprised to find someone in the Balzac house who treated them with civility. Laurent attended to the details of arranging new book contracts, acted as Balzac's liaison with various publishers and relieved him of innumerable time-consuming chores.

He also made strenuous efforts to interest various theatre owners in a production of *L'École*, and his repeated failure in no way diminished his own enthusiasm for the play. Balzac was deeply hurt, however, when theatrical managers dared to reject his work. It was absurd, he said, that someone who needed only to let it be known he intended to write a book in order to obtain a contract could not find a theatre owner willing to produce his work. He could only conclude that his enemies were at work again, and that a widespread conspiracy was preventing Paris audiences from enjoying a Balzac play.

Never one to waste time brooding, he wrote *Le Cabinet des antiques*, which is best described in his own preface:

This book is the tale of impecunious young men, the bearers of great names, who come to Paris to meet with disaster—through gambling, or the desire to shine, or the allurements of Paris life, or the attempt to increase their fortune, or through happy or unhappy love affairs. The Comte d'Esrignon is the counterpart of Rastignac, the latter another type of provincial young man, but adroit and audacious, who succeeds where the former fails.

The theme was reminiscent of *Illusions perdues*, so he went to work on the second part of that masterpiece, calling it *Un Grand Homme de province à Paris*. Almost miraculously, he was able to endow it with the same spirit, mood and style, as though he had moved directly from the writing of the first part to that of the second.

But work, even the writing of literary gems, was something he could take almost for granted. His delight was the house, on which he was already spending far too much. He had moved in as soon as the builders moved out, even though Dr. Nacquart had warned him he would be jeopardizing his health if he didn't wait for the place to dry out. The carpenters were still very much in evidence, however, as they were now engaged in a new project, that of rebuilding the simple weaver's cottage, which the lord of the manor wanted to make habitable for Fanny Guidoboni-Visconti, his patient and generous mistress-patroness. He was able to ignore the sawing and hammering as he wrote ecstatically about his new home:

My house lies on the slope of the mount or hill of Saint-Cloud, which borders halfway up on the King's park toward the south. To westward the view embraces the whole of Ville-d'Avray, and to the south I look down upon the Ville-d'Avray road which stretches along the hills to the beginning of the park of Versailles. To eastward my gaze roams beyond Sèvres and encompasses a vast horizon—behind which lies Paris. The haze of the great city veils the edge of the famous slopes of Meudon and Bellevue. In the distance lies the plain of Montrouge and the road which runs from Orléans to Tours. It is a landscape of rare grandeur and alluring contrasts.

In the immediate vicinity of my property lies the railway station on the line from Paris to Versailles, the embankment of which runs through the valley of Ville-d'Avray without, however, restricting my view in the slightest degree. So I can travel in ten minutes, and at the price of ten sous, from Les Jardies to the Madeleine in the heart of Paris! From the Rue des Batailles, from Chaillot, or from the Rue Cassini it cost me at least forty sous and occupied an hour of my valuable time.

Taking this convenient situation into account it can never be said that the purchase of Les Jardies has been a foolish move on my part since the price of the property is certain to rise enormously. The whole estate comprises five acres of land, bounded by a terrace to the south and surrounded by walls. Nothing has yet been planted, but in the later autumn we shall make a veritable Garden of Eden out of this little corner of the earth, with flowers, shrubs and fragrant odors. In Paris or its environs anything may be purchased, if one has the money, so I shall buy twenty year-old magnolia trees, sixteen year-old limes, twelve year-old poplars, birches, and etc., which can be transported with clods of earth around the roots. I shall also have vines, which are brought in baskets, and which shall produce grapes this very year!

Yes, civilization is wonderful, a miracle! It is true that today the ground is as bare as the palm of one's hand, but by next spring there will be an astonishing transformation. I intend to acquire a few more acres of land in the vicinity for kitchen gardens, groves of fruit trees, and so forth, for which I need an additional thirty thousand francs, but this sum I intend to earn this winter.

The house is steep and narrow, like the perch in a parrot's cage, three stories high, with a main room on each floor, and at the top my study, where I am writing this letter . . . A staircase almost like a ladder runs from one story to the next. Right around the house runs a covered gallery, along which one can walk, reaching up to the first floor and supported on brick piles. The whole of this little pavilion, which has an Italian air about it, is painted in brick color, the corners are of hewn stone, and the annex containing the well of the staircase is red. There is just room for me (and perhaps my assistant) in this house of mine. Sixty paces to the rear, in the direction of the park of Saint-Cloud, is an outbuilding with servant's quarters, larder, etc., on the first floor, together with stable, coach house, harness room, bath, wooden shed, etc. On the first floor there is a large apartment which might, if necessary, be let, and on the second floor there are bedrooms for the servants and guest rooms for friends.

I have a spring of water at my disposal which is as good as the celebrated spring of Ville-d'Avray, since it is fed from the same underground pool, and my property is surrounded on all sides by pleasant walks. None of the rooms is completely furnished as yet, but I shall gradually transfer all of my remaining possessions from Paris.

Here I shall remain until I have made my fortune. I already find it so much to my liking that I believe I shall one day settle down here to end my days in peace as soon as I have enough money on which to retire. Then I shall bid farewell to all my aspirations and ambitious plans, without the beating of drums and without unnecessary fanfares.

The furnishings Balzac brought from Paris were inadequate, and filled only a portion of the house, so he soon returned to the antique markets and began spending far too much money, once again buying from gullible merchants who extended him credit. That was just the beginning; Fanny's cottage had to be perfect, and the retaining walls that had to be rebuilt after every heavy downpour were a constant expense.

Stories about the Garden of Eden soon began to circulate in Paris, and before long the newspaper gossips gleefully printed stories of every mishap and minor catastrophe. So much untoward happened that many of these accounts were relatively accurate.

The publicity soon put bill collectors on the author's trail, and by the spring of 1839 they began to appear at his marble and gold gate. He quickly countered with a scheme to foil them: either he or Laurent saw the intruders from the solarium, which commanded a view of the entire property. The servants immediately removed all valuables, carrying them to the rebuilt weaver's cottage, the one structure on the property that was hidden by a screen of thick evergreens. Balzac either concealed himself in the cottage or raced, surprisingly sure-footed, to a hidden refuge on the far side of the gully.

The bill collectors were permitted to roam through the house at will, and sniffed in contempt at furniture of little value. They could find no sign of the master, either, and unable to serve him, had to return empty-handed to Paris.

For three long years this technique was effective, and during that time Balzac's expenses continued to mount. He poured money into Les Jardies at a rate that defied reason, and a conservative estimate of his major expenses during this time indicates that he spent at least one hundred thousand francs, perhaps one hundred and fifty thousand, on the place. He could have purchased a magnificent townhouse in one of Paris' best residential districts for far less.

He took an almost childish pride in his ability to outwit his creditors, and his friends were forced to listen to his boasts. But all good things eventually come to an end, and after he spent three years dodging the bill collectors, one of them discovered his allegedly foolproof system.

Some of his creditors banded together, and instead of bringing court action against the culprit himself, they filed suit against a man they knew was solvent, Count Guidoboni-Visconti. Emilio was guilty only of closing his eyes to his wife's trips from their Versailles home to the no longer simple weaver's cottage, and was embarrassed by his unexpected involvement in the quicksands of Balzac's financial affairs.

Even more important, Fanny found herself teetering on the edge of ruin. A major scandal threatened to send her plunging to the bottom of a social abyss, and as she was already weary of protecting Balzac, paying the most persistent of his creditors to save him from disaster.

The net, immediate result was the total collapse of his credit, and he was forced to dispose of his Garden of Eden, selling the property at a staggering loss while he searched for a new place to live in Paris. The experience taught him nothing, however, and until the end of his days he remained convinced that, given a little more time, he would have made his pineapple plantation a reality.

XV

Neither the distractions of being a householder nor the tribulations of dodging creditors could keep Honoré de Balzac from his writing desk. He had reached the peak of his powers, and it appeared he had become incapable of turning out anything less than a masterpiece. The books on which he worked in 1838 and 1839 were, without exception, among his finest: *Une Fille d'Ève*, *Béatrix*, *Le Curé de village*, *Qui a terre a guerre*. The breadth of his knowledge was astonishing: he understood the minds and mores of courtesans and village priests, financiers and paupers, middle-class provincials and aristocratic Parisians. He knew the ambitions of men and the emotions of women, the venality of the bourgeoisie and the helpless anger of the working classes. What is truly amazing is that he seemed incapable of applying any of what he knew to his own life.

Scores of letters that he wrote to Eveline Hanska, Zulma Carraud, George Sand and his sister over a period of years indicate that he realized he needed all of his energies and every hour of available time to complete the *Comédie humaine*, a superhuman task that no ordinary man would have set as his goal. Yet, over a period of several years beginning late in 1838, Balzac frittered away countless, precious days writing inferior plays. In the main they were comedies, most of them poor imitations of the works of Molière and Voltaire, and were so slipshod, so lacking in insights, so badly constructed that they do not seem to have been written by the author of the *Comédie humaine*.

The reason is that Balzac did not regard the theatre as a true literary outlet. Plays, unlike novels, were not serious work, but merely a key that would unlock a treasure chest containing pieces of gold. Victor Hugo had earned a fortune by writing plays, and other, far lesser men had emulated him. Therefore the great, the unique Honoré de Balzac could do far better than second-rate hack writers.

Had he wished to concentrate on the drama as a literary form he undoubtedly could have achieved outstanding success. Few authors have ever enjoyed a deeper understanding of human character, and he had become a master of concocting tight, emotion-laden plots. Unfortunately, however, he equated the writing of plays with the seeking of Roman silver in Sardinia or forming a league of subscribers to books published for large masses of people. Get-rich-quick schemes were a spare-time avocation in which he allowed himself to indulge on occasion, when his daydreams became overpowering, but at no time did they require the disciplined devotion necessary to turn out a first-rate novel that readers in many lands would hail for centuries to come.

The failure of *L'École des ménages* to find a producer embittered him, and he made up his mind to try a different approach to the theatre. Through Laurent he met Harel, the proprietor and director of the Théâtre Porte Saint-Martin, who proved to be a convivial fellow. Persuasive and enthusiastic, Balzac outlined an idea for him, the dramatization of his novel *Vautrin*. Most people were unable to resist his verbal salesmanship, and *Vautrin* was no exception; contracts were drawn, and the happy Balzac signed the papers. *Vautrin* would be produced on the stage!

It was impossible for him to live in the country when he was needed day and night at the theatre, but he was still wary of bill collectors, and quickly found a new subterfuge. The shop of Buisson, his tailor, was located a scant city block from the Théâtre Porte Saint-Martin, so he persuaded the accommodating Buisson to permit him to sleep in the back room.

Thereafter he spent every waking moment at the theatre, helping Harel assemble a cast, conferring at length with the actors regarding the characters they would play, holding discussions with the scenic artists and costumers. When Harel scheduled the start of rehearsals, however, a minor oversight was discovered: there was no play script, so the actors had no lines to learn.

But this slight matter was of no concern to Balzac, who blithely informed the producer-director that he would provide the script within the next twenty-four hours. Going to Buisson's house, he summoned a group of his close friends, and informed all of them that he had to have a play ready for Harel the following morning. The last to arrive was Théophile Gautier, whose anecdotes are noted for their accuracy, and who describes the meeting in his *Portraits:*

"So you want to ask my opinion?" I inquired, settling down comfortably in an armchair to listen to a lengthy reading.

Balzac guessed my thoughts from my attitude of ease and replied with an air of innocence, "The play isn't written yet."

"The devil you say!" I exclaimed. "Then the reading will have to be postponed for six weeks."

"Oh, no! We are going to polish it off at once and collect the cash. I have a pressing obligation to meet and can't wait."

"But you can't turn out a play by tomorrow," I protested. "There isn't even time to have it copied."

"This is how I am going to do it. You will write one act, Ourliac will write another, Laurent-Jan will compose the third act, De Belloy the fourth, I myself will be responsible for the fifth, and

tomorrow at mid-day I shall read the whole play to Harel, just as we have agreed. Each act of a drama doesn't contain more than four or five hundred lines, and anyone who knows writing can turn out five hundred lines of dialogue in a day and a night."

"Tell me the subject, give me an idea of the way you want the plot to develop, describe the characters as precisely as you can, and I will make the attempt," I replied with a certain bewilderment.

"Oh!" Balzac cried, with a magnificent disdain and a superb air of being overwhelmed by such an absurd request. "If I'm forced to tell you the entire plot we shall never be finished in time."

It had not occurred to me that I was being indiscreet in asking what the play was about, but Balzac regarded my attitude as one of mere idle curiosity.

With great difficulty I managed to extract from him a brief indication of the theme, and then sat down to draft a scenario of which no more than a few words survived in the final version. As can well be imagined, the play was NOT read to Harel the following day. I do not know how the other collaborators managed, but the only one who had a serious finger in the pie was Laurent-Jan, to whom the play is dedicated.

Balzac's helpers completed their task in thirty-six hours, and in the next day and night he buckled down to serious rewriting, somehow finishing the overwhelming task in another twenty-four hours. The reading had to be postponed for no more than a single day.

At best *Vautrin* was a hodgepodge of style, characterization and plotting, and at worst it was a catastrophe. Harel had advertised the play extensively, claiming it was a masterpiece, and could not back out; his flamboyant campaign had aroused curiosity, and the entire opening night performance was sold out. It was even reported on good authority that the Prince d'Orléans would occupy the royal box.

The cast included some of the best actors on the Paris stage, among them the celebrated Frédéric Lemaître, who was playing the principal role, that of a Mexican general. Throughout rehearsals he and his supporting cast frequently complained about discrepancies in the characterizations and gaps in plotting, so Balzac rewrote the play feverishly, scene by scene, completing the task only two days prior to the opening.

For three acts the distinguished audience sat in an embarrassed, frozen silence; there was no applause, and no one laughed at the comedy lines. Then, in the fourth act, the theatre erupted. Lemaître appeared onstage wearing a wig that made him look like King Louis Philippe, and the Royalists in the audience, thinking a deliberate discourtesy to the crown was intended, interrupted the play with loud catcalls. The Prince d'Orléans ostentatiously left his box and stalked out of the theatre.

The actors had a difficult time finishing the performance. A near-riot broke out during the fifth act, and police reserves were called to restore order. The play limped to a flabby finish before a sadly depleted audience.

Promptly the following morning the King's censors banned *Vautrin*, threatening to close the theatre permanently if the order was violated. The government of Louis Philippe was not yet as reactionary as it would become in the years immediately prior to the Revolution of 1848, and the King himself remembered what had happened to his predecessors when they had cracked down too hard. So the Ministry of Fine Arts privately offered Balzac a fee of five thousand francs to forget the matter.

A fee of several times that sum could not have prevented him from making an issue of the affair. He had a chance to turn disaster into moral triumph, and he wasted no opportunity, writing articles for *Figaro* and *La Presse* in which he roundly condemned all censorship, obtaining support from such genuine liberals as Victor Hugo, and, eventually, writing as though only a conspiracy of censors and his enemies had prevented him from enjoying a great theatrical triumph. By that time he believed his own propaganda, and the fact that thousands of Parisians knew the true story did not prevent him from trumpeting his case.

Subsequently Balzac wrote four more plays. *Paméla Giraud*

and *Les Ressources de Quinola* were a trifle better than *Vautrin,* but both failed as miserably. Another, *La Marâtre,* has survived only because it was written by Honoré de Balzac, and is generally considered his worst effort. Only his last play, *La Faiseur,* showed any indication that it was written by a great master; ironically, it was not staged until after his death, when it enjoyed a modest run, and subsequently was revived on a number of occasions. As in so many other ventures, Balzac failed in his attempt to find a pot of gold in the theatre.

But he was undeterred by the collapse of yet another dream, and during the three years he spent at Les Jardies he poured out novels, novellae and short stories, literary essays and newspaper articles. Two of his greatest books date from this period, the political masterpiece, *Une Tenébreuse Affaire,* and the super-realistic *La Rabouilleuse.* It has been estimated that he did most of the work on eleven other novels during this time, blocked out the plots of two others and wrote the fragments of at least two or three more.

He was in his forties now, and his stomach condition gave him no rest. He was deeply involved with Fanny Guidoboni-Visconti, and the affable Laurent brought courtesans to the country house from Paris for an occasional evening of sport. His creditors gave him no peace, he engaged in unremitting correspondence with Zulma Carraud and his sister, as well as a one-way correspondence with Eveline Hanska. There were numerous other troubles that disturbed his peace of mind and placed a strain on his nerves, too, but nothing stopped the steady flow of words onto paper, the unceasing piling of manuscript on manuscript as the *Comédie humaine* grew, took shape and acquired a large measure of the depth he had envisioned when he plunged in earnest into his life work.

Les Galeriens de l'amour did not jell as he had hoped, and he realized he had not done enough to disguise the identities of George Sand, Franz Liszt and Marie d'Agoult, so he threw away some hundreds of pages of manuscript and started the book again, this time calling it *Béatrix.* His narrator bore a close physical resemblance to George Sand, but he took great care not to offend his friend, and the character became one of his most sympathetic and charming. Liszt and Mme. d'Agoult became unrecognizable, the latter developing characteristics strongly reminscent of Fanny, to whom he dedicated the work under the pet name of Sarah, in order to avoid arousing the jealousy of Mme. Hanska. Nothing in Balzac's life was simple.

Neither his punishing work schedule nor the complexities of his romance-laden, debt-ridden personal life prevented him from branching out in new directions. None was more significant than the role he played in the formation of the first society of professional authors, men who banded together for the purpose of protecting their books, obtaining better terms from publishers and making certain that unscrupulous foreign publishers paid royalties when they printed an author's work. This organization, the Société des Gens de Lettres, was the precursor of the present-day Authors League of America, in the United States, and of similar groups in other nations.

The Société was formed in 1839, with Balzac among its distinguished charter members, among whom were Hugo, Sue, Dumas and Gautier. The members gathered for dinner at the Vefour, the favorite restaurant of Balzac and Hugo, and drew up a list of resolutions calculated to further the interests of all who wrote for a living. The wine flowed freely, and the wording of the resolutions was eloquent, but nothing came of the effort after copies were sent to various government ministries. The writers were busy men, and each had his own fish to fry, so no one bothered to make an effort to secure the help and co-operation of the authorities.

This failure annoyed Balzac, and with good reason: he, more than any of his colleagues, was being hurt by the lack of protection being given to the works of authors. A publisher in Brussels, acting without his permission, was bringing out unauthorized editions of virtually all of his books in French, and was flooding the market with them, not only in Belgium, but in France itself. Balzac was not paid a sou for these editions, and his own knowledge of the law convinced him there was literally nothing he could do to collect. The laws of both countries made no provision for the relief of writers under these circumstances.

Of all who were members of the profession, Balzac alone seemed to realize that if the authors of France banded together and put aside their personal differences for the common good, their organization would be one of the most potent in the nation. He wrote innumerable letters to his colleagues, urging firm, collective action, and some of these communications came to the attention of the faculty at the University of Rouen.

They invited him to deliver a talk on the subject, and although he was pressed for time he agreed, knowing that a number of authors were living in Rouen. That one speech became a series of eight lectures, in which he presented cogent arguments in favor of strengthening the Société. His audiences applauded, but no one stepped forward to join him in taking positive action.

He remained convinced, however, that the association would become effective if it grew teeth, and wrote a document familiar to virtually every member of his profession in succeeding generations. The Code littéraire de la Société des Gens de Lettres spelled out in precise, far-seeing detail what writers could do to improve their vocational lot, and included a firm stand against censorship that mirrored the Bill of Rights in the Constitution of the United States.

Victor Hugo let it be known that he approved of the Code in toto, but other authors were more critical. Men who were friends were nevertheless jealous of each other, and there was no precedent for joint efforts. A half-dozen members of the Société insisted, jointly and separately, on amending the Code or writing their own versions. Petty squabbles broke out, factions formed and some of the less successful began to criticize their more famous peers in public.

Balzac made strenuous attempts to halt this senseless feuding, but was damned for his pains by virtually everyone he approached. His own personality was not that of a peacemaker, and his colleagues found his manner irritating. He was sometimes flamboyantly enthusiastic, sometimes too brusque, and he boasted so much about his own enormous income that he offended many who earned far less. The Société degenerated into a drinking club, and the disgusted Balzac resigned; the time was not yet ripe for an effective association of authors.

Yet another activity occupied him in 1839, this one an attempt, at least in the beginning, to enhance his own reputation. Many years earlier he had been acquainted with a newspaper reporter named Peytel, who subsequently had left Paris, after becoming an attorney, and had returned to his native village. There he had married a wealthy woman, who brought with her a manservant from her parents' home. Peytel discovered that she and the servant were lovers, and one night they were murdered. The notary subsequently confessed the crimes to the police, who admittedly questioned him with great enthusiasm, and was tried in a case that made newspaper headlines throughout the country. He was sentenced to death.

Balzac decided to make his own investigation of the case. It has been said he was motivated by a desire to emulate Voltaire, who had covered himself with glory a century earlier when he had revealed the truth in a somewhat similar case, but there is no evidence to indicate that Balzac was deliberately treading in his great predecessor's footsteps. In any event, he interviewed Peytel in prison, and immediately convinced himself the man was innocent.

Thereafter Balzac spent several weeks of his own time and money—neither of which he could afford—looking into every angle of the case. Peytel's guilt or innocence is irrelevant; what matters is that Balzac believed him innocent and threw all of his enormous energy into an attempt to set the man free.

Using his own legal background as well as his talents as an author, he wrote a long appeal to the higher courts, requesting a reversal of the lower court's decision. The document may have been one of his finest writing efforts, and at the least reveals that the law lost a brilliant practitioner when he decided to earn his living as an author. But the Court of Appeal refused to accept his plea, stating that he had no official connection with the case. His intervention was extralegal, the court ruled, his arguments were not considered and Peytel was duly executed.

Once again Balzac's efforts in the realm outside the world of his own books had failed. The Paris press, regarding him as increasingly eccentric, mocked his efforts, and the immediate effect may have been a diminution of his reputation. In the long run, of course, his activities in the Peytel case have served to increase his stature, but that did him no good in 1839. He had lost time he should have been spending at his writing desk, and had done nothing for weeks to reduce his mounting debts.

His financial situation was becoming still worse, and by 1840 he owed various people the staggering sum of approximately three hundred thousand francs. Less than half of this was what he called "friendly" indebtedness; he knew that his mother, Dr. Nacquart, his tailor and others who were close to him would not sue him. But his mother was becoming less supine. She was being supported by the De Survilles, and she wrote at least two firm letters to Balzac, telling him she was ashamed of being forced to live, at the age of sixty-two, on the charity of her son-in-law. Balzac wept when he read her letters, he told her, but his tears did not influence his conscience, and he made no attempt to repay even a small portion of what he owed her.

Other creditors were even more demanding. Some of his property in the house on the Rue des Batailles, which he still owned, was seized by bailiffs, and so many bill collectors came out to Les Jardies that he was forced to find a new subterfuge. As clever in avoiding payment as he was in concocting plots for his novels, he found a new device: none of the furniture or other belongings at Les Jardies belonged to M. de Balzac, the servants told the collectors who came out from Paris in ever-increasing numbers to storm the rural citadel. Everything in the house was the personal property of Count Guidoboni-Visconti, who was allowing his old friend, M. de Balzac, to make free use of the various household goods. But the ruse was only a temporary stopgap, as Balzac well knew.

For the first time he began to entertain serious thoughts about the advisability of abandoning his suburban Garden of Eden. Fanny was growing weary of the need to supply him with cash on demand, and their affair was in the doldrums. Many changes seemed to be in the air. The correspondence with Mme. Hanska was growing less frequent, in part because Eveline was answering only an occasional letter, and even Balzac could not maintain his undying enthusiasm for a woman who didn't seem to care whether or not she heard from him.

Besides, someone new entered his life in 1839, by the way of writing him an admiring letter. The lady was Hélène-Marie-Félicité de Valette, the thirty-year-old widow of a notary named Goujeon, to whom she had been married briefly many years earlier, prior to his death. Under the terms of her husband's will she was comfortably situated but would lose her share in his estate if she ever remarried. This circumstance had caused her to lead an active extramarital life for eleven years.

In 1831 she had given birth to an illegitimate child, the offspring of Count du Moulinet d'Hardemare, with whom she was still having an affair. She was also the mistress of another wealthy, powerful and personable man, the Baron Hippolyte Larrey, a distinguished physician who held the post of chief surgeon of the Army. Each of her lovers seemed aware of his rival's place in her life, but neither seemed to care.

Hélène carried on her multiple activities from two addresses, keeping a country house in her native Brittany and maintaining a small but handsomely furnished apartment on the Rue de Castiglione in Paris. Two lovers did not prevent boredom from setting in, and she appears to have been spurred by a desire for excitement when she opened her correspondence with Balzac.

Her imagination and her ability to lie about herself matched the best he could offer. In her first letters she called herself Félicité de Valette, and neglected to mention the fact that she had been married and long had been a widow. Naturally, there was no mention of her lovers or her illegitimate child, either.

Balzac reacted as he always did to communications from unknown ladies of noble birth, and sent Hélène one of his customary, warm responses. She kept pace with him, and soon proposed that she pay him a visit at Les Jardies. He was delighted, but because of unexpected circumstances was not present when she called.

Hélène boldly stole his inkwell as a souvenir, then wrote him about the theft in detail and offered him an "antique" inkwell she had "inherited" as a replacement. The couple did not meet until 1840, by which time the lady had regaled the author with the supposed story of her life, in great detail. Not a word of her account was true.

Hélène proved to be as handsome as she was flirtatious, and the affair began in January 1840, a week or two after the couple met. Balzac discovered his new mistress was not only adept in the erotic arts but wealthy, and within a few weeks he borrowed ten thousand francs from her. By mid-March he wondered if he might be in love again. Hélène seemed to fit all his requirements, and his correspondence with Zulma Carraud indicates he was seriously contemplating marriage.

Then, late in the spring, a difficulty arose in the person of one Edmond Cador, a newspaper gossip writer and minor literary critic who wrote under a number of pseudonyms. Balzac and Hélène had been seen together in restaurants and the theatre, and their names were being coupled in print with increasing frequency. Cador came to the author, he said, because he didn't want to see the great Balzac make a fool of himself.

Mincing no words, the newspaperman told the astonished Balzac that the lady was being kept by two wealthy lovers, one of whom was the father of her illegitimate son. In the course of a long and painful interview, Cador eventually revealed his own reason for coming to Balzac: he, too, had been sleeping with Hélène, and he produced a stack of letters in her handwriting to substantiate his contention. He managed to preserve the façade of a gentleman, however, by refusing to let Balzac read the letters.

Fortunately or otherwise, the lady was paying a visit of several weeks to her country house in Brittany at the time, so the angry

Balzac had to write her a letter in which he outlined Cador's charges in full. The chagrined Hélène replied in an even longer letter, and mixed half-truths with outright lies, blending a mélange worthy of the master storyteller himself.

Balzac knew she was lying, and amused himself by trying to trap her. Her replies, which filled many pages, gave the illusion of complete honesty but actually told him nothing. Apparently Hélène decided that distance would lend greater sincerity to her protests of candor, and she remained in Brittany until the autumn.

By this time Balzac was able to view the affair with a new equanimity. By now he had abandoned any thoughts of marrying Hélène, but neither her lack of honesty nor her way of life disqualified her as a mistress. He, who himself could bend the truth with such facility, saw no reason to terminate a relationship with a woman who possessed the same knack. Hélène was attractive and helped him create a good impression when they were seen together in public. She was a spirited, skilled bedmate who challenged his ingenuity as a lover. And he could not forget, either, that he owed her ten thousand francs, a sum he would be forced to repay if he refused to see her again.

Accepting the situation for what it was worth, he went off to Normandy with her for a holiday of eleven days, and enjoyed the experience so much that in 1841 he went to Brittany with her for a still longer vacation. In the same year he dedicated *Le Curé de village* to her, but her name was removed from another edition that appeared four years later. By then the relationship had soured badly: neither amused the other any longer, and Balzac was insisting she had made him a gift of the ten thousand francs, while she was demanding that he repay the sum with compound interest.

The affair was significant because it revealed in Balzac an unexpected ability to accept the reality of a situation and conduct himself accordingly. Also, he used Hélène as the model for a number of his feminine characters, chief among them Béatrix in the novel of the same name.

The distractions of a new affair in 1840 did not prevent Balzac from doing more than any normal man's share of work, and in that year he wrote the novel that, in the opinion of various authorities, most closely paralleled his own religious feelings. *Le Prêtre catholique* was the story of a murder that had its roots in the Peytel story. A lovely woman of character marries a wealthy, detestable banker and takes a laborer as her lover. The laborer murders the husband, is discovered and sentenced to death, but pretends he is mad so the lady's name will not be dragged in. The wife, now a widow, redeems herself through her strong Catholicism and her service to the community. There is even a strong touch of latter-twentieth-century land reclamation in the novel: the area in the vicinity of the widow's village is suffering from a lack of water, but she enlists the help of a young engineer, and together they succeed in restoring the fertility of the land. Redeemed by her good works, the widow makes a public confession of her sins as she dies.

The same theme is evident in *Le Curé de village,* the next novel Balzac wrote. It is the story of the engineer who appeared in *Le Prêtre,* and stresses the belief that man wins spiritual redemption through charity and service to his fellow man. Balzac insists there is no other way, and in these two books he states his principle with such forceful sincerity that it is difficult to believe these could not have been his own views, no matter how much he may have slighted them in practice.

In 1840 he also launched another of his mad ventures, sparked by the success Alphonse Karr had enjoyed the previous year. Karr had started a new monthly magazine, a literary and political journal that had been an overnight success and within a year had become one of the most profitable enterprises of its kind in Paris. Balzac, who had learned nothing from the failure of the *Chronique de Paris,* was wildly jealous of his former employee's success, and swore he could far surpass Karr. His own interest in politics was relatively slight, but he declared in a prospectus for a new review of his own that he intended to "expose the comedy of government." He also promised to tell the truth about new books, claiming that literary criticism had sunk to a dismal, all-time low point because the men who wrote about books were "singularly lacking in both sincerity and integrity."

He called his new journal the *Revue Parisienne,* and no one argued with his bold contention that it would be unique. In fact, Paris was dumfounded by his announcement to the effect that he intended to write the entire magazine himself. It would contain hitherto unpublished short stories and novellae, he said, as well as fragments of other, major works that, for one reason or another, had never been seen by the public.

Not only would Balzac write the entire publication, but he intended to edit it, act as his own circulation manager and handle every other aspect of bringing the magazine to the public except supervise the actual printing, a task he entrusted to his only employee, a man named Dutacq, who would receive one fourth of the profits. Literary Paris shook its collective head and waited for the first issue, which appeared in the late spring of 1840.

It was a miracle that Balzac could write so much, another that his book production continued unabated, and yet another that so much of what appeared in the *Revue Parisienne* was truly brilliant. Balzac was merciless in his treatment of Sainte-Beuve and other enemies who had dared to attack him in the past, and frequently he allowed his animosity to cloud his judgments. Even when his literary reviews were unjust, however, he wrote with a style and a clarity of thought that were extraordinary.

The *Revue* has another, enduring claim to fame. Balzac was the discoverer of an author sixteen years his senior who had spent the better part of his life working in anonymity as a literary hack. Marie Henri Beyle, who wrote under the name of Stendhal, had published a novel called *La Chartreuse de Parme* the previous year but it appeared destined to suffer the fate of another novel, *Le Rouge et le Noir,* which had been published without fanfare in 1830. These works, along with a number of others, had drawn virtually no notice. The critics had ignored them, and the indifference of the reading public had been monumental.

Then Balzac read *La Chartreuse de Parme,* a study of love and contemporary manners, and hailed it in the *Revue* as the greatest romantic novel of the century, an opinion posterity has confirmed. For three issues Balzac sang the praises of the unknown Stendhal; here, he wrote furiously, was a genius whose work remained unknown because the literary world of Paris was corrupt and stupid.

His campaign enjoyed few short-term benefits, although he succeeded in arousing the interest of some readers in Stendhal, and an audience that grew larger year by year came to appreciate his judgment and concur in it. The one immediate result was the warm friendship between the two men that the review of *La Chartreuse de Parme* established. They had been acquainted for ten years, but had known each other only slightly during that time. Now Stendhal wrote a letter to Balzac, thanked him and called the review "astonishing, such as no writer has ever written about another."

For the better part of two years these two outcasts, mutually scorned by most members of the literary establishment, saw each other frequently, compared notes and freely expressed their thoughts about their enemies. Balzac had found a truly kindred spirit, but the relationship was cut short by tragedy. Stendhal was worn out by his long, unsuccessful attempts to gain recognition, and one day in March 1842, he dropped dead of a heart attack on the streets of Paris. Balzac was one of a small group of faithful friends who accompanied the body of Marie Henri Beyle to its final resting place, a paupers' cemetery in Montmartre.

By that time the *Revue* had been long forgotten. The journal was one of Balzac's worst failures, and was published for only three months, when a lack of adequate readership forced the publisher-editor-business manager-sole author to suspend publication. The best that can be said for the *Revue* is that it did little to increase the burden of Balzac's debts. His production manager had worked without wages, hoping to share in the profits, and no salaries had been paid to anyone else. Balzac had done his single-handed work at home, so he had accumulated no office expenses. And the small readership had more or less paid the costs of paper and printing.

But the *Revue* had taken up so much of his time for months that he had been unable to obtain advance royalty payments from book publishers for projects not yet initiated, and his creditors pursued him without mercy. Virtually all of them now knew about Les Jardies, and it appeared likely that he soon would lose the house.

One creditor actually believed so firmly in the fiction that the place was the property of Emilio Guidoboni-Visconti that he brought suit against the unsuspecting count. Fashionable Paris laughed aloud at the absurd development, and both Emilio and Fanny decided they had had their fill of Honoré de Balzac. Fanny was true to her own creed to the last, however, and her parting with him was gentle, amicable and civilized. She called him no names and, far more important, made no attempts to gain repayment of her many loans to him.

At a time when he most needed friends who were wealthy and influential, Balzac now stood alone to face a hostile world. But, in this hour of crisis, which erupted in November 1840, he proved that his cunning was equal to that of the creditors, bill collectors and bailiffs who, in his own mind, were representatives of all his implacable foes.

XVI

Unable to pay debts that had snowballed to about one third of a million francs, Balzac quietly declared himself bankrupt in November 1840. Les Jardies was put on the block at a liquidation sale, and this place, which had cost more than one hundred thousand francs was sold to an architect named Claret for a mere seventy-five hundred. The creditors shared this miserable fee.

Only two people knew the truth of the situation, Balzac and Claret. The former had managed to raise the money in cash and had a secret understanding with the friendly architect, who had put up the fee on his behalf. The world might think Claret was the new proprietor of Les Jardies, but Balzac himself was still its owner, and would step forward to reclaim it at a more auspicious time. In a single, brilliant move he had outwitted his enemies, ordinary mortals who clung to the strange belief that the greatest of living authors should pay his bills, just as nobodies did.

Now Balzac faced the problem of finding another place to live, and his luck was good. In the little village of Passy, then a rural retreat on the outskirts of Paris, he located a house that admirably served all his purposes. It had been built by a banker, and was on several levels above the Seine. One portion opened onto the Rue Basse, but a lower section, unseen from that street, had its entrance on the Rue du Roc, which led to the river below. If a bill collector or bailiff appeared at the main door on the Rue Basse, Balzac could leave the house by the other entrance without being seen and if necessary could travel to Paris by boat. His creditors could block the roads to the city, if they chose, but he would continue to outwit them. Just to make doubly certain his new dwelling place remained undiscovered, he placed a shingle bearing the name of a Mme. de Breugnol on the front door.

Unlike the fictitious widow of the house on the Rue des Batailles, there really was a Mme. Louise Breugnol, and when Balzac was living in the house he ostensibly stayed there as her guest. How he first met her is uncertain, although she appears to have been acquainted with a number of members of the writing fraternity prior to their association.

However they may have met, Louise admirably suited many of Balzac's purposes. She was a few years his junior, still attractive, and not only had an exceptionally keen mind but understood the publishing business. This knowledge made it possible for her to visit publishers on his behalf and handle most of his dealings with them, thereby saving his time and enabling him to keep his whereabouts secret. She was so adept that within a short time she was negotiating his new contracts, in effect acting as his literary agent, and obtained better terms than he had ever been able to work out for himself. He trusted her implicitly, far more than he had ever trusted anyone else in his business affairs, and Louise responded by bringing him the largest advance royalty payments he had ever received.

She managed the house, directing the activities of two to four servants, the number varying according to Balzac's moods and needs during any given period. She always insisted on cooking his evening meal, his one main meal of the day, with her own hands, however, and he boasted to his friends that her cooking was superb. Louise was a widow, a woman whose middle-class background was similar to Balzac's and she undoubtedly was familiar with the hearty provincial dishes he most enjoyed.

She was also his mistress, of course, and they lived together for a number of years in the closest approach to domestic contentment Balzac had ever known or would know. Louise was bourgeois in her moral approach to life, which meant that Balzac was forbidden to bring any of his courtesans or prostitutes to the house, and when he cheated on his mistress, which he did frequently, he was forced to act surreptitiously, in the manner of a husband cheating on his wife.

The couple exchanged so few letters that many facts regarding their relationship are unknown. According to a number of communications that Louise wrote after Balzac's death, it appears that she made a number of trips with him, including one to Savoy and another to several of the German states. Apparently these were relatively brief holiday sojourns, and no details have been unearthed.

One fact emerges, in spite of all the unknowns: Balzac enjoyed a tranquillity with Louise that he had never before experienced. It is also clear, from the few notes he wrote her that are extant, that he bound her to him with his usual extravagant promises of undying love, and she may have believed she would live with him as his mistress-housekeeper-business manager for the rest of their lives. If so, she was doomed to suffer the disappointment experienced by all of the other women in his life who thought they could tame him into a state of at least relative fidelity.

One immediate result of the liaison with Louise was a noble experiment. Balzac had achieved a new stability in his domestic life but was still subjected to his mother's nagging. Mme. de Balzac was sufficiently sensible to entertain no false hopes, and it is unlikely that she ever expected the return of the one hundred thousand francs she had loaned her son. But she was forced to depend on her children for her living and thought it unfair that the De Survilles, whose income was modest, should be forced to bear the entire burden. Henry, who was planning to return to the tropics with his family, was a slender reed, so she continued to hope that her famous son, who earned a minimum of one hundred thousand francs per year, would offer her more than token support.

Mama's badgering, combined with Balzac's own guilts, had compelled him to give her varying sums for a long time, but he hated to part with cash that he could use for his own indulgences, and the presence of Louise under his roof led him to believe he could bring his mother to live with them. The move, he reasoned, would reduce his expenses appreciably.

Mme. de Balzac must have been startled by the invitation, and suffered misgivings; a lady didn't live under the same roof with her son's mistress. But she paid a visit to the house in Passy, and by the time the afternoon ended her fears were dispelled. Louise Breugnol—the *de* that was sometimes added was strictly Balzac's invention—was the living embodiment of bourgeois respectability, a woman of solid virtues, thrifty and lacking in ostentation, sensible in her approach to life—and a superb cook who had herself baked the mouth-watering cake she served at tea. As Mama later informed Laure de Surville, "Mme. de Breugnol is a *good* woman . . . She is the soul of honesty . . . She loves Balzac and will look after him well . . . The poor woman has had many troubles. I assure you, she is to be pitied, and I hope that Honoré will make her life secure as soon as he can do so. It will be only fair, because she curbs his spending and restrains him from many follies."

Suitably reassured, Mme. de Balzac moved into the Passy house early in December 1840 and thereafter enjoyed the friendliest of relations with Louise. But she and Balzac found it impossible to dwell together amicably. The basic problem was that Mama totally failed to understand her son.

She not only expected him to make gestures in her behalf, but could not rid herself of the notion that she should play a central role in his life. She was hurt when he failed to join her for breakfast or noon dinner. It bothered her when she came to his study to discuss matters concerning his welfare that she deemed important and he brusquely refused to interrupt his writing schedule. She became annoyed when he ignored such excellent advice as her admonition that he was working too hard and should go into Paris more frequently to relax with his friends. And it disturbed her when he dined with her and Louise in the evenings, the only meal he ate with them, and repeatedly drifted off into an inner world of his own, forcing her to repeat whatever remarks she had just made.

Her attempts to enter and reorder his life, her efforts in behalf of changing the style of living he had chosen for himself fell on ground that was hostile as well as barren. For limited periods Balzac was able to tolerate or ignore his mother's interference, but eventually her well-intentioned carping grated hard on his nerves, and his temper erupted. He shouted, Mama shouted, and after he retired to his study, slamming the door behind him, Mme. de Balzac went to bed with a "sick headache."

The incessant conflicts with his mother soured Balzac's relations with everyone except the placid Louise, who paid no attention when he stormed. A new tone of impatient irritation crept into his irregular correspondence with Mme. Hanska, who—in her infrequent letters—dared to criticize him. In one ill-tempered letter to her he became very stern:

I beg you never to interfere, either with praise or censure, in the affairs of people who feel the waters meeting over their heads and are trying to rise to the surface! Rich people will never be capable of understanding the difficulties of those less fortunate.

In one of her brief communications Eveline Hanska gave vent to her own annoyance by making an unfortunate reference to what she called Balzac's "frivolous nature," and he immediately ripped off an outraged reply:

In what way am I frivolous? Is it because during the past twelve years I have been devoting myself without respite to the comple-

tion of an immense literary task? Is it because for ten years there has been no room in my heart for more than one love? Is it because for the past twelve years I have been toiling day and night to pay off an enormous debt with which my mother's insensate and deliberate design has burdened me? Is it because, despite so much misery, I have neither smothered myself nor blown out my brains, nor flung myself into the river? Is it because I work without intermission and try, in a variety of ingenious ways, to shorten the period of penal servitude to which I am condemned?

Please explain! Is it because I shun society, because I keep to myself, in order that I may concentrate on my one passion, on my work, and the repayment of my debts? Frivolous nature, indeed! Really, you are behaving as a good bourgeois might have done had he seen Napoleon turning to right and left and in every direction to examine the field on which he was going to give battle, and then remarked, "This fellow can't stay in one place! He has no goal."

It was remarkable that Balzac was still corresponding with Mme. Hanska. Her letters were somewhat remote and impersonal, and his protestations of love had become mechanical. Eveline's daughter, who was growing to womanhood, was becoming her confidante, so there was no longer the need to find an outlet in the sympathetic, distant author who understood women. It may be that Eveline didn't want to sever her one link with the world of civilization, culture and glamour. Life on an isolated estate in the Ukraine was still very dull, and her correspondent, after all, was one of the most renowned and distinguished of living writers.

At first glance, Balzac's reasons for maintaining the correspondence are more difficult to ascertain. His relationship with Louise Breugnol amply demonstrates that, at the age of forty-one, he had given up his dream of spending his life with a beautiful, wealthy and adoring noblewoman. In 1839 a familiar note had reappeared in his letters to Zulma Carraud and Laure de Surville, whom he asked to keep watch for a wealthy widow who might be attracted by the idea of marriage to a famous writer.

After due consideration, however, it becomes evident that Balzac was the victim of his own lifelong habits. In his youth he had become accustomed to sending long letters to Mme. de Berny, telling her of his hopes, his aspirations and his problems. For more than two decades he had utilized the ear, sympathetic or seemingly so, of one feminine sounding board after another. He needed the outlet, and it would seem that, by explaining his situation of the moment on paper, he gained the ability to put his troubles out of his mind in order to devote his complete attention to his work.

Balzac was still the actor, to be sure, and no matter how sharp their exchanges became, he could not resist the opportunity to strike a pose in order to win Eveline's sympathies. In 1841 they were bickering, each accusing the other of writing infrequently, and when Balzac reminded Mme. Hanska that she had more time than he for the purpose, she replied tartly that she would write only when she received a letter from him. His nerves already rubbed raw by his arguments with his mother, he replied to Eveline in kind, while his unbridled imagination simultaneously impelled him to reach out to the limits of absurdity in his attempt to bind her to him:

Ah! So at last I discover how incredibly petty you are, which proves to me that you are a creature of this world who lacks the spiritual graces!

Ah, so you stopped writing to me because my letters to you were infrequent. Well, they have been infrequent because I have not always had the money for postage, although I did not want to tell you this. Yes, I have sunk as deep as that, and even deeper. It is very horrible and very dismal, but it is true, like the Ukraine where you are living. Yes, there have been days when I have proudly devoured a roll as my only sustenance as I have walked along the boulevards.

Having written of his pitiful, near-starving state, Balzac happily left his study and went downstairs to enjoy the enormous five-course dinner that Louise had prepared for him. Not even the presence of his mother lessened his appetite for two or three dozen oysters, a few bowls of pea and sausage soup, several lobsters, a heaping plate of beef ragout with vegetables, a double portion of salad, an assortment of cheeses and an apple, a pear, a peach and some plums. He had also acquired the Dutch habit of emptying the contents of a silver bowl filled with salted nuts to top off the meal.

The relationship with his mother became so bitter that, in July of 1841, Mme. de Balzac decided to save her own sanity, even though her son's madness was incurable. She returned to the home of the De Survilles, still on the best of terms with Louise, although barely speaking to Balzac.

Her departure made no difference in the scheduling of household routines, and Balzac continued to spend his usual long hours at his desk. All through the many changes in his life over the period of two years, among them the termination of his affair with Fanny Guidoboni-Visconti, his move from Les Jardies to Passy, the beginning of his affair with Louise Breugnol and the intrusion of his mother, he worked more or less simultaneously on seven or eight novels and a half-dozen novellae, writing a few chapters of one, then turning to another and yet another before going on to the next round.

Among the most important of these works were *La Rabouilleuse*, *Une Ténébreuse Affaire*, *Ursule Mirouët*, *Mémoires de deux jeunes mariées*, and *La Fausse Maîtresse*. Any one of these novels would have won him a large measure of immortality, even had he written nothing else in his lifetime. His mastery of his craft was complete, and like Hugo, he was capable of achieving any effect he wanted to create. His themes extended the scope and depth of the *Comédie humaine*, his techniques were unerring and he had become a virtuoso in his manipulation of language. The compliment he prized above all others was the casual but sincere remark made by Hugo, the greatest poet of the century. "Balzac," he said, "you think of yourself as a writer of prose, and so you are, but above all you are a poet because your words capture for mankind the elusive spirit that sets humans apart from animals."

Of these new works, *La Rabouilleuse* was perhaps the most ambitious because virtually all of its characters were unattractive, making it difficult for the reader to sympathize with any. The setting was a small town near Frapesle, Issoudun, with which Balzac had become acquainted on his visits to the Carrauds. Issoudun was ruled by a group of unscrupulous men who did not bother to earn a living, many of them army officers retired on half-pay. Into their midst came one even more amoral, Colonel Philippe Bridau, whose brother, Joseph, was an artist of stature. Philippe killed a rogue named Max Gilet in a duel, then set out to win Max' mistress, Flore Brazier, from his own bachelor uncle, whom he ruined in the process. Flore, who gave the book its title, was a temptress, but Philippe destroyed her as well and managed to rob both his own brother and mother. He was surrounded by prostitutes and degenerates, using their weaknesses as a means of establishing his own strength, but his excesses were his own undoing at a time when he was on the verge of ultimate triumph.

In spite of its harsh characterizations and the cynical, dismal picture it presented of small town provincial life, *La Rabouilleuse* was a great success. The critics called it shocking, but Balzac responded with an estimate that proved accurate when he said, "The reader wants to be shocked. Then he can assure himself that all the bad things in his own life could be much worse."

Ursule Mirouët, which deals with the occult that Balzac loved, was one of his most far-fetched stories, but it was so firmly rooted in realistic details that readers accepted the far-fetched elements on which the plot depended. These included such matters as a man learning through a fortuneteller that his lovely niece was in love with a splendid young fellow, which impelled the old man to make her his principal heir. After his death a warped character, typical of Balzac's larger-than-life monsters, stole the inheritance, but the old man came back from the dead to reveal the crime to his niece, and all ended well.

The modern reader finds it difficult to swallow the story of *Ursule Mirouët,* but the fascination with the microscopic details of daily living is as great in present times as it was in Balzac's own day. It is a never-ending wonder that a man who could be so selfishly indifferent to the feelings of virtually everyone with whom he came in contact could have had an ear so sensitive to delicate nuances, an eye that recorded the minutiae in the worlds and lives of men and women of every class. The details of this novel form a complete portrait of an era, and the background alone makes the book a classic.

Une Ténébreuse Affaire is notable chiefly because it represents an abrupt change of pace for an author who was demonstrating his phenomenal ability to write books of many kinds and moods. It was an historical novel, a suspense story and a mystery, filled with elusive allusions that the reader finds impenetrable until given an explanation on the very last page. It was the story of a kidnaping and its causes, of fast-paced chases and intricate intrigues, of duels and fights and wild horseback rides, of low schemes and high adventure. But Balzac was no longer capable of writing a mere action story, and *Une Ténébreuse Affaire* reaffirmed his basic belief that regardless of a man's political persuasions or advanced civilized state, he is governed by the primitive forces in his own nature, forces that are common to all humans and that appear in times of great stress.

Every French intellectual aspired to membership in the nation's most distinguished society, the Académie, and the ambition had come to life in Balzac in 1836. Perhaps he had cherished dreams earlier, but in that year he began to mention his coming membership, and soon taking it for granted that he would be elected, spoke of the eight thousand francs per year income and the life peerage sometimes awarded to members as though they were already his.

In his more realistic moments, however, he apparently realized it would be no easy feat to enter the select ranks. Only a small minority of the nation's men of stature had accepted him as an equal, and he was still regarded as an outsider by members of the academic community, who shared the literary critics' contempt for him. But he continued to think of himself as the greatest European novelist of the age—a judgment in which posterity has concurred—and it galled him that the Académie seemed unaware of his existence.

In 1839 he initiated his campaign to win membership, and found several Academicians who were sympathetic to his cause. They submitted his name, but before the entire group had an opportunity to vote, Balzac discovered that the name of Victor Hugo also had been entered in the lists. It was unlikely that more than one author would be seated at any one election, so Balzac promptly withdrew, in part because Hugo was one of his few real friends, in part because he didn't want to make a poor showing in the balloting. Hugo was infinitely more popular, and no one was more aware of it than Balzac.

His generosity further cemented his friendship with Hugo, who eventually became his champion in the Académie and repeatedly nominated him for membership. But the majority could not regard him seriously, no matter how great his accomplishments; to them he was a grotesquely fat man who lived and dressed flamboyantly, carried outlandish walking sticks and was eccentric in his manner of living. Again and again the shortsighted Académie rejected him, to its own discredit, and membership eluded him for the rest of his life.

But Balzac's work provided its own satisfactions, and the *Comédie humaine*, which he first used in 1839 as the title for the entire body of his work, continued to grow. It is startling to note how many books, in addition to the novels, novellae and stories he wrote and published, were being developed in the planning stage. Seventy-four were actually printed, and another fifty to seventy-five were in existence in the form of notes and outlines. It is impossible to estimate how many more he would have written had he remained in good health and lived another quarter of a century.

Examining the sum total of his work as a single entity, the reader is overwhelmed by his encyclopedic knowledge. He was intimately familiar with every part of the Paris of his day, and knew not only its physical characteristics and peculiarities, but its social, economic and political structure. The same was true of scores of smaller communities stretching from the English Channel to the Mediterranean.

He has been plastered with every conceivable label, both by his contemporaries and succeeding generations, who have called him a conservative, a liberal and a radical, a monarchist, a Republican and an anarchist, a traditional Catholic and an atheist. Not until more than a century after his death has it finally dawned on students of Balzac that he was basically a reporter, a man endowed with remarkable perception and sensitivity, an observer who not only completely understood both his own era and human nature, but who possessed an uncanny ability to write objectively about people and the world in which they—and he—lived from day to day and year to year.

It is for these reasons that he has been so difficult to categorize. His work covered such a vast spectrum that he refuses to be pigeonholed. Similarly, those who have regarded him as the "king of the realists" have missed the essence of his work. He saw his world in terms of an exaggerated realism, and his portraits were far larger than life. One facet of his genius was his realization that the truly realistic was dull, so he colored and shaped his work accordingly, heightening, shading and always dramatizing. A letter he wrote to George Sand indicates his consciousness of what he was doing and best explains what he attempted so successfully to achieve:

I like exceptional beings; I myself am one, so I understand their feelings, desires and disappointments, and therefore can explain them to the reader. What is more, I need them to throw my more commonplace characters into relief, and I never sacrifice them unnecessarily. But the commonplace characters are of great interest to me, too (you don't care for them, any more than you do in real life, so you lack patience with them). I enlarge them: I idealize them in reverse, emphasizing their ugliness and stupidity. I bring

31. Balzac's house (right) on the Rue Berton in Passy.
(Roger Viollet)

32. View of the garden of Balzac's house in Passy. (Photographie Bulloz)

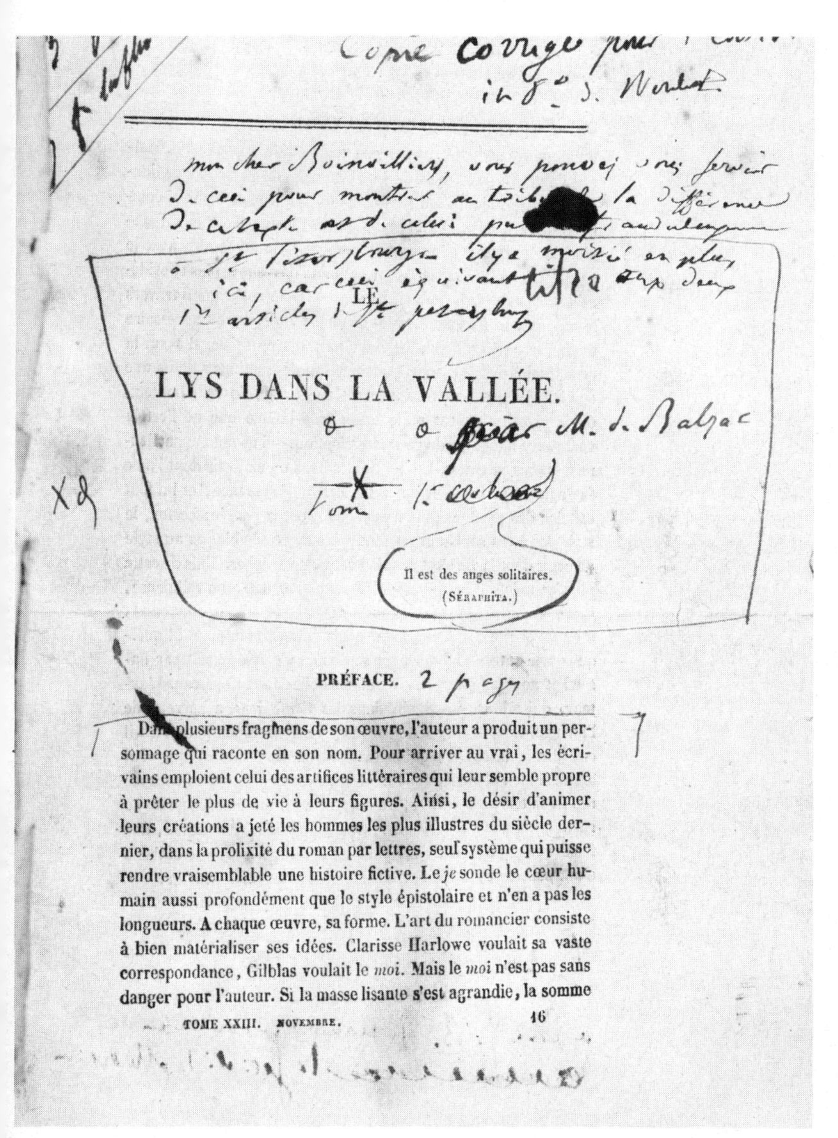

LE

LYS DANS LA VALLÉE.

Il est des anges solitaires.
(SÉRAPHITA.)

PRÉFACE.

Dans plusieurs fragmens de son œuvre, l'auteur a produit un personnage qui raconte en son nom. Pour arriver au vrai, les écrivains emploient celui des artifices littéraires qui leur semble propre à prêter le plus de vie à leurs figures. Ainsi, le désir d'animer leurs créations a jeté les hommes les plus illustres du siècle dernier, dans la prolixité du roman par lettres, seul système qui puisse rendre vraisemblable une histoire fictive. Le *je* sonde le cœur humain aussi profondément que le style épistolaire et n'en a pas les longueurs. A chaque œuvre, sa forme. L'art du romancier consiste à bien matérialiser ses idées. Clarisse Harlowe voulait sa vaste correspondance, Gilblas voulait le *moi*. Mais le *moi* n'est pas sans danger pour l'auteur. Si la masse lisante s'est agrandie, la somme

TOME XXIII. NOVEMBRE. 16

34. (Above) A revised page proof, in Balzac's hand. He had already made between fifteen and twenty-five drastic revisions of this material. (Photographie Bulloz)

33. (Left) The fireplace in Balzac's house on the Rue Basse in Passy. (Photographie Bulloz)

35. Balzac in his coach. Charcoal sketch. (The Bettmann Archive)

36. A sketch of Balzac in his late years. (Historical Pictures Service, Chicago)

37. Balzac and Countess Hanska. A caricature of the time. (Collection of M. Marquet de Vasselot) (The Bettmann Archive)

38. Balzac's house on the Rue Fortunée (today Rue Balzac). The photo was taken in 1899 before its demolition. (Roger Viollet)

39. Balzac's sister as an old woman. (Musée Balzac; Roger Viollet)

to their deformities (physical, moral, mental) an added dimension of the horrifying or grotesque. The ordinary reader is not interested in characters like himself, but in my enlarged creatures he recognizes elements of his own nature, and it is this recognition that enables him to accept my magnified versions of the commonplace.

It becomes clear, then, that Balzac was engaged in a deliberate, sensitively conscious process of artistic creation. It would appear probable that this process of enlargement and exaggeration became so much a part of him that he applied it to his own life, until he could no longer distinguish between the real world and the magnified world of his own imagination. Even when sleeping with a woman, quibbling with his mother or eating an enormous meal prepared for him by his housekeeper-mistress, he never thought of himself as no ordinary mortal, but as an incomparable genius, a member of the literary elect whose every word and deed would be remembered for centuries. He played the role to the hilt, relishing it so much that it became a part of him and influenced his life style accordingly.

Enough of his daydreams had materialized to convince him that all of them were true. One eluded him, however, and it must have been difficult for him to maintain any enthusiasm for his correspondence with Eveline Hanska. Sometimes he wrote as often as monthly, but she replied so infrequently that he became inclined to allow as long as three months to elapse between letters. He continued to assure her of his undying constancy, but years of repeating the same phrases had made his protestations dispirited. And Mme. Hanska, who had learned about most of his romantic escapades, taxed him with his infidelity on the rare occasions when she wrote to him, so the correspondence had been reduced to dreary rote. But Balzac stubbornly refused to relinquish it, and made it a point to send off a copy of each of his books to the Ukraine as soon as it was published. The gesture cost him nothing, and he still entertained vague thoughts about a possible future relationship with the handsome noblewoman who had been his mistress for such a short time. One never knew what tomorrow might hold in store.

Soon after the beginning of 1842 Balzac's foresight paid its first dividends. On January 5 he received a formal, black-edged notice, written two months earlier, informing him that Baron Hanski had died. The news electrified him, instantly reviving the glorious future of which he had dreamed seven years earlier. The handsome, wealthy aristocrat—who had claimed she loved him and had gone to bed with him to prove it—was now a widow. The most persistent of his daydreams, that of marriage to just such a woman, was at last within his grasp. Eveline was a blueblood, skilled in the erotic arts, and she had inherited so much property from her husband that she was undoubtedly one of the wealthiest widows in Christendom. Marriage would enable him to pay off all his debts, give up the various mistresses who offered him only fleeting satisfaction—and spend the rest of his days with the perfect mate.

XVII

As soon as Balzac received word of Baron Hanski's death he retired to his study and composed a letter to Eveline. It was no easy task, far more delicate than the most subtle of his efforts in shaping his novels. In it he was required to achieve a precise balance, striking an appropriately sympathetic note, while at the same time informing her that his own love for her was undiminished and that he could at long last look forward to the permanent union with her that had been only a dream for seven years. He wrote:

Insofar as I am concerned, my dear adored one, although this untoward event brings within my reach that which I have so fervently desired for nearly ten years, I can, in justice to you and in the sight of God tell you that in my heart I have never held or cherished any thought other than one of complete submission, accepting the situation you and I faced. Even in the most cruel moments of my life I have never sullied my soul by entertaining evil wishes.

But one cannot prevent oneself from indulging in occasional, involuntary fancies. I freely admit to you that I have often said to myself, "How much happier my life would be with her."

One cannot preserve one's faith, one's most intimate being and integrity, somehow keeping one's spirits alive, without hope. Those motives which the Church regards as virtues have sustained me in my struggles. But you know, I am quite sure, because you know me, that I deeply sympathize with you in your time of great and abiding grief.

Balzac gave his imagination free reign, and it was all too easy to think of himself as already married to Eveline. But nagging doubts bothered him, and his own volatile, impatient nature made it impossible for him to sit back and remain silent while he awaited her reply.

What worried him more than anything else was the picture of himself he had so consistently painted when she had accused him of having affairs with other, attractive women. He had written to her that his hair had turned white, that he was badly overweight, suffering from a large variety of illnesses, and that, in sum, he was a tired old man who lacked the ability as well as the desire to engage in sexual relations with a woman, any woman. It would be catastrophic if Eveline accepted his words literally, so a scant three days after writing his first letter, he sent another to correct any lasting impressions he might have created:

There are only a few white hairs here and there on my head, and as a result of my studious way of life I am exceptionally well-preserved, aside from my congestion of blood, which is inevitable in view of my sedentary occupation. I do not think I have changed since Vienna, and my heart is so young that it has kept me young in body in spite of the monastic austerity of my quiet existence. I still have fifteen years of youth left to me, more or less, just as you have, my dear one, and at this moment I would gladly give at least ten years of my old age to hasten the day when we will see each other again.

The torrent of one-sided correspondence continued unabated. Balzac proposed that he repair to Dresden, the closest civilized metropolis to the Ukraine, and spend as many months there as might be necessary in order to be relatively near his beloved. Perhaps she would prefer that he travel to Russia and reside there at his own expense until she deemed it appropriate to marry him.

Was Eveline afraid he might embarrass her by revealing the intimacies of her correspondence with him? She could forget the letters she had written to him. They were in his safekeeping, and in the event of his sudden, unexpected death, he had instructed Laure de Surville, the executrix of his will, to burn every letter.

Was Eveline afraid he intended to live on the fortune she had inherited? Never! His books were selling as never before, and he had attained financial independence. In fact, he would refuse to touch her inheritance under any circumstances, and she would be free to do with her money as she pleased, saving it or spending it or giving it away. Money, Balzac declared passionately, was the least of his concerns.

Contradicting himself, he found it necessary to tell her how to handle her estate, men being far wiser and shrewder than women in matters of finance. Russian real estate had a low market value in the rest of the world, so he suggested she sell her property in the Ukraine and invest in the high-yield bonds issued by a stable government. He had no particular love for Great Britain, but the economy of the British Isles was booming, and she would be far-sighted if she followed his mythical example and put her funds into British bonds.

He also took it upon himself to deal with the future of her daughter, Anna, at that time fourteen years of age. The girl should be married as soon as possible, he said, and a husband should be found for her who was hard-headed, wise in the ways of the world, and—above all—wealthy. Well aware that the government of the Czar disapproved of the spending of income from various properties in foreign lands, Balzac suggested that Eveline sign over to her daughter whatever might be left of her estate, and in return obtain a fixed income from the man who would become her son-in-law.

The letters produced no response, and although Balzac didn't realize it, Mme. Hanska faced serious problems of her own. Her late husband's uncle, a fierce, proud man, was horrified by the thought that vast estates would pass into the hands of a woman, and after her death would go to her daughter. Although he wanted none of the property for himself, the uncle wanted to make certain that the land would be inherited by male descendants of the Hanski line. He petitioned the crown, asking for a decree to that effect, and Mme. Hanska knew her own position was precarious since the Czar and his ministers had no affection for members of the Polish nobility.

There were personal complications as well. Eveline's sister had disgraced herself by engaging in an affair with Pushkin, but at least the poet was a Russian and a genuine aristocrat. The family would not be able to tolerate a permanent liaison with a miserable foreigner, a Frenchman who had risen to his present position of questionable eminence from the depths of the despised middle class.

But the fear of the Czar's displeasure and the disapproval of her relatives were secondary factors. What Balzac failed to take into account was Eveline's own basic attitude. Her marriage had been neither passionate nor romantic, but over the period of two decades she had grown genuinely fond of her gentle, scholarly husband, and her grief for him was genuine. So she was irritated and perhaps a little shocked by the premature insistence with which her French suitor pressed his case. Also, she was no wide-eyed hero-worshiper dealing with a famous author for the first time. Experience had taught her that Balzac was a mercenary opportunist, a lecher and a habitual liar. Certainly the prospect of becoming his wife did not appeal to her.

Even more important, she was devoted to her adolescent daughter, and Balzac erred grievously when he urged her to marry off the girl. Eveline resented his callous interference in a matter that was none of his business, and she was further angered by Balzac's expectation that she would throw herself into his arms.

The weeks passed slowly, and for the first time in his life Balzac found it almost impossible to concentrate on his work. He continued to work long hours, but discovered that most of the words he put onto paper were worthless gibberish. His long-range future was hanging in the balance, and the ink caked on his pen.

Finally, late in February 1842, he received his first communication from Eveline, whose reply, he said, was written with "glacial calm." She was blunt, mincing no words, and her rejection left nothing to even the wildest imagination. "*You are free,*" she told him.

She knew him well enough to realize that this blunt, simple statement would not silence him, so she elaborated in detail. She no longer trusted him. He had proved to her that he was a liar and a cheat. In seven long years he had never as much as suggested the desire to visit the Ukraine, but in that time he had traveled extensively in Italy and France, finding both the time and money for his extended holidays. What was more, he had not traveled alone, and even in Paris had engaged in several long-term, notorious affairs. His protestations of innocence had been absurd, and had convicted him doubly in her sight, so she wanted no more to do with him. She was no longer interested in romance, having reached a mature age, and planned to devote the rest of her life to her daughter, who had become the core of her existence, her very reason for living.

Balzac was shattered by Eveline's attempt to terminate their relationship. Never had any woman rejected him with such finality or cruel candor, never had anyone exposed his weaknesses with such brutality. He sent her a relatively brief reply in which he tried to recover what was left of his dignity and aplomb: "*Disinterest, devotion, faith and constancy are the four keystones of my character, and between these four there are only tenderness and good will.*"

He had no intention of taking her at her word and abandoning his suit. Not only were fabulous rewards awaiting him at the far end of the rainbow, but Eveline had challenged him, and he accepted the call to battle. He, the acknowledged master who knew more about the psychology of women than any other man of the age, refused to bow his head in defeat. He weighed various possibilities: perhaps he would surprise her by traveling to Russia and pressing his suit in person; on the other hand it might be wiser to play a waiting game. The stultification of the dreary life she led in Russia would be certain to influence her in his favor, in the long run.

It was fortunate for Mme. Hanska that he did not choose the former course. The Imperial court in Kiev ruled against her in the case brought by her husband's uncle, and she was forced to submit a personal appeal to the Czar for a reversal. The appearance of the bourgeois French author on her property would have ruined her case as well as her reputation.

For a short time he licked his wounds in silence, but in the spring of 1842 he learned from friends in the Austrian embassy that she had moved from the Ukraine to St. Petersburg so she could attend to her case in person, and the news spurred him into renewed action. St. Petersburg was a seaport, and a civilized man could travel there without subjecting himself to the hardships that a journey to the remote Ukraine would entail. He opened a new barrage, bombarding Eveline with love letters that called all of his genius as a wordsmith into play.

The most remarkable feature of these communications is their ring of sincerity. It has been argued that Balzac exerted his greatest efforts because he was fighting for a fortune, but this explanation is insufficient. As always in his relations with a woman, he became the victim of his own daydreams: he convinced himself that his love for Eveline was genuine, so his suffering, his longing, his heartbreak were real.

He was not applying undue pressure, he told her, and was willing to wait as long as she deemed appropriate to set her own house in order. All he asked in return was that she set a date, no matter how distant, when she would consent to become his wife:

Alas, my beloved angel, it is no great boon that I have asked of my Eva. I have only wanted you to say, "In eighteen months, in two years we shall be happy together." I have only wanted you to say "we" and to fix the terms of my waiting.

His imagination built a fire within him, and he poured his emotions onto paper:

Oh, my beloved, to live at last heart to heart, each for the other, with nothing to fetter us! There are moments when the thought makes me foolish, and I ask myself how these years have passed, with me here and you so far away! How vast is the power of money! What a sad spectacle it is to see the most beautiful sentiments depending upon it. To see oneself chained, nailed down in Passy when one's heart is five hundred leagues away.

There are days when I abandon myself to dreams. I imagine to myself that all of our difficulties have been dispelled, that the wisdom, the discretion, the skill of "the Queen" have triumphed, that word has arrived from her, bidding me, "Come!"

And I pretend to myself that I am on my way to you. On such days my friends do not recognize me. They ask me what is wrong, what has gone amiss. I laugh as I reply, "My troubles are about to end. At last I have hope."

And they say, "He is mad."

Reverting to his habits in the earliest days of their relationship, Balzac wrote to Eveline daily. No matter how heavy his work load, he poured words onto paper, filling pages, writing endless versions of the same theme.

A woman totally lacking in sensitivity would have been flattered, and Eveline was not devoid of delicate feelings. The communications she was receiving with such regularity were written by her onetime lover, the man who had made her empty life in the Ukraine bearable for so long. Other influences also were at work. Thanks to the agitation of her relatives against Balzac, her cultivated friends in St. Petersburg learned of his interest in her and were impressed. French was the second language of every educated Russian, and Honoré de Balzac was recognized in the Czar's capital as a novelist without a peer. The mere fact that he professed to be in love with a woman gave her a distinction of her own.

Other pressures also were at work on Eveline. The lawsuit brought by her husband's uncle had reminded the Imperial court that she was Polish, not Russian, so she was received coldly in official circles. She needed no one to tell her that no matter how steadfast her loyalty to the Czar might be, she would be regarded as an outsider at court for the rest of her life. This meant that, regardless of how great her inheritance might be, no ambitious gentleman would want to run the risk of acting as her escort, and she was doomed to remain a widow for the rest of her life. At best she might become the mistress of some prominent nobleman, provided she consented to live on his estates or her own and absented herself from St. Petersburg.

The germs of some new thoughts began to take shape in her mind. She might be wise to make a settlement with her husband's uncle, accepting the best terms she could obtain, and then leave Russia forever with her daughter. The thought of homeless exile did not appeal to her, but if forced to accept it she might do worse than find some measure of social standing as Honoré de Balzac's wife. If she could do better, to be sure, she would not hesitate to reject him, but in the meantime perhaps it was a mistake to terminate their relationship.

So, after considerable hesitation, she wrote to him again, opening the door a few inches. And, although Balzac did not appear to realize it, his goddess was less self-assured than she seemed. After all, seven years had passed since he had last seen her, and she had grown older and heavier in that time. So she sent him a miniature painted for the purpose, and told him that when he saw it he would probably end their correspondence.

Predictably, Balzac became even more fervent in his declarations of love. He was willing, he told her, to apply personally to the Czar for Russian citizenship and the right to marry her. If she gave her approval, he would leave immediately for St. Petersburg. The lady, herself contemplating permanent removal from Russia, was alarmed by his impetuous offer and begged him not to leave France.

Balzac realized the odds were against him and that he needed allies rather than foes in his attempt to storm Eveline's citadel. He knew, too, that only an enhanced social position and an improved financial situation might cause Mme. Hanska's relatives to relent in their opposition to him. So he launched several new campaigns simultaneously. The Académie was the most renowned company in all of Europe, and even in barbaric Imperial Russia it was regarded with awe, so he renewed, in vain, his efforts to win a seat in that august body.

Experience had taught him that his books would not make him solvent, no matter how many he wrote or how great their success, so he made another attempt to emulate Victor Hugo, who had won another fortune for himself in the theatre. The public had already demonstrated its lack of interest in drama by Balzac, so he wrote a comedy which he called, *Les Ressources de Quinola*, the story of an inventor and the scheming, sometimes bumbling valet who tried to help him.

The management of the Théâtre de l'Odéon liked the play and agreed to present it. The casting proved difficult and there were various other tribulations, but it was presented in the spring of 1842, and the reaction of the public matched that of the critics, who were universal in their merciless denunciation of the effort. The disappointed Balzac was forced to write Eveline that his enemies had triumphed again. In return for his great efforts the play earned him less than five thousand francs.

The failure sent him back to the books he continued to produce at his usual undiminished pace. Among the more important in 1842 and the first months of the following year were *Un Début dans la vie, Albert Savarus, Les Paysans, Honorine, La Muse du département,* the second part of *Les Deux Frères* and *La Rabouilleuse.*

The last of these was too advanced for its day, and created a scandalous sensation. In it he boldly utilized a theme no other author of stature other than De Sade had ever attempted, that of sexual bondage. It was the story of a physician in his seventies who brought up a girl of thirteen to be his mistress, teaching her perversions he found pleasing, but he planted the seeds of his own ruin when his son, in whom all of his hopes for the future were centered, willingly made himself a slave to the girl's whims.

Un Début dans la vie was unique because it was not based on a story that Balzac developed himself, but on a detailed plot written by Laure de Surville. Her brother returned the compliment by dedicating it to her, and although *Un Début* lacked depth, it was a financial success.

Albert Savarus is significant because, like *Louis Lambert,* it is basically a self-portrait by the author, and presents Balzac, as he saw himself in 1842, with remarkable, objective clarity. Savarus is a genius, deeply in love with an Italian duchess, who sets out to win a political triumph in the hope that an impressive victory will persuade her to marry him. He succeeds, but in the process inadvertently snubs a younger woman, who maliciously interferes in his romance. The duchess turns away from Savarus, marrying another, and the brokenhearted hero renounces the world by entering a monastery.

In his correspondence with Eveline, Balzac made no attempt to hide his identity as Savarus or hers as the duchess, and even began their romance in Geneva. The words he put in the mouth of Savarus were aimed directly at the elusive lady in St. Petersburg: "*I'm at the end of my strength; if you should fail me, I shall collapse permanently in one way or another.*"

Mme. Hanska was not duly impressed, and if she understood his message she chose to ignore it. He sent her the first copy of the book as soon as it came off the presses, but she wrote that it did not appeal to her, principally because she considered it a man's novel and could not become interested in the principal character.

Balzac drove home his point in a series of increasingly frantic letters, telling her repeatedly that his need for her was urgent. Eveline, knowing him, would not have been surprised to learn that, even while begging for her sympathy, he was in the process of consummating the biggest and most important business deal of his life.

He believed the time had come for him to make the *Comédie humaine* a reality, and publicly revealing his title for the first time, he let it be known that he wanted to bring out a new collection of his works, to which he would add annually. The task of printing so many new editions would have strained the resources of any one publisher, so three firms, those of Furne, Hetzel and Dubochet, banded together and offered the author a tempting contract, which he accepted. He received an advance royalty payment of fifteen thousand francs, and, after forty thousand volumes were sold, would be paid a royalty of fifty centimes per volume. Therefore, as he fully realized, he would be assured of a steady income for the rest of his life.

The publishers estimated that Balzac would earn at least fifteen thousand francs per year under the agreement, and their assurances sparked a new daydream. He would earn an additional twenty thousand annually with his pen, and would live at Les Jardies in comfort with his bride. In his letters to Eveline he painted glowing pictures of their future, blithely ignoring the advice of an attorney, Maître Gavault, who was trying to reduce the chaos of his financial situation. Les Jardies was a ruinous financial burden, Gavault told him repeatedly, and had to be sold at once if Balzac hoped to avoid bankruptcy proceedings. Gavault soon learned that his client did not suffer the fear of being in debt that afflicted ordinary mortals, so he tried a different approach. The estate would bring a good price, he informed his client, and he held out the bait of an investment that would bring a handsome return.

Balzac promised to think about the matter and, retiring to the study of his rented house, wrote *Honorine*, a short novel. It was a simple, charming love story, and he later claimed to have turned it out in a miraculous three days, but his notes indicate that he probably spent two weeks at the task, itself an incredibly short period of time. Confident that Eveline would summon him to St. Petersburg when her year of official mourning ended, he occupied himself by completing *La Muse du département* and the second part of *Illusions perdues*, then going on to write *L'Envers de l'histoire contemporaine* and *La Torpille*, all of them major works.

He borrowed freely from the life of Caroline Marbouty in his plotting of *La Muse*, a savage commentary on society in which he stressed that the love of any man and woman was doomed if the couple failed to abide by conventions. Society, he said, would mock a love of which it did not approve, and pressures, both public and private, would destroy it.

Refusing to accept his own dictum, however, Balzac continued to pursue his own unconventional love, and his daydreams became wilder. His election to the Académie was assured, he wrote Mme. Hanska, but he showed no embarrassment when his candidacy again was rejected, and he glossed over his defeat.

Eveline's year of mourning passed, but she continued to hold her persistent suitor at arm's length, insisting that he refrain from joining her. He spent his time writing a number of stories that would appear in *Splendeurs et misères des courtisanes*, and celebrated his forty-fourth birthday in May 1843, by working around the clock on a third portion of *Illusions perdues*, which continued to grow, and which he called *Les Souffrances de l'inventeur*.

By now his letters sounded desperate, and Mme. Hanska apparently concluded that he would come to Russia with or without her approval, so she decided he would be easier to handle if she granted him permission to join her. Balzac received her letter in mid-June, and immediately undertook the formidable task of gathering funds for his journey. He borrowed from the old friends who were his only remaining sources of credit, and even sold the original manuscripts of a number of books in order to raise cash.

At the end of June he left Paris, and after suffering a number of delays caused by the breakdowns of shipping, he endured a miserable sea voyage and arrived in St. Petersburg at the end of July. His tribulations were far from ended. The demands of propriety made it impossible for him to stay at the Koutaizoff Palace, the Hanski home in the Russian capital, so he took lodgings nearby, and quickly discovered that the place was infested with bedbugs.

But he shrugged off such inconveniences. He and his beloved were reunited at last! Balzac had gained weight and his hair was now gray, while Mme. Hanska looked plump and middle-aged, but there is no honest account of what they really thought of each other. Eveline kept her opinions to herself, while Balzac predictably insisted that she had become more ravishingly beautiful than ever.

Certainly he must have realized that his open attentions were compromising Mme. Hanska, making her the center of the aristocracy's gossip, but he plainly didn't care. Each day, promptly at noon, he called on her at her palatial home and remained there for several hours; returning to his lodgings for an interlude of work, he stopped writing at eight in the evening and presented himself at the Koutaizoff Palace for dinner.

Fortunately for Mme. Hanska's reputation, the situation was not as bad as it might have been. The Czar was not in residence in St. Petersburg, and many nobles had gone off to their country estates for the summer, which relieved social pressures somewhat. All the same, the presence of Honoré de Balzac in Russia, combined with his unabashed interest in the lady, could not be kept secret. After all, the entire court, the government bureaucracy and the small middle class all read, wrote and spoke French fluently, and Balzac was the most widely read and admired French author in the country, so his mere presence created a considerable stir.

But he went to such pains to indicate that his visit was strictly private that he received relatively few invitations, and actually rejected those that interfered with his main purpose, the wooing of Eveline. A number of high-born ladies were disappointed when the word was quietly passed, presumably by Mme. Hanska herself, that he would not accept invitations to dinners or teas, luncheons in his honor or receptions.

But some functions could not be avoided, particularly when Czar Nicholas I took an unexpected interest in him. Nicholas, who had succeeded his cultured brother, Alexander, in 1825, was widely regarded as Europe's most authoritarian despot. He was anti-intellectual, suspicious and cold, and hated liberalism in any form; the best that could be said about him was that he was exceptionally handsome. Convinced that he ruled by Divine right and that his decisions were inspired by Divine revelation, he was nevertheless thin-skinned, and knew that his educated subjects considered him a barbarian. So the presence of Balzac in his realm gave him an opportunity to demonstrate that he wasn't completely lacking in appreciation of literature.

It is unlikely that the Czar had ever read any of Balzac's books, and certainly he would not have liked them or approved of their earthiness, much less their insistence that every man had the right to seek happiness in his own free way. But Nicholas saw no need to study Balzac's work when a mere gesture would suffice.

So, about two weeks after Balzac's arrival in St. Petersburg, he received an invitation to attend a royal military review at Krasnoye-Selo. The overweight author spent the entire day on horseback beneath a broiling sun, and the experience was so exhausting that he was confined to his bed for the next twenty-four hours. He was presented to the Czar, however, and chatted with him for more than a half hour.

No one knows what the ill-matched pair said to each other, and Balzac displayed rare tact in his subsequent references to Nicholas. Obviously aware that Mme. Hanska's financial future rested on a royal decision that the Czar might make personally, he took pains to praise the Emperor of all the Russias in the only way he could. In a letter to George Sand—that he knew would pass through the hands of the royal censor—he said, "*Everything that has been written about the Czar's remarkable good looks is the truth. Not one man in Europe can compare with him.*"

With the exception of a few such diversions, Balzac devoted himself exclusively to Mme. Hanska. He spent many evenings reading aloud to her and to Anna from the more romantic of his novels, which he knew both mother and daughter would enjoy. He exercised his charm, wit and talents as a conversationalist to the utmost, never losing sight of the fact that what he had achieved in Geneva so many years earlier could be repeated now, when Eveline was older, less attractive and more vulnerable.

When Mme. Hanska tentatively presented him with an idea of her own for a novel, he leaped at the opportunity to become her "collaborator," and developing the theme in his own way, wrote *Modeste Mignon*, which was published early in 1844. It was, appropriately, a highly romantic story, and Balzac called it "the conflict between poetry and reality, between illusion and society."

In all, he concentrated on his goal, Mme. Hanska, in the same way he ruthlessly put everything else out of his mind when he worked on a manuscript. Before long he was sleeping with her again, and his battle was half won. If Eveline had forgotten the pleasures of sex, he reminded her of them. If she had forgotten how it felt to be flattered, he recalled to her that she was a remarkably attractive woman. It was unnecessary to tell her that her lover was no ordinary man but one of the most renowned authors in the world, since this was the tie that, slender though it had been for years, had still bound her to him.

Using his new advantage, Balzac did his best to persuade her to marry him, and Mme. Hanska no longer completely rejected him, as she had done immediately following her husband's death. She could make no commitment until she won or lost her battle for her inheritance, she told him, and above all she would not consider marriage—to anyone—until Anna became a little older and was herself safely and happily married.

This meant a wait of another two years, perhaps, and Balzac was content. As he had written her in so many letters during the year and a half that had passed since Baron Hanski's death, he did not care how long he had to wait for her, provided he knew that she would marry him some day and would give him at least a tentative date.

Suffused with the glow of a romantic victory that made all the daydreams of his youth come true, he left St. Petersburg in early October, and arrived back in Paris at the beginning of November.

A number of problems directly connected with his trip troubled him. The sensation-mongering press, trying to find a motive for his journey, printed stories to the effect that he had become a paid agent of the Czar, a charge that infuriated him. It was also said in print that he was involved in a spectacular romance with a great lady, and various names were mentioned, including that of a prominent Italian princess. But he had kept his secret so well that no one, including various fellow authors and literary critics, guessed Eveline's identity.

Balzac was not disappointed to discover that his attorney's attempts to sell Les Jardies for a good price had failed. The idea of setting up permanent housekeeping there with Eveline still appealed to him, and he mentioned the possibility to her in a number of letters.

Louise de Breugnol awaited the returning author at the rented house in Passy, and he immediately resumed relations with her, untroubled by his commitment to Mme. Hanska. Why Louise continued to live with him is something of a mystery, since she undoubtedly knew his reason for going off to Russia. She was on friendly terms with his mother and sister, and Laure de Surville, who was becoming more of a termagant with each passing year, was insistent in her promotion of Louise's candidacy for the honor of becoming Mme. Honoré de Balzac. Here, perhaps, is the clue to Louise's puzzling behavior. Her lover's long-distance romance with the lady in distant Russia had persisted for years, but she was on the spot, living with him under the same roof, and may have subscribed to the bird-in-hand theory, perhaps believing that, when the time came, Eveline would refuse to marry him.

The most persistent and annoying of Balzac's problems was that inspired by an old obligation. Henriette Borel, Anna Hanska's governess, who had been Balzac's go-between in his earlier correspondence with Eveline, had decided to seek a new life for herself. Still troubled by the role she had played in the illicit romance, she had made up her mind to become a nun, and before leaving St. Petersburg, Balzac had rashly promised to give her all the help he could, and had invited her to make her home with him while she made her necessary arrangements.

Mlle. Borel arrived in Paris on his heels, and he was forced to give her a room in the Passy house. Her presence not only made it more difficult for him to pursue his affair with Louise, for fear Henriette would send incriminating details to St. Petersburg, but the garrulous, dyspeptic visitor interfered with his work schedule.

She remained at the Passy house for several months, to his increasing annoyance, before she finally found a place for herself in a convent. To the surprise of Louise and Laure de Surville he occasionally visited Henriette there, but it was obvious that he made the calls for only one reason, to impress Eveline.

Plunging into work with renewed vigor in spite of his unsatisfactory domestic situation, Balzac completed *Modeste Mignon* and then turned out another novel, *Les Petits Bourgeois,* both of which were serialized in what may have been the best French publication of the period, the *Journal des Débats*. He also completed *Splendeurs et misères des courtisanes,* perhaps the most "untidy" of his major works, which was romantic and cynical, realistic and in places so melodramatic that it became almost ridiculous.

No one recognized the faults of the work more clearly than the author himself. As always, his need for money verged on the desperate, so he wanted the additional funds that he would earn if the book were serialized before being published in hard covers. That meant he needed melodramatic plotting, combined with the sensationalism in dealing with sex that had become his trademark. Eugène Sue and Alexandre Dumas were commanding higher prices for the serialization of their novels than he was being offered, and recognizing the danger signs, he was determined to beat them at their own game and reassert his primacy in the field.

He also made the time to continue work on *Les Paysans*, the story of a great landowner, a reactionary, and his troubles in dealing with a younger, more liberal generation, a book which he considered one of his most important. But the strain of overwork was beginning to tell on him. He suffered an attack of jaundice shortly after his return from Russia and impatiently returned to his labors too soon. Coffee no longer stimulated him as it had through the years; he suffered blinding headaches that drove him from his desk, and occasionally the muscles in his face twitched involuntarily.

Balzac made no secret of the alarm he felt when he could not drag himself out of bed one morning, and instead gave in to the temptation to sleep. Never before had he reacted to the challenges of his work in this way, and he wrote gloomily to Eveline that only their marriage would save his life. He refrained from adding that Dr. Nacquart also considered his health precarious and had urged him to cut down drastically on his insane schedule. He paid no attention to the advice, shrugging it off as he had in the past, and for the same reason: he needed more and more money, particularly as he required vast sums for the expensive furnishings he was already buying for his marital love nest.

In the summer of 1844 a letter from Eveline containing unexpected news stunned him. The Czar had reversed the verdict of the lower courts and had ruled in her favor. She was now her husband's sole heir, and all of his property belonged exclusively to her.

Her wealth was staggering, but Balzac reacted with magnificent indifference. All of her fortune should be saved for Anna, he wrote her; he intended to be her sole support after they were married, and he promised she would continue to live in the same luxury she had always known.

XVIII

Balzac's firm resolve to support his future wife without her financial help vanished within a month, dissolved by the rosy mists of his unbridled dreams. A noble lady of wealth and stature who married the world's most prominent living novelist could not be expected to live in a middle-class dwelling like Les Jardies, which he convinced himself would bring a high price when sold. Eveline needed a home in the most fashionable residential district of Paris, the Champs Élysées, and a house purchased there would be a splendid investment, as land values in the neighborhood were sure to rise.

Undaunted by his chronic indebtedness, Balzac persuaded himself he could supply eighty thousand of the one hundred thousand francs he believed he would need to purchase a suitable dwelling for his blue-blooded bride-to-be. So, solely for the sake of her future happiness, he would swallow his pride and allow her to advance him the additional twenty thousand francs, which he would accept only as a loan. He informed her of his wise, generous decision, and when she answered by bombarding him with page after page of specific questions regarding possible properties he had in mind, how much repairs, alterations and furnishings would cost, what they would be required to spend for upkeep and other mundane matters, he replied in a lofty tone. Women had no understanding of financial matters, he declared, and the intelligent wife allowed her husband to handle her purse for her. He even congratulated her because she was marrying a man whose enormous earnings proved he was sagacious in dealing with money.

The gulf that separated illusion from reality was great. Girardin had purchased the serial rights to *Les Paysans*, paying the full sum in advance, even though the book was not yet completed, and Balzac struggled to finish his manuscript while ignoring headaches and muscular spasms in his face that caused him to weep so copiously he could not see the paper on his desk.

Suddenly Eveline's situation changed. She left St. Petersburg with Anna and took up residence in Dresden, and although Balzac didn't yet know it, Anna had become engaged to marry a wealthy young nobleman, Count George Mniszech, who lived there.

All Balzac needed to learn was that Eveline had moved to Dresden, and he proposed to join her at once. For reasons of her own that have never been fully explained—perhaps an attack of cold feet as she contemplated marriage to such a patently unstable man—Mme. Hanska ordered him, on the pain of her most severe displeasure, to remain in Paris.

Her lover and would-be husband responded with one of his more harebrained ideas, suggesting that she and Anna pay an incognito visit to Paris. The notion was as daring as it was mad, because a subject of the Czar was permitted to visit France, the hotbed of perpetual revolution, only when provided with a special permit bearing the personal signature of Nicholas himself. If Mme. Hanska came to Paris without the Imperial approval her estates would be confiscated, in toto, and she would not be allowed to return to Russia. Eveline was shocked and rejected the scheme.

In February 1845, Balzac finally learned of Anna's betrothal, and sensing that the time of his own marriage was at last drawing near, he became so insistent he come to Dresden that he wore down Mme. Hanska's defenses; in April she relented. Blithely casting aside his vocational obligations, including the completion of novels already appearing in print in serial form, Balzac collected what cash he could scrape up and left Paris at once. Immediately prior to his departure he was heartened by the first official recognition of his talents ever bestowed on him by the French government, his appointment to the rank of Chevalier in the Legion of Honor, but he was disappointed because no cash award accompanied the honor.

When he reached Dresden he found Eveline elusive and uneasy, so he tried new tactics and tried to reach her through Anna and her count. George Mniszech was typical of the young Polish nobility, and was dashing and handsome, an ardent patriot, rather coarse and almost totally lacking in intellectual qualities. But his sense of humor was strong, so Balzac appealed to him and to Anna by playing the clown, and the young couple became devoted to him.

Mme. Hanska observed his antics with a jaundiced eye, and in the frequent letters she wrote to her daughter—even though they slept in adjoining bedrooms—she invariably referred to her supposed future mate as "poor Balzac." The term is indicative of her real opinion of him.

She resumed their affair, all the same, and Balzac quickly fell into the habits of the very rich who were unacquainted with the meaning of work. Mme. Hanska developed a desire to travel, Balzac happily fell in with her plans, and they made a tour of the German states, visiting Hamburg, Kannstadt and Karlsruhe. For two ecstatic months Balzac totally ignored his work and did not write a single word, enjoying the first complete holiday he had ever known after a quarter of a century of ceaseless, grinding toil.

In July the party reached Strasbourg, and a few days later, after

George went off to Belgium to attend to some family business, Balzac achieved a victory by persuading Eveline and Anna to accompany him to Paris. The ladies traveled incognito, and Balzac took delight in handling the details. He secured a passport for Mme. Hanska in his sister's name, and obtained another for Anna as his niece. Renting a small furnished house for them in the Rue Basse, he staffed it with servants, then set about the happy task of showing them his city. They took carriage rides and walked; they visited every monument, museum and library; they attended concerts, the Opera and the theatre; they strolled down the boulevards and dined at Balzac's favorite restaurants. Balzac probably knew Paris better than any man alive, and was an incomparable guide, so the month spent in the city was an unending joy.

August came, and the holiday went on, with Balzac escorting the ladies to Fontainebleau, Orléans, Bourges and his birthplace, Tours. Still resolutely ignoring his manuscripts, indifferent to the *Comédie humaine* and the concluding chapters of serials, he accompanied Eveline and Anna to Rotterdam, then went on with them to The Hague, Antwerp and Brussels, where George rejoined the party. In September they went to Baden-Baden, where they remained for several glorious weeks, and at the end of the month they turned up in Marseilles, where they engaged passage to Naples on a ship. Everywhere they stayed at the best hotels, enjoying the most luxurious accommodations, and everywhere they dined in the most expensive restaurants, shopped at the finest stores and enjoyed the services of expert, locally hired servants.

Had Balzac been paying his own way he would have been forced to terminate his holiday after spending only a week in Dresden, and even then he would not have been living on his own money. Obviously Mme. Hanska was paying the bills, and Balzac apparently did not object to her largesse. Nothing is known of the financial arrangements the couple made, whether they found some method of preserving Balzac's pride or whether he simply did not care. After a lifetime of almost unimaginable hard work he did nothing but enjoy himself; he believed he owed himself the prolonged respite and, aside from his outraged publishers, no one who knew him could deny him the right to cultivate pleasure.

Girardin hounded him, so he interrupted his idyll for a few days early in September to write the final portion of *Béatrix* and a few chapters of *Les Paysans,* but he allowed nothing else to interrupt the euphoric days and nights he spent with his mistress-future wife, who compounded his joy by paying all of the bills. It may be that, for the first and only time in his life, he knew complete happiness during the six months he played truant.

Clearly Mme. Hanska enjoyed the sojourn, too, and did not mind providing the funds. Her companion was socially amiable and amusing, an incomparable bedmate, and his renown won them respectful consideration wherever they went. She liked the flurry of excitement their arrival created in every city and town, and preferred it to the anonymity of wealth she had known in her previous travels. In addition, she was spared the problems, financial and personal, that would be certain to complicate her existence if she became Mme. de Balzac. She was experiencing the rare treat of simultaneously having and eating her cake, even though its cost came out of her own pocket.

All good things eventually end, and Balzac's carefree holiday was no exception. By the autumn of 1845 his relations with his publishers were so strained that he realized he would have difficulty in finding anyone to print his books unless he began fence mending immediately. So he reluctantly returned to France, arriving in Paris in mid-November.

By this time he had reached a firm understanding with Mme. Hanska, who had foolishly shown her good faith in him by giving him the large sum of one hundred thousand francs for the purpose of buying a house. Evidently he had forgotten his previous boast to the effect that he would pay four fifths of the cost of their joint home himself.

The fortune burned a hole in his pocket, and he could not resist spending several thousand francs on jewelry for Eveline; he sent her the gifts at once, but neglected to mention that he had used her money for the purpose. Then, his conviction that he was a financial as well as a literary genius undiminished by a lifetime's rueful experiences, he decided to "quadruple" Mme. Hanska's funds by investing in the stock market. Convincing himself that shares in the new Northern Railway would rise astronomically in the immediate future, he sank the better part of the fortune in the railroad's stock.

Oddly, his own financial affairs had improved somewhat during his six-month absence from Paris, principally because royalties had been accumulating during that time and he had not spent any of the money. At Mme. Hanska's urging he reduced a number of his debts, but neglected to pay as much as a sou to his mother. Nevertheless he felt hurt when Mme. de Balzac complained about the situation.

The long holiday had done wonders for his health, too, just as Dr. Nacquart had predicted. His facial tic had disappeared, his headaches had vanished and his stomach pains had diminished enough to have become bearable. He had greater energy and zest for life than he had felt in years.

A number of post-journey problems created complications, of course. Laure de Surville had reached the conclusion that his treatment of their mother was shameful, and quarreled so bitterly with him that they were barely on speaking terms. And Louise de Breugnol was proving difficult after awakening to the realization that her lover-employer's relationship with "the Russian woman" was truly serious, and that she herself would be forced to abandon her high hopes.

For a short time Balzac thought he was in luck. Louise found someone else she thought she might marry, and her former lover was relieved of all responsibility for her. But she soon changed her mind, and returning to Balzac's house, demanded that he set her up in business so she could become self-supporting. She wanted to open a shop in which, among other things she would sell postage stamps and the seals that made legal documents official, and needed an elusive government permit for the exercise of this privilege. Balzac was forced to spend entire days seeking the help of friends and acquaintances who enjoyed influence in government circles, and the impatient Louise badgered him so unmercifully that he regretted the day he had first taken her under his roof.

The knowledge that his dream of marriage to Mme. Hanska would become a reality sustained him, however, and not only enabled him to forget day-to-day unpleasantnesses but sent him off on the wildest, most prolonged buying spree of his life. No one, down to the present day, has ever been able to estimate with any degree of accuracy how much he spent, in 1845 and 1846, on paintings and furniture, bric-a-brac and bogus antiques.

Never before had his mania been less controlled, his buying more compulsive. In spite of his renewed, exceptionally busy work schedule, he made the time to go shopping every afternoon, and added useless, expensive items to a collection that soon had to be stored in a warehouse. He bought a porcelain dinner service that, he wrote to Eveline in triumph, had come from China, but soon thereafter discovered it had been made in Holland and was forced to admit that "it is no more Chinese than I am."

A snuffbox that supposedly had been the property of the Empress Josephine turned out to be an item of cheap, local manufacture. A silver drinking goblet allegedly used by King Henry VII of England turned green within a week, and its "royal crest" fell off the side.

One day he ruefully admitted to Mme. Hanska that collecting bric-a-brac was a "science," but his optimistic ebullience soon reasserted itself, and he was buying additional bargains, boasting that "people do not know their Paris. With time and patience there is nothing you cannot find here, and cheap to boot . . . I am ransacking every corner of the city. The really good things are doubling in price every day."

Eveline was not impressed by his bargain-hunting, and urged him to restrain his enthusiasm. He was hurt, and protested that he was investing in their future. In fact, he declared, virtually everything he acquired was worth at least triple or quadruple what he paid for it, so he was furnishing the home he hadn't yet located at no cost. She would live like a queen, he told her repeatedly, and he wanted her to realize what a good manager and businessman she was marrying.

Balzac's ability to recognize genuine antiques and works of art was unique, or so he told Mme. Hanska, but what was truly extraordinary was his ability to fool himself. At a single glance he knew that a desk he found at the rear of a dealer's shop had belonged to Queen Henrietta of England, that a clock in a state of disrepair had told the time for the Medicis, and that scores of other items were so valuable they belonged in the Louvre. His powers of self-delusion were monumental.

What makes his collection remarkable is that literally not one piece of bric-a-brac or furniture had any real value. Many years later, when all of his possessions were sold at auction after Eveline's death, everything that Balzac had purchased with such pride went to a low bidder. He had not bought one real antique, one item that had increased in value by as much as a sou.

His real problem in 1845 and 1846, however, was his inability to concentrate on his work. Writing had become a torture, the words refused to flow onto paper, and after he struggled at length with a manuscript he was so dissatisfied with the results that he destroyed what he had done.

Les Paysans, which he was anxious to complete, refused to jell, and he had to abandon it repeatedly, turning to other, lesser works. Only *Splendeurs et misères* gave him relatively little trouble, and it expanded far beyond his original concept. He had already done two long parts, and now, after adding a third, made extensive notes for what would become a fourth.

Mme. Hanska, who had never known anyone else forced to work for a living, showed him no understanding and little sympathy. She had no financial problems and consequently regarded his complaints as tiresome. Travel made life worth living after one had been buried for the better part of one's life in the remote Ukraine, so, in February 1846, she suggested he join her in Rome for a tour of the Italian states and Switzerland.

Balzac needed no urging, but his departure was delayed by Louise de Breugnol, and he was forced to exert himself to the utmost in order to obtain the government stamp privilege for her. He left Paris in mid-March and spent the next six weeks with Eveline, Anna and George, returning home at the end of April. One concrete result of this journey was Eveline's firm decision to marry him. Even though he found it difficult to write he had not lost his powers of persuasive speech, and talked her out of her last hesitations.

They made specific plans for the future, and Eveline, almost as impractical as her future husband, thought it would be pleasant to buy a château somewhere in the French countryside, where they would spend half of each year, and either buy or rent a house in Paris for the other six months.

Balzac discovered it was easier to write again, now that the future was assured, and his mind was further relieved when Mme. Hanska wrote him that George Mniszech's father had died; the old man had opposed his son's marriage to Anna, but no obstacle now stood in the path of that union.

Another letter from Eveline contained even more spectacular news: she was pregnant.

Balzac immediately took command. The baby, he informed her, would be a boy, and they would name him Victor-Honoré, after the two greatest writers of the age, so there could be no doubt that he would become an author, too. One matter required immediate attention, and could not be neglected: there would be too many complications if the child was illegitimate, so it would be necessary for his parents to be married without delay.

The problem was complicated by the possibility that Mme. Hanska would lose the Russian estates responsible for her income if she married a foreigner without first obtaining the written consent of the Czar, who had been known to delay for many months before rendering a decision in such a matter. But Balzac knew how they could get around Nicholas; the wedding would be performed in some small French town, where a token payment to the authorities would guarantee that the publication of the banns, which was required by law, would be concealed in a mass of other documents.

In order to have the ceremony performed, however, they would be obliged to present Eveline's birth certificate, and her husband-to-be urged her to send for it without delay. What he failed to realize, and what Mme. Hanska did not want him or anyone else to know, was that she had been lying about her age for many years. She had actually been born in 1800, and therefore was only one year younger than Balzac, not the seven years she pretended. Her vanity made it impossible for her to admit the truth, and rather than allow it to be revealed, she decided to have the baby in private, preferably in one of the minor German principalities, then let Balzac take care of the child until such time as she could straighten out her financial affairs without fear of incurring the Czar's wrath.

Her desire for secrecy appealed to Balzac, but he had a few ideas of his own on the subject, and acted accordingly. First he bought more shares in the Northern Railway "to secure the financial future of our little family." Then, in September 1846, he bought a house at 14 Rue Fortunée, off the Faubourg Saint-Honoré, which he considered perfect for their needs.

He spent "only" fifty thousand francs for the place, and a few "minor repairs" would cost another ten thousand, so he had struck a great bargain. Real estate values in the neighborhood were soaring so rapidly that the property would be worth at least one hundred and fifty thousand francs within a year. She could consider herself fortunate that he had acted promptly.

The dwelling, a mansion built in the time of Louis XVI by a wealthy member of the court, was perfect for their present as well as their future needs. On the second floor was a secret apartment, secluded from the rest of the house, and Eveline could not only give birth to her baby there, but could live with the infant in the apartment for as long as might be necessary. No one would know of her presence.

The house boasted other features that made it perfect. The inner courtyard was completely enclosed, and had a garden that could not be seen from the street. The grand staircase was made of marble, six of its fireplaces were of carved alabaster, and, best of all, the house had a private chapel so lovely that it resembled a "miniature Pantheon." Murals lined the staircase and graced a number of rooms, so what more could a couple starting housekeeping together ask in the way of a home?

There were a few "minor" inconveniences, he admitted. The coach house, stables and servants' hall had been sold separately the previous year, so they would be forced to build some "small" additions. The house had not been used in so many years that the interiors of the brick fireplaces would have to be replaced, and a few of the bedchambers needed carpentry.

But no matter. From the street the mansion looked like an ordinary dwelling, and only when one went inside were its marvels revealed. Most of the rooms were small, so the atmosphere was positively cozy. He already had enough furniture and bric-a-brac to furnish twelve rooms, and would speed his purchases of what they needed for the rest of the place, so all would be in readiness when Eveline arrived.

Mme. Hanska not only failed to appreciate Balzac's thoughtfulness, but was horrified. She recognized her own extravagances when she committed them, but he was mad, completely untroubled by the compounding of his already staggering debts.

Balzac laughed at her fears. He was working again, wasn't he? Several books were taking shape, and even the wretched *Les Paysans* was showing progress. Every publisher in Paris was clamoring for his work, the journals were offering him huge sums for serial rights to books that were still in the planning stage, and the golden flow into his coffers was being resumed. He wished she would realize he was an even more accomplished man of business than he was an author, but he supposed this was difficult for anyone, even his beloved, to grasp. Never mind, she would soon learn, and then she would trust him implicitly, as she should.

He would join her in Germany for the marriage of Anna and George, and after he explained his transactions in greater detail, Eveline would understand that he was a financial as well as a literary genius. He was already moving his priceless antiques and other recent purchases into the house, and laborers were hard at work on repairs. Unfortunately, the cost of competent help was rising outrageously, so the essentials would cost approximately thirty thousand francs, instead of the ten thousand he had estimated. He was being so sensible, however, that every sou counted, and he was being steadfast in his refusal to add unnecessary frills. Granted that the place would be a veritable museum, so dazzling that it would stagger their friends, but he was adhering to the principle of maintaining the simplicity that both of them wanted in a home, and he felt certain she would rejoice with him when she saw the house.

But Eveline became increasingly uncertain, each time she received another letter, that she wanted to see the house, marry the man and settle down with him. He had an opportunity, he wrote her, to buy the finest collection of books on the theatre to be found anywhere in the world, and would have to pay a mere twenty-four thousand francs for a treasure worth at least four times that amount. When she reminded him that he didn't have even a fraction of the sum needed for a down payment, Balzac sulked. Books, he said, earned him his living, so he knew them; he had wanted to share this stroke of good fortune with her, but if she insisted on finding grounds for a quarrel, he wouldn't tell her about his triumphs. She would enjoy the benefits, but he would spare her the details of his victories.

Circumstances that grew out of his incessant spending made it impossible for him to maintain his dignified, remote stance. Northern Railway stock was still falling, his debts continued to mount, and he urgently needed another twenty-five thousand francs. No one but Eveline was in a position to give him the money, and he was forced to ask her for it.

Her reply reasserted her independence. She had already written off the entire sum of one hundred thousand francs she had advanced him, and didn't expect to see any of that money again. But she had no intention of loosening the purse strings now, and would make him neither a gift nor a loan. If he had squandered one hundred thousand francs, that was his misfortune, but she would not permit him to fritter away her inheritance.

The spigot had been turned off, and Balzac knew that only by returning to the backbreaking habits of a lifetime might he be able to pay off the most pressing of his debts. But something was missing, and he could no longer spend twenty productive hours out of twenty-four at his desk. He became sleepy, hungry and tired, and the flow of words had been reduced to a trickle.

Les Paysans was proving particularly stubborn. A serious story of the conflicts between city and rural dwellers, their mutual suspicions and inability to recognize a different way of life, the book required the drive and dedication he had previously taken for granted. Forced to put it aside again, he wrote a number of short stories, which required the expenditure of relatively little effort.

He also turned out *La Cousine Bette*, a light novel dealing with a woman who is a poor relation, and who compensates for her chronic unhappiness by making life miserable for the members of her family with whom, in turn, she makes her home. The book was first published by *La Presse* in serial form, and to Balzac's own surprise it was hailed by the critics as a literary gem.

At almost the same time, in the autumn of 1846, the third section of *Splendeurs et misères*, which he called *L'Instruction criminelle*, was published and achieved instant popularity. The first volumes of the collected *Comédie humaine* appeared, too, and even the most antagonistic of reviewers were forced to admit that Balzac was a man of extraordinary talents.

So Balzac was able to forget his troubles when he went off to Wiesbaden, in October, for the marriage of Anna Hanska to George Mniszech. It had not yet occurred to him that his productivity was permanently impaired, and that he would never again be able to pour out his books in an unending stream. No sooner did he reach Paris than he wrote to Eveline that he was planning twenty new novels and at least two or three plays.

Their personal problem continued to preoccupy him, to be sure. Various friends told him he would not be able to keep a small town marriage secret, so he abandoned the idea in favor of an even more drastic scheme. Writing Eveline a long letter, he urged her to give her entire fortune to Anna; then she would no longer have any reason to fear the Czar's displeasure, and could marry him openly and immediately. He earned enough money to support even a wealthy noblewoman accustomed to every luxury, and he promised he would give her no cause to regret her dependence on him. Mme. Hanska, having observed the financier in action at close range, procrastinated and wrote vague replies.

In December 1846, twin blows that struck in quick succession almost destroyed what remained of Balzac's equanimity. France was suffering from the increasingly unsettled economic conditions that would lead directly to the Revolution of 1848, and Northern Railway stocks plunged to a new low, making them worth only a small fraction of what he had paid for them.

Two days later he received a curt letter from Eveline, written from the house she had rented in Dresden. She had fallen ill, and had given birth prematurely. Less than an hour later the infant had died. In a brief postscript, free of malice, she indicated that the child had been a girl.

Balzac wept, and his tears were genuine. He had been looking forward to the birth of a boy, and grieved for the loss of Victor-Honoré, conveniently overlooking the fact that he had sired a daughter rather than a son. He lost his appetite and could not sleep, and George Sand was shocked when she met him by accident on the street one day. He had lost fifty pounds, and she almost failed to recognize him.

When Eveline recovered her health she wrote that she was thinking of returning to the Ukraine for a time, and Balzac's panic overwhelmed him. Unless she married him before the end of the coming summer, he told her, he would not be responsible for what became of him. For the first time in his life he was threatening suicide, and well may have meant what he said.

Work was no longer his salvation, and he added to his own turmoil by returning to the manuscript of *Les Paysans*. A fortnight later he received word from Eveline that she would be traveling to the Ukraine by the time he read her words, and his muse completely abandoned him. For an entire week he stared miserably at a blank sheet of manuscript paper, unable to write more than a few awkward sentences.

Trying to keep busy, he supervised the workmen who were swarming over the new house, and even purchased linen for the place. Apparently he was trying to assure himself that, regardless of all appearances, Eveline had not abandoned him and still planned to marry him.

But he was whistling shrilly in the dark, trying to convince himself that all was well when his entire world was crumbling around him. Although he may not have known it, he stood on the lip of an abyss, and was on the verge of a complete mental and physical breakdown.

Another, unexpected letter from Eveline granted him a miraculous reprieve. She had changed her mind, and instead of proceeding directly to the Ukraine, was coming first to Paris for a stay of approximately two months. She gave no indication of what had prompted this abrupt switch in her plans, and Balzac's biographers are unanimous in their agreement that she hadn't been overcome by a desire to spend several weeks in his company. It may be that she wanted to find out for herself whether she could salvage any portion of the one hundred thousand francs she had given him for purchase and furnishing of a modest home.

Balzac's recovery was miraculous, and he discovered he could write with the concentrated fury that had been his habit thoughout his entire career. He ripped out a companion story to *La Cousine Bette, Le Cousin Pons,* which the critics ultimately called superior to the former, and completed the final portion of *Splendeurs et misères.* Only the final part of *Les Paysans* continued to elude him before he went to Frankfurt, in February 1847, to escort Mme. Hanska to Paris.

Pons, Bette and the characters surrounding them are among the most memorable Balzac ever sketched, and both novels avoid the melodrama and false sentimentality that sometimes marred his earlier works. It might be noted that *Bette* and *Pons* were written after a long period of rest, the only real holiday he had ever known, and both show a freshness of approach frequently lacking in his other work. Not one false note spoils the author's mood of grim realism as he deals with the petty triumphs and heartbreaking disappointments, the false illusions and self-confining mores of middle-class French men and women living in the reign of Louis Philippe. Obviously no qualitative judgment can be made of the work of a man who wrote so many masterpieces, but the reviewers who were Balzac's contemporaries could not have been far wide of the mark when they called *Bette* and *Pons* his most mature and powerful novels.

Balzac had good cause to be pleased with himself and his accomplishments when he went to Frankfurt. The tide had turned in his favor again, and thanks to the brisk sale of the collected *Comédie humaine,* his pockets were stuffed with francs, which enabled him to avoid embarrassment while entertaining the woman he considered the love of his life.

Eveline settled into the apartment Balzac had rented for her, and then accompanied him on an inspection tour of the house on the Rue Fortunée. How often he had pictured this scene in his imagination and correspondence! She would clasp her hands in ecstasy, close her eyes and weep. The beauty of the place would render her inarticulate, and only her gasps would indicate her pleasure. But Mme. Hanska did not lose her voice, her perspectives or her powers of rendering independent judgments.

Balzac was stunned when she blistered him with criticism. There was so much marble in the house it looked like a graveyard. He had used far too much brass in the decorations, from chandeliers to cupboards, making most rooms gaudy and gloomy at the same time, a remarkable achievement in bad taste. She had envisioned a delicate, decorous little palace, and instead saw a dreadful middle-class museum. As she later wrote to Anna, the house was both "sinister and comical."

Her temper rising as her disappointment mounted, Mme. Hanska accused Balzac of squandering her money on a place totally unsuitable for any self-respecting woman. She had been devoted to him for years, but he was repaying her fidelity by making her ridiculous.

Balzac was so crushed that Eveline belatedly realized she was dealing with a sick man and relented. Her criticism had been overly caustic, she told him, and she appreciated the house far more than she had indicated. There had been a time when he would have seen through her lies, but he was so anxious to win her approval that he was mollified.

This was not the Balzac Mme. Hanska had known, and she privately consulted Dr. Nacquart, who told her that her lover's health was precarious. Balzac needed a long period of rest, free of all stress, if he hoped to recover his strength and equilibrium.

During Eveline's visit, which was extended from eight weeks to ten, he did no work, but spent the entire period acting as her proud escort. They attended the theatre and the Opera regularly, dining at his favorite restaurants, and for the first time he presented some of his friends and colleagues to her. Gautier found her a plump, cheerful woman of faded beauty and no particular intellectual prowess, while George Sand disposed of her in a single sentence: "Were she middle class, Honoré wouldn't have looked twice at her."

Not once during the two and a half month sojourn did Eveline meet Balzac's mother or sister. The author dreaded such a confrontation, apparently afraid that his sharp-tongued relatives would insult his beloved and create new complications for him. All three of the ladies found his attitude curious, and all three requested that a meeting be arranged, but Balzac temporized, and when he escorted Mme. Hanska back to Frankfurt, she had yet to set eyes on Mme. de Balzac and Mme. de Surville.

Balzac returned to Paris from Frankfurt, and it soon became evident to everyone who knew him that he was on the verge of a collapse. Often he wept without reason, unable to control his tears, and not only was he mentally unable to return to his manuscripts, but his hand trembled violently, making it difficult for him to hold a pen.

The vindictive Louise de Breugnol chose this particular time to make life more difficult for her former lover-employer. Entering his house during his absence, she had stolen Mme. Hanska's letters to him, and was demanding five thousand francs in gold for their return. Balzac wanted to call in the authorities, but was reluctant to embarrass Eveline, and paid the blackmail. He had kept Louise's note, in which she admitted stealing his property, and believed this would neutralize any future attempts to make use of several of Mme. Hanska's letters, which she had carefully removed from the packet. The incident soured and unsettled him, aggravating his condition.

He moved into the house on the Rue Fortunée, and spent hours each day rearranging bric-a-brac, moving objects from one room to another. Eveline had given him firm instructions, forbidding him to buy anything more for the place, but he could not resist the temptation to pick up a few "priceless" pieces, all of which, he wrote, were magnificent antiques. His letters to Eveline became longer, and he also resumed the correspondence with Zulma Carraud that had lagged in recent years, but these efforts filled only a small portion of his time, so he finally returned to his work, dreading the moment when he would pick up his pen and discover he could not write.

His worst fears were justified, perhaps because he once again elected to attack *Les Paysans*. Not only was he unable to add a single paragraph to the book, but was so dissatisfied with his previous efforts that he could not force himself to read the earlier portions.

The domestic upheavals in many European countries and principalities that would become known as the Revolutions of 1848 were already brewing, and nowhere was the atmosphere more tense than in France. Laborers in rapidly expanding industries were demanding higher wages and better working conditions but were being exploited by members of the growing middle class who were becoming wealthy and powerful. Commerce and industry were growing too quickly, placing credit in jeopardy. Ineffectual rulers—and there were few as inept as Louis Philippe—tried to maintain their controls by curbing the civil liberties of their subjects, and in France men of every class were so incensed they spoke openly of overthrowing the monarchy. Talk of establishing a republic was in the air, and the poor of Paris threatened to establish a new kind of world, in which all goods would be shared.

Balzac seemed only vaguely aware of what was going on around him. He had developed a vague contempt for Louis Philippe and wasted no sympathy on him. A stronger King, or even a competent President, he wrote Eveline, could have prevented the erosion of financial credit that had caused the decline of Northern Railway shares to a small fraction of their previous value. In another letter he briefly mentioned the menace of communism that was threatening France and the Italian states, indicating his contempt for the doctrine, but he did not seem unduly concerned. He cared about nothing except Eveline, and filled page after page each day, expressing his longing for her.

Whether Mme. Hanska had developed a genuine love for Balzac or merely pitied him is a question that could be debated endlessly without finding a definitive answer. Whatever her motives, his letters touched her, and after a separation of four months, she wrote to him in August 1847, giving him permission to join her in the Ukraine. Balzac's sun, which had been hidden for four long, unfruitful months, suddenly emerged again, dispelling the darkest clouds he had ever seen.

XIX

An overland journey from Paris to the Ukraine ordinarily took at least two weeks, but Balzac, who left on September 5, was so eager to reach the Hanski estate that he completed the trip in eight days. He had been warned to expect hardships on the road, so he carried a huge picnic basket that contained a dozen and a half loaves of rye bread, a smoked tongue, a smoked ham, coffee, sugar and two bottles of cognac. His provisions were virtually untouched, however, because he was recognized on trains and stagecoaches and received royal treatment.

Wierzchownia, the country seat from which George Mniszech managed his mother-in-law's estate and his own, adjoining property, staggered the imagination of anyone unaccustomed to Russian aristocratic living. The manor house, according to Balzac's description, was a somewhat smaller version of the Louvre, with an entrance that resembled a Greek temple. Endless sitting rooms, salons and parlors were filled with superb antiques that made his own purchases appear shabby, and he was given a suite, one of a dozen or more, that consisted of a sitting room, bedchamber, study and dressing room. For days he marveled at the porcelain, glassware and silver, the heavy drapes of purest silk and the magnificent rugs. Not even in his most unconfined dreams had he pictured such luxury.

Several thousand serfs worked on the two estates, living in sod huts that Balzac described with embarrassment. He had been assured that these dwellings were warm enough for comfortable human habitation in winter, he said, but added rather dubiously that he didn't believe anyone could enjoy true comfort in such cramped quarters. What impressed him more than anything else were the flat fields that stretched to the horizon in every direction. The soil was black, "fifty feet deep," and so rich that fertilization was unnecessary.

Many of the refinements that Frenchmen took for granted were lacking. There were mirrors ten feet high, but wallpaper was unknown; the estate's hospital, staffed by a German father-and-son team of physicians, was the only place within a radius of more than two hundred and fifty miles that the sick could be treated; there were so few trees in the area that they were precious, and the manor house was heated by straw, which was burned in stoves.

For many years after Balzac's death it was believed that he was required to spend hours every day entertaining the pleasure-loving Eveline and Anna, but this was not the case. Mme. Hanska encouraged him to return to his work, and he spent eight to ten hours each day at his desk. It is true that this was far less than his lifelong average, but Eveline's proximity enabled him to write rapidly and smoothly again.

He wrote a new novel, *L'Initié*, a study of virtue, and although it was obviously the work of a man no longer in his prime, its plotting and characterization were still the product of a master's pen. It was published in Paris the following year.

He also worked on *Les Petits Bourgeois*, which he hadn't yet completed, began *La Femme auteur* and turned out the opening portion of what was planned as one of his largest and most complicated works, *Le Deputé d'Arcis.* Life in the Ukraine was dull, and he spent his evenings reading his day's output to an enthralled Eveline, her daughter and her son-in-law. His audience told him he had never done better work, and he may have believed the praise, even though he was exhausted by the time he dropped his pen after a day's work.

There were no bill collectors or bailiffs in the Ukraine, Eveline was on hand day and night, and a huge staff of servants anticipated Balzac's every need and desire. So he was reluctant to leave, but urgent business made it imperative that he return to France. Another payment was due on the Northern Railway shares he had purchased, and the entire investment would be lost if he failed to make the payment in time.

Eveline gave him ninety thousand francs for the purpose, along with additional funds that would enable him to enjoy a few luxuries in the months ahead, and he left in late January, during the coldest weather of the Russian winter. His health already frail, Balzac suffered on the journey, and was forced to halt so frequently that he spent three debilitating weeks on the road.

He returned to a Paris that was seething on the brink of a revolution that, people of every class agreed, could no longer be avoided. The middle class, which had been the mainstay of Louis Philippe's regime, had deserted the bumbling monarch, there were daily riots in the streets which the Garde Nationale could not or would not quell, and the breakdown of authority was evident on every hand. Louis Philippe was in danger of losing his crown, perhaps his life. Only a few days after Balzac's return he watched a mob sack the Tuileries; royal troops fired on a crowd of demonstrators, and twenty-three persons were killed. Barricades were established in the streets, and Louis Philippe immediately abdicated, escaping into exile.

A republic was established, and a provisional government came into power, one of its members being Balzac's friend and fellow author, Alphonse Lamartine. Co-operative industrial workshops were set up, and plans were made to elect a national Constituent

Assembly in April. The moderates and conservatives won an overwhelming victory in that election, the co-operatives were abolished and the citizens of Paris again rioted. Suppressed by the army after three days of bloody fighting, the spirit of the rioters was broken when their leaders were either shot or sent into exile. With peace of a sort restored, the Constituent Assembly drew up a constitution for France, and the Second Republic came into being.

Balzac was, in the main, an observer rather than a participant in the events that shook his native land to its foundations. He took sensible precautions and left his house in late February and early March only when necessary. He worried about the decline of money markets, and was upset when Northern Railway shares continued to fall, but at the same time he saw an opportunity to make a fortune and wrote to George Mniszech, urging him to make funds available at once for investment. The young count failed to heed his advice, and Balzac was annoyed, particularly when he discovered that everyone he knew was buying land, real estate and stocks.

He noted with interest that the theatres, which had closed for several weeks, were opening again. He had never forgotten that an author could make a quick fortune with a successful play, and the time seemed ripe for a new effort. Learning through friends that Marie Dorval, one of the leading actresses of the period, was looking for a new play, he dusted off an unfinished work, *La Marâtre*, and took it to her. She was interested, and the Théâtre Historique agreed to do the play, with her in the principal role.

Balzac's eyes were bothering him, and when he wrote for more than an hour or two at a time he suffered double vision, but opportunity was beckoning wildly, and he would not let a physical handicap deter him. Returning to his old disciplines, he completed the play in two weeks, and rehearsals were scheduled for April.

At this unlikely juncture he took his only leap into active politics. To an extent, at least, he was motivated by the conviction that France would perish unless she established an authoritative, stable government, but there appear to have been other reasons for his move, too. "If Lamartine, who writes abominably, can become one of the principal officials of our government," he told Victor Hugo, "think of how much more an author of real stature could accomplish."

One week before the election he submitted his name as a candidate for the Constituent Assembly, and sent a long letter to one of the more conservative newspapers, the *Constitutionnel*, outlining his position, a demand for a government that would use every means at its disposal to assure the restoration and preservation of order.

On April 23 the voters went to the polls, and more than a quarter of a million Parisians cast their ballots for Lamartine. Balzac received precisely twenty-one votes, and immediately retired from politics.

He was needed at the Théâtre Historique for the rehearsals of *La Marâtre*, a romantic play whose theme was the conflict between an attractive young woman and her stepmother, and he revised a number of scenes. The management made no attempt to interfere, and his attempts to heighten the dramatic effect were so successful that the entire cast was convinced the play would be a great success.

The reviews were glowing. Théophile Gautier rejoiced because a great novelist had entered a new field, and said the theatre would be enriched. Gautier was the playwright's friend, of course, but other critics applauded just as loudly. Even reviewers who had shown marked antipathy toward Balzac for years agreed that he had written a first-rate play, and his dream of earning a fortune in the theatre appeared on the verge of coming true.

The second night's performance was sold out by noon, and then fate intervened. Street rioting broke out again in the wake of the election, and only a few seats at the Théâtre Historique were occupied, as most of those who had purchased tickets were afraid to leave their homes after dark. The following morning the management regretfully decided to close down the theatre until a more permanent peace was established.

Balzac earned a grand total of less than five hundred francs for his effort, and once again a dream eluded his grasp.

It was small wonder that he felt depressed, and he eagerly accepted an invitation from Jean de Margonne to visit Saché, where he had done some of his best work. Putting the turmoil of Paris behind him, he enjoyed the country air and the bounty of the Margonne table, but he made little headway in his attempts to complete *Les Petits Bourgeois*. By the time he returned to the city in July, however, he managed to polish another old play, *Le Faiseur*, for which the Comédie Française paid him an advance of five thousand francs.

The tensions and disturbances of Paris were too great for him, however, and his health was further weakened by chest pains and a shortness of breath, which Dr. Nacquart diagnosed as a heart condition. Once again complete rest was prescribed, and Balzac knew of only one place he wanted to go, the Ukraine. Mme. Hanska had agreed to transfer her property to her daughter, thus removing the major obstacle to their marriage, and had sent a formal application to Czar Nicholas, asking for his consent.

A few arrangements had to be made, chief among them placing the house on the Rue Fortunée in the hands of someone reliable. Balzac could think of only one person on whom he could rely, his mother, and the old lady agreed to live in the mansion and supervise the activities of the servants during his absence. Having lived in genteel poverty for many years, she may have relished the prospect of dwelling in luxury for a few months.

In mid-September 1848, Balzac started off on what would be his last major journey from France. At Mme. Hanska's insistence he carried with him an accounting of what the house on the Rue Fortunée had actually cost, and was himself somewhat surprised to learn that he had spent more than three hundred thousand francs—almost all of it Eveline's money—restoring and furnishing the place. He was convinced, however, that the results had been worth every sou; he was the master of a magnificent home, and would be proud to bring his bride there.

His health made it necessary for him to travel by slow stages, and he did not reach Wierzchownia until the end of the first week in October. Eveline's presence revived him, but it was obvious to his hostess that he was not in good health, and a manservant was assigned to take care of him.

During the early months of his stay, which extended through the rest of 1848 and all of the following year, Balzac tried to overcome his disabilities and bear down on the labors that had been all-important to him for the better part of his life. He worked on four or five different manuscripts, shifting from one to another as his mood dictated, but his progress was maddeningly slow. He had to be content with writing a single sentence in the time it had taken him to turn out several pages, and his efforts were so tiring he sometimes fell asleep at his desk.

Eveline was notified whenever he dropped off, and promptly put him to bed, insisting he stop work for the day. She was always within call, making herself available whenever he needed her, and when physical discomfort kept him awake at night, she sat beside his bed. Nothing better illustrates her changed, softened attitude toward him than her approach to money: his mother forwarded the most pressing of his bills, and Eveline paid them for him without complaint.

The reasons for her new consideration are difficult to determine. As his health and ability to work deteriorated, Balzac became more dependent on her and may have aroused whatever maternal feelings she possessed. Perhaps she felt increasing pity for him as she watched a great novelist floundering in a physical and emotional morass. It is even possible that, after their long association, she had learned to love him.

Whatever the reasons, her loyalty was tested. Balzac suffered an attack of bronchitis that left him in a weakened condition, and Eveline faithfully fed him the medicines prescribed by Dr. Knothe, the estate's physician, who learned there was no task more difficult than that of keeping the patient quiet. Hoping to spare him unnecessary effort, Mme. Hanska handled the bulk of his correspondence for him, replying to letters in her own words after learning the gist of what he wanted to say.

Balzac refused to remain in bed and occasionally he roused himself, displaying a burst of energy. He lost patience when the Czar failed to respond to Eveline's repeated requests for permission to marry a foreigner, and sent Nicholas a long, eloquent appeal under his own signature. His fervor finally dispelled the fog of imperial lethargy, and on March 10, 1850, the Czar granted permission for the marriage of his loyal subject to the renowned Frenchman.

The wedding was a very private affair, and took place at the Church of St. Barbara in the little town of Berdichev at 7:00 A.M. on March 14. Anna and George Mniszech were the witnesses, and the party returned to Wierzchownia immediately after the ceremony, arriving late that night. The bride and groom were so tired that Dr. Knothe administered sedatives and put them to bed in separate rooms.

In the next few days Balzac sent the happy news to France, writing long letters to his mother, his sister and Zulma Carraud, which were followed by shorter communications to a score of friends. Now that Eveline was at last his wife he wanted to complete the dream by transporting her to the Paris mansion he had prepared for her, but his memories of his previous journey across Russia and Poland in the dead of winter chilled his ardor, and he agreed to wait until the April thaws made travel more comfortable.

By the time they left the Ukraine at the end of April, Dr. Knothe was convinced that Balzac was a dying man, a diagnosis Dr. Nacquart unhappily confirmed when the couple finally reached Paris the better part of a month later. At Balzac's insistence his mother moved out of the house on the Rue Fortunée a few hours before the bride and groom arrived. He had not been able to conquer his dread of an unpleasant scene his mother might cause, and he also made it plain that he was less than anxious to arrange a meeting between his bride and his sister.

But Balzac no longer had a voice in the management of his affairs. His eyesight was badly impaired, he frequently lost consciousness, and Dr. Nacquart gave strict orders confining him to his bed. Eveline spent most of her waking hours nursing him, and in this time of crisis his mother and sister rallied to her side. If the elder and younger Mmes. de Balzac failed to develop any warm relations, at least they observed the amenities, and Balzac's fears were proved groundless. Eveline and Laure de Surville quickly became good friends, and maintained a close relationship for years after Balzac's death. But he knew nothing of their rapport during the brief time left to him; they were afraid of exciting or upsetting him, and refrained from telling him they had even met.

In June Balzac rallied and actually left the house on a few occasions, attending to minor errands or driving down the boulevards of his beloved Paris for short periods. Friends who had been reluctant to call now appeared to meet Eveline and wish her husband a rapid recovery. Victor Hugo, who openly declared that Balzac was his only equal as a writer, was one of the first. Mme. Hugo, who was not on the best of terms with her husband, made a separate visit the following day. Gautier came, as did George Sand, and the Girardins appeared together, all of them later commenting on Eveline's gallantry and courage. Her good-natured calm was unflagging, and only when Balzac was asleep would she leave his side to take a short stroll in the garden. He had shown rare good judgment, his friends agreed, in his choice of a wife.

In late July Balzac suffered a relapse. He was sent to bed again, and several medical specialists, summoned to a consultation by Dr. Nacquart, agreed that his condition was hopeless. Eveline had a cot moved into his sickroom, insisted on nursing him herself and would not leave his side.

No one appreciated her efforts more than Laure de Surville, who later wrote at length about her to various friends and relatives. Balzac had been so ill at the time of the wedding, she said, that it was probable he and his bride never enjoyed marital relations. Eveline had known she was marrying a man too ill to recover, but—strictly for the sake of giving him happiness in his last months—she had married him, willingly giving up both her country and her fortune for him. He had never tried to hide his muddled financial affairs from her, so she had known he was riddled by debts, and he still owed manuscripts to a number of publishers who would be certain to tie up what little estate he might leave. She had married him, Laure said, for no reason other than her desire to give him what joy she could before he expired.

On the morning of Sunday, August 18, Balzac's condition was so alarming that Eveline sent for a priest, who administered the last sacrament. Dr. Nacquart came, bringing a nurse with him, and during the afternoon Balzac's mother arrived.

That evening Victor Hugo called, and posterity is indebted to him for his account of Balzac's last hours. The dying man was stretched out on his bed, gasping for breath and unconscious, while the nurse stood watch. The physically and emotionally exhausted Eveline had gone off to her own room to snatch a few hours of sleep, and Balzac's mother sat hunched in a corner of the sickroom, unmoving and unspeaking.

"He will die at dawn," the nurse said.

Hugo returned home, where he found a number of guests awaiting him. "Gentlemen," he told them, "Europe is about to lose a great spirit."

Honoré de Balzac died at 5:00 A.M. on the morning of August 19, 1850. Eveline was still asleep, and only his silent mother and the nurse were in attendance.

The funeral service was held two days later and was completely lacking in pomp. A number of distinguished citizens attended, but the crowd was small, and most of those present were printers and compositors who had worked on Balzac's books. The first novelist of his age, perhaps the greatest in the history of literature, was buried in the cemetery of Père-Lachaise, and Victor Hugo delivered an oration so stirring that Alexandre Dumas wept.

Never one to stint in the presence of an audience, Hugo spoke for more than a half hour, and several newspapers reprinted his address. Neither Balzac's widow nor his mother shed tears until they heard his final words:

It is not night, but light. It is not the end, but the beginning.

It is not nothingness, but eternity. Do I not speak truth, all you who are listening? A tomb such as this is a proof of immortality.

Old Mme. de Balzac survived her son for another four years, quarreling incessantly with her daughter and son-in-law. Somewhat to her own initial surprise she was supported by Eveline Hanska de Balzac, who made certain she lived in comfort, if not luxury. No matter what she was given, the old lady greedily demanded more, and Eveline frequently was forced to remind her that the gifts she received were freely given by a woman who had been her daughter-in-law for only a few months and who owed her nothing.

Eugène de Surville, who lived until 1867, left a considerable estate, but Laure, whose resemblance to her mother had become remarkable, claimed she was poverty-stricken. She managed to live comfortably for many years, however, and often gave expensive gifts to her daughters and grandchildren.

Zulma Carraud knew real poverty after her husband's death in 1864, but enjoyed a success of her own late in life. She wrote a number of books for children which enjoyed considerable popularity, and earned enough to support herself in modest style until her death in 1889.

Honoré de Balzac's will, which named his wife his only heir, acknowledged a debt to her of one hundred and thirty thousand francs, which was approximately one third of what he actually owed her. He left mementos and manuscripts to various friends, among them Mme. Carraud, Dr. Nacquart and Alexandre de Berny, the son of his first mistress. He had nothing else to leave.

Eveline de Balzac decided to remain in Paris after her husband's death, refusing the offer made by her daughter and son-in-law to rejoin them. So they sold their estates and came to Paris, building a house of their own near the mansion on the Rue Fortunée.

Although she was not responsible for Balzac's debts, Eveline was determined to honor them, and after spending months wading through bills and account books, paid off all of his creditors. She also proved herself a remarkably able businesswoman, and not only arranged for the publication of new editions of the *Comédie humaine*, but also made a working agreement with a professional writer, Charles Rabou, to complete two unfinished works, *Les Petits Bourgeois* and *Le Député d'Arcis.* She supplied him with the necessary plotting and characterization, and citing herself as the ultimate authority in all matters regarding Balzac's writing, said to his publishers, *"I have lived more with the characters in* La Comédie humaine *than in the real world."*

Both books ultimately were serialized, and both enjoyed great success; they were presented as the products of Balzac's pen, and Rabou's name did not appear on either work. The publishers of Paris were so impressed by Eveline's efforts in clearing up her late husband's debts that they made every effort to co-operate with her, and in time various fragments, correspondence and previously unpublished stories saw the light of print. Honoré de Balzac's reputation continued to grow rapidly after his death, and all of these books earned considerable quantities of money, as did the *Comédie humaine*. Within a decade of his passing she was receiving annual royalties in excess of fifty thousand francs.

She also knew great personal happiness. In 1852 or thereabouts she became acquainted with Jean Gigoux, one of the period's most successful painters of portraits and historical scenes. She had no desire to marry again, but formed a liaison with him, and they lived together until her death in 1882, spending most of their time either at his Paris studio or, after she sold the mansion on the Rue Fortunée, at the château she bought at Villeneuve Saint-Georges.

To Eveline, in her last decades, came the honors and wealth that Balzac had sought. All of Europe and the New World paid homage to her, his widow, and she had the satisfaction of watching his fondest dreams belatedly come true. Occasionally someone remarked to her that it was a shame he had not lived to see the enhancement of his fame, but she could only shrug in reply. After all, Honoré de Balzac always had been ahead of his time.

PRINCIPAL BIBLIOGRAPHY

Arrault, Albert, *Madame de Berny*, Paris, 1945.
Arrigon, L.-J., *Les Années romantiques de Balzac*, Paris, 1927.
——, *Les Débuts littéraires de Honoré de Balzac*, Paris, 1924.
Balzac, Honoré de, *Correspondance*, Paris, 1876.
——, *Correspondance inédite avec Madame Zulma Carraud* (ed. by Marcel Bouteron), Paris, 1935.
——, *La Comédie humaine*, London, 1895, 11 vols.
——, *Letters to His Family* (ed. by W. S. Hastings), Princeton, 1934.
——, *Letters to Madame Hanska*, Paris, 1899–1950, 4 vols.
——, *Oeuvres complètes*, Paris, 1853–5, 20 vols.
——, *Works* (*édition definitive*), Paris, 1869–75, 24 vols.
Barrière, Pierre, *Les Romans de jeunesse d'Honoré de Balzac*, Paris, 1928.
Béguin, Albert, *Balzac visionnaire*, Paris, 1946.
Biré, E., *Honoré de Balzac*, Paris, 1897.
Bouteron, Marcel, *La Véritable Image de Madame Hanska*, Paris, 1929.
Brunetière, F., *Honoré de Balzac*, Paris, 1897.
Cabanes, A., *Balzac ignoré*, Paris, 1899.
Descaves, Pierre, *Les Cent-Jours de M. de Balzac*, Paris, 1950.
Faguet, Emile, *Balzac*, Paris, 1913.
Floyd, J. H., *Les Femmes dans la vie de Balzac*, Paris, 1926.
Gautier, Théophile, *Honoré de Balzac*, Paris, 1861.
Green, F. C., *French Novelists*, London, 1931.
Hanotaux, G. and Vicaire, G., *La Jeunesse de Balzac*, Paris, 1904.
Le Breton, André, *Balzac*, Paris, 1905.
Marceau, Felicien, *Balzac et son monde*, Paris, 1955.
Maurois, André, *Prometheus, the Life of Balzac*, New York, 1965.
Picon, Gaétan, *Balzac par lui même*, Paris, 1956.
Preston, E., *Recherches sur la technique de Balzac*, Paris, 1926.
Prioult, A., *Balzac avant La Comédie humaine*, Paris, 1936.
Sand, George, *Histoire de ma vie*, Paris, 1851.
Wedmore, F., *Life of Honoré de Balzac*, London, 1890.
Wurmser, André, *La Comédie inhumaine*, Paris, 1964.
Zweig, Stefan, *Balzac*, New York, 1946.

INDEX

N